Oxford Applied Mathematics and Computing Science Series

General Editors
J. N. Buxton, R. F. Churchhouse, and A. B. Tayler

OXFORD APPLIED MATHEMATICS AND COMPUTING SCIENCE SERIES

I. Anderson: *A First Course in Combinatorial Mathematics*

D. W. Jordan and P. Smith: *Nonlinear Ordinary Differential Equations (Second Edition)*

D. S. Jones: *Elementary Information Theory*

B. Carré: *Graphs and Networks*

A. J. Davies: *The Finite Element Method*

W. E. Williams: *Partial Differential Equations*

R. G. Garside: *The Architecture of Digital Computers*

J. C. Newby: *Mathematics for the Biological Sciences*

G. D. Smith: *Numerical Solution of Partial Differential Equations (Third Edition)*

J. R. Ullmann: *A Pascal Database Book*

S. Barnett and R. G. Cameron: *Introduction to Mathematical Control Theory (Second Edition)*

A. B. Tayler: *Mathematical Models in Applied Mechanics*

R. Hill: *A First Course in Coding theory*

P. Baxandall and H. Liebeck: *Vector Calculus*

D. C. Ince: *An Introduction to Discrete Mathematics and Formal System Specification*

D. C. INCE
Open University

An Introduction to Discrete Mathematics and Formal System Specification

CLARENDON PRESS · OXFORD

Oxford University Press, Walton Street, Oxford OX2 6DP

Oxford New York Toronto
Delhi Bombay Calcutta Madras Karachi
Petaling Jaya Singapore Hong Kong Tokyo
Nairobi Dar es Salaam Cape Town
Melbourne Auckland

and associated companies in
Berlin Ibadan

Oxford is a trade mark of Oxford University Press

Published in the United States
by Oxford University Press, New York

© *D. C. Ince, 1988*
First published 1988
Reprinted 1990

British Library Cataloguing in Publication Data
Ince, D. C.
An introduction to discrete mathematics and
formal system specification
1. Finite mathematics—For computer sciences
I. Title
510
ISBN 0-19-859667-7
ISBN 0-19-859664-2 pbk

Library of Congress Cataloging in Publication Data
Ince, D. (Darrel)
An introduction to discrete mathematics and formal system
specification / D. C. Ince.
— (Oxford applied mathematics and computing science
series)
Bibliography: p.
Includes index.
1. Electronic data processing—Mathematics.   2. System design.
I. Title.   II. Series.
QA76.9.M35153   1988   004'.01'51—dc19   87-37583
ISBN 0-19-859667-7
ISBN 0-19-859664-2 (pbk)

Typeset and printed by The Universities Press (Belfast) Ltd

Preface

Formal specification is the name given to the use of discrete mathematics for describing the function of both hardware and software systems. It is a subject which is gaining popularity in the United Kingdom and the United States; it was recently made a major component of the British Government's Alvey software engineering strategy. It is now starting to impinge upon the undergraduate and postgraduate curricula.

Unfortunately, few books cover the subject at an introductory level. The books that have been written tend to assume a moderately high level of mathematical sophistication and plunge into the description of formal methods of specification immediately. This book takes a much more gentle approach; it assumes only an O-level or high-school knowledge of mathematics and teaches the mathematics of specification in an informal and relatively relaxed way.

It is split into three parts. The first part describes current approaches to developing software systems and the problems of requirements analysis and specification. In particular, it concentrates on the inadequacies of natural language. This section has been included because I have found that there is a degree of prejudice against formal methods which can only be overcome by detailed criticisms of current system-specification methods and notations.

The second section teaches the discrete mathematics necessary to specify complex systems exactly. The emphasis in this section is on modelling reality using mathematical structures. Rather than teach the mathematics in an abstract way (something which I have found tends to put computer scientists off the subject very quickly), the book draws upon real examples of software and systems.

The third section is an introduction to one notation, Z. This is a notation based on typed set theory which has been demonstrated to be an excellent medium for unambiguously specifying computer systems. The notation is taught in a more formal way than the underlying mathematics in the second section.

The book is intended for two classes of reader. The first class is students of computer science. A foundation for many computer-science degrees is a course in discrete mathematics. Very often this is taught as a service course with little regard to its utility and, consequently, students shy away from formal methods. This book can be used as a text for such an introductory course or as a text for a second- or third-year course in formal specification.

The second class of reader for which this book is intended is staff currently working on software projects who are interested in learning and applying formal methods of specification. Many such staff studied mathematics at O- or A-level when the syllabus was heavily biased towards calculus or was intended as a preparation for calculus. Consequently, little discrete mathe-matics was taught. Formal specification requires a background of discrete mathematics. Unfortunately, it can only really be studied in courses lasting more than a week or two. Many companies are loath to send key personnel on such courses; I would hope that this book would be an adequate substitute.

The book contains both worked examples and exercises. The former are enclosed in boxes and consist of a question followed by a detailed explanation of the answer. You would be advised to cover up the answers with a sheet of paper and attempt the example before proceeding with the rest of the book. The exercises are divided into short rote-type questions and longer questions designed to facilitate understanding concepts. They are mainly concentrated in the second section of the book. Again you would get full value from this book if you attempted these questions before proceeding with your reading.

There are a number of technical difficulties with formal specification. However, these difficulties shrink into insig-nificance beside the difficulty of technical transfer arising from the lack of sympathetic material. I hope that this book will go a long way towards alleviating this.

I would like to thank a number of people who have helped in the preparation of this book. First, Steve King and Bernard Sufrin of the Programming Research Group at Oxford University who commented on an early version of the book. Any errors are, of course, my fault not theirs. Second, my wife Stephanie who put up with my all too frequent absences during the writing of the book.

Milton Keynes
May 1987

D.C.I.

Contents

Part I

1 COMMERCIAL SOFTWARE DEVELOPMENT — 3

1.1 The software life cycle — 3
    1.1.1 Software requirements analysis and system specification — 3
    1.1.2 System design — 6
    1.1.3 Detailed design — 7
    1.1.4 Coding — 8
    1.1.5 Integration — 8
    1.1.6 Maintenance — 8
    1.1.7 Validation and verification — 9
1.2 Current problems in software development — 10
1.3 Formal methods of software development — 11

2 CUSTOMER REQUIREMENTS, SYSTEM SPECIFICATION, AND NATURAL LANGUAGE — 15

2.1 The contents of the statement of requirements — 15
2.2 Deficiencies in statements of requirements and specifications — 18
2.3 The qualities of a good systems specification — 23
2.4 A procedure for requirements analysis and specification — 25
2.5 An example of requirements analysis—a reactor monitoring system — 28
    2.5.1 The statement of requirements — 28
    2.5.2 An examination of the statement of requirements — 30
2.6 Mathematics and system specification — 34
2.7 Problems with formal system specification — 38

Part II

3 PROPOSITIONAL CALCULUS   43

3.1 Propositions and propositional operators   43
3.2 Contradictions and tautologies   53
3.3 Requirements analysis, system specification, and propo-
     sitional calculus   54
    3.3.1 Simplification   57
    3.3.2 Reasoning   65
        3.3.2.1 Reasoning using transformation to im-
     plication form   68
        3.3.2.2 Inference using invalid argument   74
3.4 The detection of inconsistencies   80
3.5 An example of the use of propositional calculus in the
     specification of a coupled computer system   84
3.6 Summary   90

4 PREDICATE CALCULUS   92

4.1 Propositions as predicates   93
4.2 Quantifiers as predicates   97
    4.2.1 Existential quantification   97
    4.2.2 Universal quantification   102
4.3 Proof and deduction   111
4.4 Reasoning about natural numbers   117
4.5 Predicate calculus and design specification   119
4.6 Requirements analysis and specification as the construc-
     tion of informal theories   127

5 SET THEORY   131

5.1 Sets and subsets   131
    5.1.1 Set specification   134
    5.1.2 The empty set   138
    5.1.3 Subsets and the power set   139
5.2 Set operators   141
    5.2.1 Set equality   141
    5.2.2 Set union and set intersection   142
    5.2.3 Set difference   144
    5.2.4 The cross-product   144
    5.2.5 Set cardinality   145
5.3 Reasoning and proof in set theory   145
5.4 Modelling a filing system   147

6 RELATIONS AND RELATIONAL
  OPERATORS   155
  6.1 Relations as sets of ordered pairs   155
  6.2 Relation composition   162
  6.3 The identity relation   165
  6.4 Relation restriction   167
  6.5 The transitive closure of a relation   173
  6.6 Theorems involving relations   177

7 FUNCTIONS AND SEQUENCES   180
  7.1 Functions   180
  7.2 Higher-order functions   187
  7.3 Modelling a version-control system using higher-order
       functions   190
  7.4 Functions as lambda expressions   194
       7.4.1 Curried functions   196
  7.5 Sequences as functions   196
  7.6 Applying sequences in specifications—a print spooler 199

8 INDUCTION AND RECURSIVE
  SPECIFICATION   204
  8.1 Recursive specification   204
  8.2 Numbers and induction   209
  8.3 Set induction   214
  8.4 Sequence induction   217

Part III

9 THE SPECIFICATION LANGUAGE Z   221
  9.1 Schemas   221
  9.2 The structure of Z specifications   226
       9.2.1 Schema inclusion   226
       9.2.2 Events and observations in Z   227
  9.3 Some examples of schema use   234

10 OPERATORS AND OBJECTS IN Z   238
   10.1 Numbers and sets of numbers   238
   10.2 Sets   240
   10.3 Relations   242
   10.4 Functions and sequences   246

10.4.1 Functions   246
10.4.2 Sequences   249
10.5 Modelling a back-order system   254
10.5.1 The statement of requirements   255
10.5.2 Specifying the static properties of the system   257

11 THE Z SCHEMA CALCULUS   266
11.1 Schemas as objects   266
11.2 Extending and manipulating schemas   269
11.3 Z schema conventions   273
11.4 Logical operators and schemas   280
11.5 Using the schema calculus—a simple query system for a
     spare-parts data base   281

12 Z SPECIFICATIONS IN ACTION—THE
    UNIVERSITY OF LINCOLN LIBRARY
    SYSTEM   287
12.1 The statement of requirements   287
12.2 The static properties of the system   293
12.3 The operations   300
12.4 Presenting a Z specification   319
12.5 Postscript   324

APPENDIX: DEFINITION OF Z
    OPERATORS   327

REFERENCES   341

INDEX   343

Part I

1 Commercial software development

Many readers of this book will only be familiar with programming as a software development activity. This chapter provides an introduction to a number of the more important software development activities and places the rest of the book firmly in the context of an engineering approach to software.

1.1 The software life cycle

Producing a major software system with a large number of staff, each of whom will have a wide range of competence and skills, is one of the most complex activities the human race currently undertakes.

About 20 years ago programs were very small. Perhaps the largest occupied a few hundred lines of code. Software systems now contain hundreds of thousands of lines of code and a much more disciplined engineering approach to software development has had to be adopted. It involves splitting the development process into a series of phases, each phase being associated with a distinct activity. These phases are **requirements analysis, system specification, system design, detailed design, coding, integration, operation,** and **maintenance**. Figure 1.1 shows a summary of the activities of the software life cycle.

This book is an introduction to one particular approach to the early parts of the software project. It is based on mathematics and is quite different from the majority of current techniques. In order to put the approach into context and also to point out difficulties with current software-development techniques this chapter looks in a little detail at current good practice on large software projects.

1.1.1 Software requirements analysis and system specification

The software life cycle starts with requirements analysis and system specification. The input to requirements analysis and

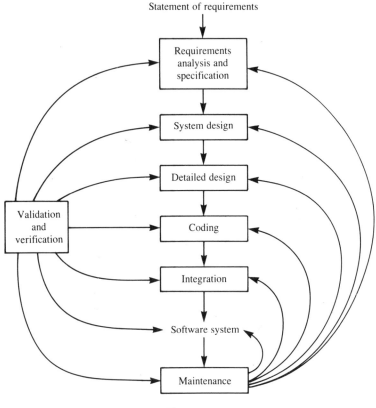

Fig. 1.1

specification is a **customer statement of requirements** (e.g. Fig. 1.2) and the output is a **software specification**. The former is the customer's idea of what a system is to do; the latter is an unambiguous version of the former.

The process of requirements analysis and system specification consists of removing errors in the statement of requirements. The end-product of this activity will be a system specification. Such a document will contain both **functional** and **non-functional** requirements.

A functional requirement is a statement of what a software system is to do. Typical functional requirements are shown

7. Storage of water-level readings

> 7.1 The software should store the hour-by-hour readings from sixteen sensors for the last three months.
>
> 7.2 The water level readings should be stored on magnetic tape which should be continually mounted.
>
> 7.3 A reading of zero indicates that a malfunction in a reservoir sensor has occurred. If more than six malfunctions occur in a day, then an error message should be displayed.

8. Query facilities

The software should enable water engineers to query stored water-level data.

> 8.1 The software should enable the average daily water level for the past three months to be displayed for any day.
>
> 8.2 The software should enable the average monthly water level for the past three months to be displayed for any of these months.
>
> 8.3 The response to these queries should be of an acceptable duration.

Fig. 1.2

below.

> When the DISPLAY command is executed the program should calculate and display the average of the last 10 transducer readings and display this figure on the operator's console.
>
> The monitoring subsystem should produce at the end of every minute an up-to-date display of reactor pressures for all those reactors connected to the primary circuit.

Non-functional requirements are those which are concerned with practical constraints upon the software developer. Typical non-functional requirements are shown below.

> The command and control subsystem should always be
> resident in main memory.
> The response to MONITOR commands should be less than
> 0.4 s—even at peak processing time.
> The system should be programmed in COBOL 74.

A critical determinant of project success is the system specification. Poor specifications have led to project overruns and major budget problems; in some cases they have led to cancellation. Early attempts have led to graphical notations (Weinberg 1980; Schoman and Ross 1977), special purpose languages (Bell *et al.* 1977; Teichrow and Hershey 1977), and notations based on mathematics (Bjorner and Jones 1982; Guttag and Horning 1978).

1.1.2 *System design*

System design is the process of defining an architecture which satisfies the system specification. It involves the designer partitioning the software into functionally related groupings known as **modules**. Such modules will consist of constants, variables, types, and program units (functions and procedures) which provide resources to carry out a series of related tasks.

The result of the system design phase is a system architecture which expresses the relationships between individual program units in a proposed system. A very simple example is shown in Fig. 1.3. It is expressed in a graphical notation known as a structure chart and shows the design of a temperature monitor. This reads temperatures from a thermocouple and displays an error message when an out-of-range value occurs. The system design uses four program units. Two of these, *get_temp* and *check_temp*, are part of the module *temp_ops* while the program unit *display_error* is part of the module *IO_ops*. *Main* represents the main program which calls the program units. The interface between the program units is represented by the data items *temp* and *error_flag*. As with all system designs the one shown in Fig. 1.3 is hierarchic: the program units *get_temp, check_temp,* and *display_error* are subordinate to *main* by virtue of the fact that they are called by *main*.

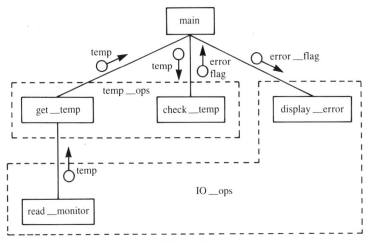

Fig. 1.3

A second task in system design is to design the data base which the developed software will use. This involves the specification of: the structure of the data base; the access methods used; and the control, security, and protection features that are to be employed.

1.1.3 Detailed design

Detailed design is the process of transforming a system design into a form in which it can be given to a programmer and implemented. It involves the design of the individual algorithms that are to be used in the developed system.

An example of a detailed design notation is shown in Fig. 1.4. It represents the design of a program unit *addup* expressed in a program design language (Cain and Gordon 1975). Such a language consists of the normal control constructs found in a programming language augmented with natural language. The function of *addup* is to read a series of 60 temperatures and find the sum of those which are between zero and one hundred degrees. As well as refining the system design, the data-base design should also be refined. This involves expanding entities

```
PROCEDURE addup (sum)
Initialize sum
FOR i TO 60 DO
    Read a temperature
    IF the temperature is between 0 and 100 THEN
        add the temperature to sum
    END_IF
END_FOR
END_PROCEDURE
```

Fig. 1.4

such as *salesman, hostile_plane, budget_deficit,* and *reactor_
record* which were defined in abstract terms during system design
into more concrete descriptions. For example, a detailed design
which dealt with an entity called *city* might define it as an
alphabetic field of a record which would contain no more than 25
characters.

1.1.4 Coding

Coding is also known as programming. It consists of processing a
detailed design and producing program code which reflects that
design. This is an almost automatic process, since the detailed
design phase will have defined the control structures and
processing that is to occur in the final system.

1.1.5 Integration

Integration is the name given to the process of taking a coded
program unit or module and adding it to a software system
during the course of construction. A developer will integrate
modules and program units into a software system gradually.
Each time that a module or program unit is integrated the
developer will have a high degree of confidence that errors
present will occur only in the module or unit that has been
integrated.

1.1.6 Maintenance

Maintenance is the term given to the changes made to a software
system after it has been put into operation. There are a number

of reasons for these changes. First, errors will have been committed which have only been discovered during operation. Second, the environment in which a software system is placed often changes during operation. For example, a new version of an operating system may be installed or a new instrument interface may be added to an existing system. Third, the requirements for the implemented system may change. For example, a customer who currently uses an accounting package may require changes to that package in order to cope with new rules for reporting VAT payments.

The increasing pressures of software maintenance place a requirement on the software engineer to devise better notations for system specification. First, in order to reduce maintenance activities due to eliminating residual errors which arise from poor specification. Second, in order to help the developer understand an existing system before modifying it in response to maintenance changes which are not due to errors.

1.1.7 Validation and verification

At certain times during a software project the evolving software product will be described by documents which specify a set of properties of the software: the customer statement of requirements will describe the customer's view of what the software should do; the system specification will describe the software developer's view of what the software should do; the system design will describe the gross architecture of a software system which satisfies the system specification; the detailed design will represent the final design of a software system; and, finally, the program code will represent the realization of the system. Each of these documents will be expressed in separate notations. A major activity that occurs throughout a software project is the detection and rectification of errors that occur in these documents. This is known as **validation and verification.**

Verification is concerned with checking that one phase in the software project accurately reflects the intentions of the previous phase. Thus, checking that the detailed design of a program unit matches its specification in the system design is an example of verification. **Validation** is concerned with checking that the product of a phase matches customer requirements. Thus, system testing, the process of executing a complete system to check that it meets requirements, is an example of validation.

Boehm (1981) characterized the process of validation as activities dedicated to answering the question 'Are we building the right product?' and verification as those activities dedicated to answering the question 'are we building the product right?'

Testing is a subset of validation and verification. It consists of processing the program code of a software system in order to carry out validation and verification. Since testing requires the use of program code, it can only occur late in the software project. Normally, the term 'testing' is associated with the multiple execution of a software system with test data. However, new techniques such as symbolic execution (Clarke 1976), static analysis (Osterweil 1983), and dynamic analysis (Miller 1977) have enlarged the range of testing strategies. Nevertheless, the majority of software projects still rely on exercising a software system with data.

1.2 Current problems in software development

A number of major problems afflict software projects. Many arise from the unsatisfactory nature of the notations used to describe a software product as it progresses through its life cycle. Typically, a developer processes a statement of requirements in natural language, produces a specification expressed in natural language, constructs a system design in a graphical notation heavily annotated with natural language, refines this design into a detailed design consisting of a set of control constructs and natural language, and then codes the system in a programming language.

In the next chapter the deficiencies of natural language will be studied in detail. At this stage it is sufficient to say that it is a medium in which it is very difficult to be precise, to state essential qualities of a software system without being cluttered by detail, and to reason with. Unfortunately, those notations which are most heavily dependent on natural language are those which occur at the beginning of the software life cycle where undetected errors can lead to massive over-runs or even total cancellation.

A second problem occurs because of the fact that developers

use a variety of notations in a software project. Often a different notation is used for each phase. This results in errors at the interface between phases.

In order to overcome many of the problems associated with current software development an increasing number of computer scientists have been turning to mathematics as a notation for describing a software product. The use of mathematics to aid in software development is known by the generic term 'formal methods'.

1.3 Formal methods of software development

The term 'formal methods' is a general description of the use of mathematical notations such as logic and set theory to describe system specifications and software designs together with techniques of validation and verification based on mathematics.

Formal methods have their roots in research on program proving during the late-1960s and early-1970s. Researchers attempted to define the function of software system using mathematics and then prove that the program code of the system met the specification.

The ultimate aim of formal methods researchers in the 1970s was the development of fully automatic proof systems. Such systems would be able to automatically decide whether a program met its specification without any testing taking place. Automatic proof systems were felt necessary because manual proof was discovered to be extremely difficult. For anything but the smallest programs, manual proof tended to be error-prone and complex. In many cases the actual proof exceeded the size of the program. Unfortunately, the complexity of the proof procedure defeated the developers of automatic proof systems, although a number of semi-automatic systems currently exist (Gerhart *et al.* 1980; Luckham *et al.* 1979; Constable and O'Donnell 1978).

The comparative failure of program proving has not diminished interest in formal methods. What it has done is to move the emphasis away from formal proof towards the notations used and towards informal demonstrations of correctness. Research in the past 10 years has concentrated on mathematics-based languages for system specification and design, together with development methods for the transformation of a software system expressed in such notations into a concrete software system.

Before examining the inadequacies of natural language in detail it would be useful to examine what formal notations can and cannot do for the software developer and also state some misconceptions that surround formal methods.

Formal methods eliminate the need for testing

Wrong, there will always be a need to test a software system. First, the customer will always require a demonstration with live data to show that a system works before he takes responsibility for it. Therefore, the developer will always have to carry out system testing and the developer and customer jointly will have to carry out acceptance testing.

There will also be a need to perform some testing during development in order to carry out a little empirical checking that errors have not been made in the mathematics used to describe the system. What can be said is that formal methods greatly reduce the amount of conventional testing required and enables errors to be discovered much earlier in the software life cycle than the coding phase.

Formal methods eliminate the need for natural language

This is another misconception. It is often stated by both the proponents and opponents of formal methods in order to support their case. The software developer will always start with a natural-language statement of requirements couched in terms of the application area. To expect otherwise would be grossly unrealistic. Also, formal specification documents will contain natural language. However, its role will be different from the role of natural language in current-project documents. In formal-specification documents natural language is used to amplify the mathematics in the same way that comments amplify program code. In current documentation natural language is the medium used to reason, to validate, and to verify. What can be said is that natural language in formal methods plays a subsidiary role to the mathematical notation rather than, at present, playing the only role.

You need a PhD in mathematics to understand formal methods

Many people believe that the use of mathematics in software development is just the invention of academics with little else to do but produce techniques and methods which represent an unattainable ideal. They believe that to employ mathematics on a software project ignores the fact that many staff will be unable to use and understand such a notation.

There are a number of answers to this. First, academics are in business to put forward ideals and to criticize the *status quo*. That is part of their job description. However, the ideals of today often end up being the working practices of tomorrow. Computer science and mathematics are full of examples of this. Research into formal language theory is now being used in the development of fast compilers for programming languages. Academics have produced results in number theory which are used in highly secure cryptographic systems. In software development academics were at the forefront of the structured programming movement.

A more serious objection is that the mathematics used is too difficult. At first sight this seems true. A formal specification document will contain Greek letters, inverted capital letters, and symbols such as $\cap$, $\exists$, and $\mathbb{P}$ which are unfamiliar to the majority of software staff. However, a formal notation is just another notation in the sense that a programming language is just a notation. I can still remember the sense of apprehension that I felt when I saw my first formal specification. It was exactly like the sense of apprehension that I felt when I saw my first program written in a language whose use I now regard as second nature.

What can be said is that the notations used in formal specification are not opaque but just unfamiliar; with sympathetic teaching such notations can be used by the majority of software staff. It has been the weakness of formal methods workers that they have not generated enough tutorial level material for readers without a mathematical background. It is the aim of this book to do just this. It teaches the mathematics in a relaxed way and introduces the application of such mathematics in one particular specification language.

If I adopt formal methods, then I will have to change my development methods

Again this is a misconception. Formal methods can be slotted into any life cycle-oriented method of software development. Of course, it will mean a developer abandoning his current notations, a task not to be underrated! However, many more techniques of validation and verification become enhanced or are more feasible with a formal notation. For example, reviews are much more effective when the participants can argue about correctness more effectively. The use of formal notations also enables prototyping to be carried out more easily since a formal specification is an exact description of the function of a software system expressed in a language with precise semantics. Such a description can be made executable or can be converted into an executable model.

2 Customer requirements, system specification, and natural language

The aim of this chapter is to examine some of the faults found in customer statements of requirements and software specifications written in natural language. The purpose in doing this is twofold. First, the document given to staff who produce the software specification is the customer statement of requirements. It is important that such staff realize the nature of such documents. Second, the inadequacies of natural language as a specification medium are most manifest in statements of requirements and software specifications. Before attempting to describe the use of mathematics in system specification, it will be useful to describe the faults that it should eliminate.

The starting point in the vast majority of software projects is the customer statement of requirements. This is an informal description of the properties of a new system or an addition to an existing system. Normally it is written in natural language; it is expressed in terms of the application area rather than computing terms. Thus, it will contain words such as: 'invoice', 'reactor', 'valve', and 'radar range' rather than words such as: 'parameter', 'module', and 'real type'.

The statement of requirements will normally require considerable processing before it becomes a viable document for development staff. The document produced is the system specification. It should be clear, consistent, and unambiguous as it forms the major reference document for subsequent activities in the software project. For example, it will be extensively used to generate acceptance tests which are used by the customer and developer to check that a completed system meets user requirements.

2.1 The contents of the statement of requirements

The statement of requirements will contain statements which detail what a system is to do. They are known as **functional**

requirements. Some simple examples of functional requirements follow.

> When the SUMMARY command is typed the average reactor temperatures of all current functioning reactors is displayed.
>
> The purpose of the command and control system is to monitor the activities of mobile units which are organized according to NATO directive NS/TC/107/ALL.
>
> The function of the report subsystem is to produce management reports on salesman performance over the current financial year.

As well as statements of function the statement of requirements will contain directives which will constrain the software developer in subsequent activities in the life cycle. They are often referred to as **non-functional requirements**. Typical examples of such requirements follow.

> The response to the CLOSE_DOWN command should be no slower than four seconds.
>
> The system should be capable of being restored to normal within one minute of a local hardware fault in any duplicated hardware unit.
>
> The programming language used should be ISO standard Pascal.
>
> All access to the 2960 filestore should be via operating system subroutines.

All the above statements constrain subsequent activities. The first requirement directs the system designer to develop an architecture which is efficient enough to respond to a command in 4 s. The second non-functional requirement directs the system designer to include a facility for dumping the state of the system to a filestore. The third and fourth non-functional requirements constrain staff involved in implementation.

A statement of requirements will also contain sentences which are **design directives** or **implementation directives**. Typical examples are

> The monitoring system should consist of a validation subsystem, a command subsystem, and a reactor monitoring subsystem.

The function of the DISPLAY command is to retrieve the salesman names contained in the main indexed sequential file and display them on the vdu [visual display unit] from which the command was typed.

When the operator types the TRAFFIC command all the traffic statistics for the last three hours will be transferred to the host computer's main memory and subsequently displayed on the vdu on which the command was typed.

The first statement is an outline of a system design. The second statement constrains the designer to use one particular file-based data structure. The third statement constrains the designer to use an algorithm which transfers *all* processed data into main memory rather than an algorithm which carries out the transfer in discrete blocks.

Such statements should be discouraged. They may overconstrain the system designer and result in an non-optimal system which, although it carries out its intended function, is not the best solution. For example, the third design instruction above may result in a system which just satisfies all its requirements. If this design instruction were eliminated and data transferred in chunks, then main memory could be released and used to hold more memory-resident software and hence increase response time.

Statements of requirements are not usually written by staff who are good designers. Such staff are unable to judge the impact of such instructions on the overall design of a system. However, there are occasionally good reasons for statements of requirements containing design instructions. For example, the second design instruction above could have been written because the salesman file may have already been implemented as part of an existing system.

A statement of requirements will often contain **goals**. These are statements which guide the software developer where choice exists. Typical goals are

In developing the system the response time should be minimized.

If possible, the amount of main memory used by the system should be as small as possible.

Such statements are used by a system designer in selecting alternative designs and making trade-offs between properties such as response time and memory utilization.

Finally, a statement of requirements will contain references to data used by a proposed system. Normally, these references are manifested in statements such as

> An employee record consists of a name, address, tax code, department, and current salary.
>
> The system should maintain the current status, temperature, and pressure of all functioning reactors.

or indirectly as

> The command PLANE_STATUS, when executed, will display at the master console the identity of each squadron together with the combat status and the number of planes undergoing routine maintenance.
>
> On receipt of the ready signal the medium-speed communication line should respond with the identity of the user currently logged into the communication terminal attached to the line.

2.2 Deficiencies in statements of requirements and specifications

Life would be uncomplicated for the software developer if both the statement of requirements and the system specification consisted of a series of sections marked

1. Functional requirements;
2. Non-functional requirements;
3. Goals;
4. Data requirements;
5. Implementation and design directives

each of which were consistent, unambiguous, and complete and where the statement of requirements would be expressed in user terms and the system specification in computing terms. Unfortunately, this very rarely happens. The purpose of this section is to outline how reality deviates from the ideal.

In general, a statement of requirements will be vague,

contradictory, incomplete, and will contain functional requirements, constraints, and goals randomly mixed at different levels
of abstraction. Often it will either have a very naive and
over-ambitious view of the capabilities of a computer system or a
view which was current a few decades ago.

Vagueness

A statement of requirements can be a very bulky document and
to achieve a high level of precision consistently is an almost
impossible task. At worst it leads to statements such as

> The interface to the system used by radar operators should
> be user-friendly.

> The virtual interface shall be based on simple overall
> concepts which are straightforward to understand and use
> and which are few in number.

The former is at too high a level of abstraction and needs to be
expanded to define requirements for help facilities, short versions
of commands, and the text of user prompts. The latter is a
platitude and should be removed from the statement of
requirements.

Contradiction

A statement of requirements will often contain functional and
non-functional requirements which are at variance with each
other. In effect they eliminate the solution space of possible
systems. Typically, the sentences that make up these contradictions will be scattered throughout the statement of requirements.
An extreme example of such a contradiction is the statement

> The water levels for the past three months should be stored
> on magnetic tape

(which may form part of the hardware requirements of a future
system) and the statement

> The command PRINT_LEVEL prints out the average water
> levels for a specified day during the past three months. The
> response of the system should be no longer than three
> seconds.

Obviously, if a slow-storage medium such as magnetic tape is

used, then the response time will hardly be in the range of a few
seconds.

A more subtle error occurs with the statements

> Data is deposited into the employee file by means of the
> WRITE command. This command takes as parameters: the
> name of the employee, the employee's department, and his
> salary.
>
> The ENTRY_CHECK command will print on the remote
> printer the name of each employee together with the date on
> which the employee's details were entered in the employee
> file.

which are functional requirements, together with the non-
functional requirement

> The hardware on which the system will be implemented
> consists of: an IBM PC with 256 k store, asynchronous I/O
> ports, keyboard, monitor, and 20 Mb hard disc.

Here the assumption made is that the employee file will contain
an entry date for each employee. Unfortunately, the WRITE
command does not take an entry date as a parameter and the
hardware specified does not include a calender/clock.

A system cannot be developed which satisfies these contradictory requirements. If this were regarded as a pure example of a
contradiction, then the ENTRY_CHECK command should be
deleted. However, the contradiction could have arisen from a set
of incomplete requirements. In this case the WRITE command
should be amended to take the entry date as a parameter or the
hardware requirement expanded to include a calendar clock.

Incompleteness

One of the most common faults in a statement of requirements is
incompleteness. An example of this follows. It shows part of the
functional requirements of a system to monitor chemical reactor
temperatures.

> The system should maintain the hourly temperatures from
> sensors which are attached to functioning reactors. These
> values should be stored for the past three months.
>
> The function of the AVERAGE command is to display on a

vdu the average daily temperature of a reactor for a specified day.

These two statements look correct. However, what happens if a user types in the AVERAGE command with a valid reactor name but for the current day? Should the system treat this as an error? Should it calculate the average temperature for the hours *up to* the hour during which the command was typed? Alternatively, should there be an hour threshold below which the command is treated as an error and, above which, the average temperature for the current day is displayed?

Mixed requirements

Rarely will you find functional requirements partitioned neatly into non-functional requirements and data requirements. Often statements about a system's function are intermixed with statements about data that is to be processed.

Naivety

Another common failing of a customer statement of requirements is that it will contain naive views of what a computer system can chieve. This will be manifested in two ways. First, the statement of requirements will contain directives and statements which underestimate the power of the computer. The most frequent transgressors seem to be electronic engineers with little experience of software who insist on hardware requirements which could be easily satisfied by software at much lower cost.

Another example of customer naivety occurs in statements of requirements for systems which can never be built within budget. Such systems are normally specified because of the low technical expertise of the customer. The most common example of requirements for an impossible system is the specification of a particular hardware configuration and a set of functions which will never meet performance requirements.

Another example of naivety occurs when a customer suffers from a grossly ambitious view of what a system is capable of. One consequence of the recent rise of interest in artificial intelligence has been a rash of statements of requirements which make the predictions of the wilder members of the artificial intelligence community seem almost sage-like!

Ambiguity

Statements of requirements written in natural language will almost always contain ambiguities. Natural language is an ideal medium for novels and poetry; indeed, its success depends on the large number of meanings that can be ascribed to a phrase or a sentence. However, it is a very poor medium for describing a computer system with precision. Some examples of imprecision are

> The operator identity consists of the operator name and his password; the password consists of six digits. It should be displayed on the security vdu and deposited in the login file when an operator logs into the system.

> When an error on a reactor overload is detected, the *error 1* screen should be displayed on the master console and the *error 2* screen should be displayed on the link console with the header line continuously blinking.

In the first statement does the word 'it' refer to the password or the operator identity? In the second statement should both consoles display a blinking header line or should it only be displayed on the link console?

Mixtures of levels of abstraction

A statement of requirements will contain sentences which are at different levels of detail. For example, the requirement

> The system should produce reports to management on the movement of all goods to and from all warehouses

and the requirement

> The system should enable a manager to display, on a vdu, the cash value of all goods delivered from a specific warehouse on a particular day. The goods should be summarized into the categories described in section 2.6 of this document.

are at different levels of abstraction. The second requirement forms part of the first requirement. In a well written statement of requirements the document should be organized into a hierarchy of paragraphs, subparagraphs, sub-subparagraphs, etc. Each level of paragraph represents a refinement of the requirement embodied in the next higher level of paragraph. In a poorly written statement of requirements connected requirements will be spread randomly throughout the document.

2.3 The qualities of a good specification

The software specification is the document produced from requirements analysis. It represents the acceptable face of the statement of requirements and is the base document which is used by all subsequent developmental activities. As such, it should demonstrate properties which should be the opposite of those outlined in the previous section. For example, where the statement of requirements is vague and incomplete the system specification should be totally precise and include answers to every conceivable question the system designer should ask.

Rather than restate the opposites of the qualities described in the previous section, it shall be taken as read that a good specification should embody the opposite qualities described in that section. However, there are some additional qualities which the system specification should have.

Customer understandability
The document should be used as a medium of communication between the developer and the customer. The software specification is a document which completely describes the characteristics of a computer system as perceived by the developer. The only way to check that requirements analysis has been carried out correctly, is by asking the customer to check the software specification. This checking can be carried out in a number of ways. First, the customer could read the specification and check it against his statement of requirements. Second, the developer could frame a number of questions to which he has already decided tentative answers. These questions would be asked of the customer and his response checked with the tentative answers. Typical questions are

What should happen if an intruder leaves primary radar space and enters secondary radar space?

Should an invoice be rejected if it doesn't contain an order
number?

If the system is in the READY state and then is switched to
the ACTIVE state while the data base is being updated what
should happen to the recovery log?

Partitionable

The system specification should be partitioned. This should
include both **vertical** and **horizontal** partitioning. Horizontal
partitioning is the separation of the system specification into
functional requirements, non-functional requirements, data requirements, hardware requirements, and goals. It also means
that each of these categories should be partitioned into logically
equivalent sections. For example, all the functional requirements
in a stock control system concerned with management reporting
should be grouped together and separated from functional
requirements for other parts of the system.

The major reason for horizontal partitioning is that it makes
validation a much more manageable proposition. For example, if
all the data requirements are grouped together, it is much easier
to check for completeness and consistency than if they were
scattered throughout hundreds of pages of a system specification.

Horizontal partitioning is also important in medium-to-large
projects where one person from the developer's staff cannot be
expected to understand all of a proposed system. It allows
customer staff with specialized skills to be involved in a well
defined part of the system specification. For example, a stores
manager would only be interested in, and knowledgeable about,
parts of a specification which concerned the movement of goods
to and from his warehouse, and would not be knowledgeable
about financial accounting functions which the company accountant would be interested in.

Vertical partitioning involves organizing a software specification into a series of levels. Each level corresponds to a level of
abstraction in the statement of requirements. This enables the
specification to be examined by staff at different levels in the
development team. For example, the designer in charge of
overall system architecture may only be interested in the highest
levels of detail, while staff engaged in specifying system tests may

only be interested in the lower levels of the specification. A software specification should be written in such a way that it can be accessed by the developer's staff without having to worry about the intrusion of higher-level or lower-level concerns. Each chunk of the specification should be readable and understandable in isolation in the same way that the individual program units in a coded software system can be understood in isolation.

Testability

A central question that should be asked by every software developer during requirements analysis is: how can I test that this requirement or set of requirements can be met by the developed software? No matter what notation is used for system specification—informal or formal—a developed system will have to undergo a series of acceptance and system tests to ensure that it meets user requirements. If the requirements embodied in the software specification are expressed in such a way that it is unclear whether an adequate test exists which validates these requirements, there is something drastically wrong. It usually means that the requirements are ambiguous or incomplete.

2.4 A procedure for requirements analysis and system specification

Requirements analysis and specification consists of a series of stages. These are shown in Fig. 2.1. First, the customer statement of requirements should be examined in order to check that the proposed system is technically feasible, that is, that it can provide every function required subject to non-functional requirements and that the developer will make an adequate profit from the enterprise.

If the system is not feasible, the developer should negotiate a modified set of requirements. This will involve removing some of the functions of the proposed system or relaxing constraints such as system performance, hardware configuration, or the cost of developing the system. If the customer agrees to the changes, the detailed requirements analysis can begin. If the customer disagrees, the project is cancelled. In a commercially tendered project this usually takes one of two forms. The first is to decline to make a bid. The second is to overbid.

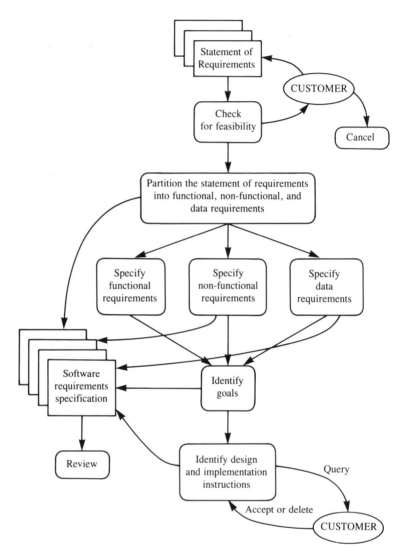

Fig. 2.1

Once the statement of requirements has been checked for feasibility, detailed requirements analysis and specification starts. This not only involves processing the customer statement of requirements, but also involves interviewing the customer's staff and examining any current manual and automated systems used by the customer. The major activity at this stage is to partition the requirements into functional, non-functional, hardware, and data requirements.

Each of these requirements should be specified as clearly as possible. Unfortunately, there are no adequate exact notations for non-functional and hardware requirements so natural language is invariably used. However, a number of exact notations are available for functional and data specification. The developer should select an appropriate notation. This book takes the view that discrete mathematics is the best one to employ for these parts of the specification.

The next stage is to identify any goals in the specification and rewrite them so they are unambiguous and complete. Next, the design and implementation instructions in the statement of requirements should be identified. It should be pointed out to the customer that by insisting on these he is reducing the probability of an optimal system being produced. The customer should then be asked to delete as many design and implementation directives as possible from the statement of requirements, preferably all of them! If any remain, they should be noted in the system specification.

A final activity is to validate the system specification to check that it is an adequate reflection of the customer's requirements. This validation is carried out jointly by the developer and the customer at a series of review meetings. It usually means the developer posing sets of questions representing stimulii and checking that his perceived response of the proposed system is not at variance with that of the customer.

One important activity which tends to get ignored during requirements analysis is the eliciting of future requirements from the customer. Software maintenance is a major developmental activity; a large part of it consists of modifying an existing system in order to respond to changing user requirements. We have now reached the position where we can design systems which are able to respond adequately to change. However, to be totally effective during the design process, the developer will need at least a partial knowledge of future requirements. The original developer of a software system will normally be in a favourable position for a future maintenance contract. Thus, it is only prudent to identify future requirements so that a robust design can be developed.

If the developer is to elicit future requirements from a customer, the activity is best left to the very last stages of requirements analysis and specification. It is difficult enough to discover current requirements without having the dialogue between the developer and the customer cluttered up with a discussion of future growth of the system.

2.5 An example of requirements analysis—a reactor monitoring system

Part of the statement of requirements for a system to monitor the state of a series of chemical reactors in a chemical plant is shown below. It is reproduced for two reasons. First, to reinforce earlier comments on the inadequacy of natural language as a medium for specification. Second, in order to illustrate the type of questions that the specifier should be asking during the process of requirements analysis. These questions are annotated in the margins of the statement of requirements.

2.5.1 The statement of requirements

Requirements for monitoring system at Ixburgh

Chemical plant 3

1. The function of the monitoring system is to **monitor** and **report** on the operational state of the **six** chemical reactors at Ixburgh Nitrogen Works.

functions any more?

2. Monitoring consists of checking that the temperature and pressure of each reactor does not exceed specified <u>limits</u>.

where are they?

3. Reporting consists of allowing process workers to interrogate a stored <u>file</u> of temperature and pressure readings stored over the past 48 hours.

function

4. Readings of pressure and temperature are transmitted along a serial line to a PDP/11 40 computer;

the format of a reading is

chemical reactor no. sensor no. flag <u>value</u>.

what are
their size?

It consists of a reactor number, the number of the
sensor which originated the reading, a zero or one
depending on whether the reading is a temperature or
a pressure, and, finally, the value of a <u>reading</u>. Each
reading is issued every second.

what
about
malfunc-
tions?

5. On receiving a temperature or pressure reading
that is outside safety limits the system should close
down the offending reactor and display its name on
the operator's console.

New
function!

6. The system should allow the plant operator to check on the
state of operation of each reactor over the past 48 hours.

(a) The operator should be able to display on his vdu the
average temperature or pressure from a specified sensor for
any number of hours.

(b) The operator should be able to display on his vdu the
number of sensor malfunctions for a specific sensor over any
number of hours.

(c) The operator should be able to display on his
vdu the name of those reactors which are currently
functioning.

Any non-
function-
ing?

7. The operator interface should be as flexible as
possible.

Platitude!

8. The system should display on the <u>subsidiary
console</u> the current temperature and pressure of all
functioning reactors for every sensor together with the
average temperature and pressure over the past 60
seconds.

what's
that?

9. The system <u>response</u> should be the maximum
possible achievable.

ambiguous

10. The system should be programmed in RTL/2. All
file handling should be performed by calls on
operating system routines. The fixed price for the
contract will be £20 000. Legal details of the contract
can be found in appendix 3.

constraints

2.5.2 An examination of the statement of requirements

Although the text seems to be liberally covered with questions indicating a poor statement of requirements the standard is not untypical of the general level encountered by industrial software developers. A description of the deficiencies of each paragraph follows.

Paragraph 1

This states what the system is to do. It is a functional requirement. Moreover, it is a functional requirement at a high level of abstraction. At this stage it is worth noting the fact that six reactors are to be monitored and ask the customer about expansion plans later in the requirements analysis phase. If there is a high possibility of more reactors being built, it may be worth noting this down so that the system designer could allow for this in the size of the system files used to hold temperature and pressure values.

Paragraph 2

Again this is a functional requirement. It is a little more specific than that described in paragraph 1. It mentions the fact that temperature and pressure should not exceed specified limits. Unfortunately, this paragraph does not specify what the limits are or refer to another part of the document which contains the limits. Also, how should the limits be communicated to the proposed system? Should they be part of the computer programs or should they be entered by the operator? If the reactors are to handle a wide variety of chemical processes, it will be worth asking the customer whether he wants an extra command to be implemented which would allow the operator to communicate the limits to the system.

Paragraph 3

This again is a functional requirement. It is at the same level of abstraction as that in paragraph 2. It also contains a design instruction. The customer has asked for pressure and tempera-ture values to be stored in a single file. Almost invariably, these values will have to be stored in backing storage but there is no reason why they cannot be stored in two separate files. Indeed, if they were stored in one file, it would involve the developer in unnecessary program complexity. The customer should be strongly advised to eliminate this requirement.

Paragraph 4

This is a data specification. It also mentions, as an aside, a hardware constraint. This data specification is incomplete. It does not give the size of each reading, it does not detail how many sensors there are, and it does not give the size of each field in a reading. Moreover, it does not specify whether a pressure reading will occupy the same number of bits as a temperature reading.

A large number of readings have to be stored in the temperature and pressure file and so the developer should check that the hardware requirements allow for this.

The paragraph also states that the readings of temperature and pressure will be transferred along *one* serial transmission line to the monitoring computer. If we assume that, say, two temperatures and two pressure sensors are attached to each of the six reactors, will the pattern of readings transmitted along the line be of the form

> Reactor 1 Temperature 1
>
> Reactor 1 Temperature 2
>
> Reactor 1 Pressure 1
>
> Reactor 1 Pressure 2
>
> ⋮
>
> Reactor 6 Pressure 1
>
> Reactor 6 Pressure 2?

This may seem a trivial question but monitoring equipment malfunctions, particularly in the harsh environment of a chemical reactor. One manifestation of such a malfunction is an impossible reading such as a negative value or a missing reading. A later section of the requirements may ask for some function to be carried out if a malfunction occurs. Thus, it is vitally important to discover the pattern of readings in order to detect a malfunction.

Paragraph 5

Potentially, this paragraph is the most dangerous in the whole statement of requirements. It could lead to massive increased costs on the project. In paragraph 1 it was stated that the function of the proposed system was monitoring and reporting. Paragraph 5 introduces a completely new major function: control. If this involves sending a simple signal to an existing and already programmed computer, this should be relatively straightforward. However, if the customer is also expecting the developer to produce the control software which causes the shut-down of a reactor, it introduces an added massive complexity into the system.

Another question that the developer should ask concerns the safety limits. One manifestation of a sensor malfunction is that it produces a reading that is outside safety limits. For example, a sensor which measures a temperature between 20 and 1000° may produce an intermittent reading of 0° when it malfunctions. At this stage the software developer should establish what are reasonable values for readings and what values can be regarded as indicating a malfunction.

This paragraph also contains the first reference to a reactor name. Previously in paragraph 4 the reactor number had been referred to. It makes good sense for the interface to the system to be in terms of reactor name *and* sensor names. In which case how are these names to be associated with the corresponding reactor numbers and sensor numbers? Should the system dynamically allow the operator to assign and de-assign names and numbers? Finally, the paragraph mentions an 'operator'. Is this the same as the term 'process worker' used in requirement 3?

Paragraph 6

This is a series of functional requirements which are an expansion of those requirements in paragraph 3 and hence lie at a lower level of abstraction. Requirements 6(a) and 6(b) contain an ambiguity. It is associated with the phrase: '. . . for a specific sensor for any number of hours'. Does this mean that an operator types in two hours and information about either temperature, pressure, or sensor malfunction is displayed for the time between these two hours? This begs a further set of questions.

What should the operator type if he wants to display information about temperature, pressure, or sensor malfunction for just one hour?

What should happen if one of the hours typed is the current hour?

What should the format of the hours typed be?

At first sight requirement 6(c) looks innocent. However, it mentions the fact that some reactors may not be functioning. If the reason for a non-functioning reactor is that it has been closed down because of a dangerous pressure or temperature reading, then this is consistent with paragraph 5. However, there may be other reasons for a non-functioning reactor. For example, a reactor may have closed down for routine maintenance. If other reasons exist, they may be hidden in later sections of the statement of requirements together with functions associated with closing down a reactor. There may even be a function concerned with starting up a reactor. Already paragraph 5 has alerted us to the fact that the proposed system may not be as simple as paragraph 1 had led us to believe.

This paragraph also contains the first reference to a sensor malfunction. No doubt a later paragraph will detail the function to be carried out when such a malfunction is detected!

Paragraph 7

This means nothing at all. The customer should be asked for a precise formulation. It possibly means that short versions of each command should be recognized by the system and that optional parameters should be catered for. It could also mean that some form of help facility should be provided. However, whatever the meaning, it should be made precise.

Paragraph 8

This is a functional requirement and is also the first reference to a subsidiary console. In paragraph 6 an operator's vdu was mentioned; it looks very much like two vdus are required for the system. The final line of the paragraph also contains an ambiguity. Should the average pressure or temperature for the last 60 seconds be displayed as an average of all the sensors in a particular reactor? Perhaps the 60-second average should be displayed for each sensor?

Paragraph 9

This is a goal. Unfortunately, it is not specified exactly as the words 'system response' are ambiguous. Does it mean the speed at which the system responds to operator queries or does it mean the speed with which a reactor can be closed down?

Paragraph 10

This consists of a series of constraints which reduce the possible solution space of system designs which implement the requirements of the system.

2.6 Mathematics and system specification

The previous section described in some detail the painstaking approach that a software developer has to adopt in analysing customer requirements. Even with the small number of paragraphs shown, a large number of questions were asked and a large number of faults, ambiguities, and vague statements discovered. Many statements of requirements are much longer than 10 paragraphs of text. Consequently, the process of requirements analysis is the most difficult activity carried out by the software developer.

The system specification so produced should represent an amplification of the statement of requirements with all the faults removed. Because of the need to be precise such documents are often extremely bulky. The system specification for a recent American fighter plane occupied over 23 volumes of text. Theoretically, the system specification represents a correct and amplified version of the statement of requirements. What actually happens in practice is that, because of the nature of natural language and the size and complexity of current systems, many faults remain. In a sense, these faults are much more serious than those found in a statement of requirements: they tend to be spread out more in a bulkier document and are hence more difficult to detect during validation. In an attempt to alleviate many of the problems associated with requirements analysis and specification and the use of natural language, software engineers are turning to mathematics. Mathematics has a number of properties which are desirable for system specification.

It is easy to represent levels of abstraction

A simple example can demonstrate this. Assume that a mathematician wishes to differentiate the expression

$$\sin(x^2 + \exp(x^3 + 4)).$$

He thinks of the expression as

$$\sin(u)$$

where u is $x^2 + \exp(x^3 + 4)$. Differentiating $\sin(u)$ gives

$$\cos(u)u'.$$

The mathematician now has to differentiate u which is

$$x^2 + \exp(x^3 + 4)$$

to find u'. He thinks of this as

$$x^2 + \exp(w)$$

where w is $x^3 + 4$. Differentiating this gives

$$2x + w' \exp(w),$$

which is

$$2x + 3x^2 \exp(x^3 + 4).$$

Substituting back for u then gives the differential as

$$\cos(x^2 + \exp(x^3 + 4))(2x + 3x^2 \exp(x^3 + 4)).$$

In order to carry out the fairly complex operation of differentiating a large expression, the expression has been represented at various levels of abstraction. These are

$$\sin(u)$$
$$\text{where } u = x^2 + \exp(w)$$
$$\text{where } w = x^3 + 4.$$

By doing this the mathematician has controlled the complexity of the problem by enabling the problem to be expressed as tractable pieces of mathematics.

As will be seen later in this book, the power of mathematics for representing levels of abstraction and for manipulating parts of expressions in isolation makes it an excellent medium for system specification.

It is easy to reason in mathematics

One of the characteristics of mathematics is its ability to deduce useful results, or to check results from propositions using rules of reasoning and theorems. Many of the readers of this book will remember learning geometric proofs which have chains of reasoning containing sentences such as:

> A triangle is a bounded figure which has three sides.
>
> If a figure is a triangle and the angle between two sides is a right angle, the triangle is a right-angled triangle.
>
> If a figure is a triangle and all the sides are equal, it is an equilateral triangle.
>
> If a line is drawn from the vertex of an equilateral triangle and this line bisects the opposite side, the two triangles so formed will be right-angled triangles.

There is no difference between these statements and those that are used when reasoning occurs during system specification. For example,

> If a reactor is shut down because of a malfunction or because of maintenance activity, the reactor can be regarded as closed down.
>
> If a reactor is closed down and an operator types the STATE command, a state error occurs.
>
> If a state error occurs, an error message will be displayed on the operator's console and a state error entry written to the error log file.

No mathematician would use natural language to represent such statements in a chain of reasoning and in justifying conclusions. Similarly, the need for precisely representing a specification and justifying chains of reasoning requires mathematics during the software project.

Mathematics is concise

Natural language is verbose. It contains a large number of noise words. Whenever long concepts are described or referred to they have to be written in full. Thus, terms such as 'the last currently malfunctioning reactor', 'the current ready state of the functioning reactors', and 'the last update transaction which has originated from a remote accounting location' may occur many times throughout a system specification. Even with paragraphs which express relatively straightforward functions the effect of such verbosity is to mask the essential details of a function.

More importantly, mathematics contains concepts which can be used to represent complicated relations that can only be expressed in a very large number of words.

Mathematics has well-defined and unambiguous meanings

Already this book has given a large number of examples of imprecision in natural language. Mathematics lies at the other end of the spectrum. A small and rather simple example of how mathematics is able to give more precision to a specification is shown below with the sentence

The lamp voltage will always be a whole number of volts between 3 to 6 volts

and the mathematical expression

lamps >= 3 AND lamps <= 6.

The former is ambiguous, does it mean that the voltages will include 3 volts and 6 volts?. The mathematical equivalent answers this question as there is no possibility of a number of interpretations.

Mathematics can be used to model reality

One characteristic of an engineering process is the use, by its practitioners, of mathematics to model reality. The electronic engineer uses circuit theory and idealized models of elements such as resistors and capacitors to design circuits; the civil engineer uses statics and dynamics to calculate stress and the peak loading of structures which have to carry traffic. In both cases mathematics is used to reason about a simplified but useful model of reality. If software engineering is to be regarded as a true engineering discipline, the same process ought to hold. The second part of this book describes a branch of mathematics which is used to model complex computer systems. The mathematics is taught in the context of describing real software systems. By the time that you have completed that section you should be convinced of the utility of mathematics in practical software development.

Mathematics can be used to suppress unnecessary detail.

This occurs for a number of reasons. A very trivial one is the fact that a symbol can stand for a complex structure. A more important reason is the abstract properties of pure mathematics. Mathematicians are more interested in properties of objects rather than concrete values. Thus a geometer is more interested in the fact that a square has equal sides rather than in the values of these sides. Mathematics can be used to describe entities such as files, tables, and queues without worrying about concrete details such as the medium on which the entities are stored or the capacity of these structures, concerns which are not important during the functional specification process. A good specification notation should be sufficiently abstract to leave the system designer with a large solution space of possible designs without constraining him with concrete details which will emerge from the design process. Mathematics is the ideal medium for this.

Mathematics is constant

The mathematics taught in the next part of this book has been used for at least a century. It will always be taught in colleges, universities, and schools as it forms the basis of pure mathematics. We are currently afflicted with many new notations for specification and design, many of which have proved transitory. Mathematics holds out the hope that it will provide a stable notation to describe the functionality and data of complex systems

2.7 Problems with formal system specification

Before concluding this section it is only fair to point out some current problems and criticisms that have been voiced about formal methods of specification.

The customer cannot understand the software specification

A software specification which is expressed in mathematics can, at best, be only understood by the developer's staff. Clearly, it is impractical to expect an accountant or a middle-level manager from the customer's staff to understand pure mathematics.

The proponent of formal methods will say that deriving a software specification expressed in mathematics enables him to ask the customer a series of penetrating questions and that these questions are much more useful and lead to a clearer specification than if a natural-language specification was used. This is true up to a point. Requirements analysis becomes a much more goal-oriented activity using mathematics; our limited experience of formal methods has shown that deeper questions about the properties of a system can be easily formulated leading to the discovery of major errors.

However, there is still a problem and it is this: a software specification is often a major reference document for the customer as well as the developer and often forms part of a binding contract; there must be a way of animating such a document so that a customer can understand it.

Very little work has been carried out in this area. One promising approach is to make a mathematical specification executable. This would enable the developer to prototype a system immediately after system specification is complete.

There is a major technology transfer problem

This problem is more serious than the preceding one. While the mathematics of system specification is not particularly difficult, it is unfamiliar to the bulk of development staff. Even those staff who have studied mathematics to an advanced level in school will find this notation strange since many of our mathematics courses are still dominated by real-number mathematics such as calculus. There is evidence that the mathematics that is required for system specification is gradually percolating through to the schools; nevertheless, the vast majority of software developers regard it as unfamiliar and over-academic.

There is a second problem which is connected with technology transfer. Those books which describe formal methods pay little attention to the mathematics. At best such books contain a mini-course of a few pages; at worst, they contain a reference to bone up on a particular pure mathematics book. This is understandable: the writer of a formal methods book wants to write a book on formal methods not a mathematics book. However, it does presuppose the existence of adequate preparatory material.

This book has been designed to alleviate the problems connected with such technology transfer. It teaches the mathematics in an informal and sympathetic way and shows how mathematics can be embodied in a particular specification notation known as Z. It would be easy to teach the mathematics involved in fairly abstract way as most pre-computing texts do. This course has been rejected. The mathematics taught is always applied. Whenever a new concept is introduced, it is illustrated with reference to requirements analysis and specification.

Part II

3 Propositional calculus

The process of system specification and requirements analysis involves examining the behaviour of a proposed software system and asking questions which enable a correct system specification to be developed. For example, the text of a statement of requirements may contain sentences such as

> If the reactor is on-line and the operator has typed a query command, the query log will be updated.

> If the operator has typed a query command from a secure terminal, then the command is allowed; otherwise a security error will have occured.

> If the system has been configured as being highly secure, then a message will be flashed on the master console when a security error occurs; otherwise, a violation message will be written to the violation log file.

The requirements analyst may take statement such as those above and formulate queries such as

> What events cause the query log to be updated?

> If a reactor is off-line and an operator types a query command then what will happen?

In the example above the queries may need to be answered by examining fairly dense prose. What is required is a compact representation of the sentences, together with a means for enabling staff to reason about the proposed system. This is the role of the branch of pure mathematics known as **propositional calculus**.

3.1 Propositions and propositional operators

A proposition is a statement that can be either true or false. Typical examples from natural-language system specifications are

The system is in shut-down mode.

The ALARM command has been typed.

An update file has been created.

No sign-off messages have been received in the past hour.

Such propositions can be represented as propositional variables which can be manipulated in the same way as algebraic variables. For example, the proposition 'the escape valve is open' can be represented by the propositional variable *esc_valve_open* and the proposition 'the reactor is in an error state' can be represented as the propositional variable *in_error_state*. Such propositional variables can have true (T) values or false (F) values.

More complex propositions can be built up from propositional variables and a series of operators. These are

negation	**not**	or ¬
conjunction	**and**	or ∧
disjunction	**or**	or ∨
Exclusive disjunction	**exor**	or $\vee_e$
implication	**imp**	or ⇒
equality	**equals**	or ⇔

Each of these operations can be represented by the words shown in the second column or the symbols in the last column. Throughout this book the latter course will be adopted.

Negation creates the opposite of a proposition. Thus, if *valve_open* stands for the proposition: 'the escape valve is open' then ¬*valve_open* stands for: 'the escape valve is not open'. The operator ¬ is an example of a **monadic** operator because it is applied to one argument.

The conjunction operator joins two propositions together to form another proposition; because of this it is known as a **dyadic** operator. The effect of the conjunction operator is to place the word *and* between its two arguments. Thus, if *valve_closed* stands for the proposition 'the escape valve is closed' and *shut_down* stands for 'the reactor has been shut down', then *valve_closed* ∧ *shut_down* stands for: 'the escape valve is closed and the reactor has been shut down'.

The disjunction operator is dyadic. The effect of this operator is to place the word *or* between its arguments. Thus, if *valid_command* stands for the proposition 'a valid command has been typed in at the console' and *error* stands for 'an operator error has occurred', *valid_command* ∨ *error* stands for the proposition 'a valid command has been typed in at the console or an operator error has occurred'.

The exclusive disjunction operator is dyadic. It is similar to the disjunction operator; however, it differs in one respect. It states that either one of its operands may be true but not both at the same time. Thus, *valve_closed* ∨ *shut_down* asserts that either *valve_closed* is true or *shut_down* is true or both *valve_closed* and *shut_down* are true while *valve_closed* ∨$_e$ *shut_down* asserts that either *valve_closed* is true or *shut_down* is true but that both are not true.

The implication operator is dyadic. It describes that fact that one proposition implies another. The standard interpretation of the proposition

$$a \Rightarrow b$$

is 'If *a* then *b*'. For example, if the propositional variable *functioning* stands for 'the reactor is functioning normally', the propositional variable *valid_command* stands for 'a valid command has been typed', and the propositional variable *executed* stands for the proposition 'the command will have been executed', then

functioning ∧ valid_command ⇒ executed

stands for the proposition

> If the reactor is functioning normally and a valid command
> has been typed, then the command will have been executed.

The left-hand operand of the implication operator is known as the **antecedent** and the right-hand operand is known as the **consequent**. Thus, in the example above, *functioning* ∧ *valid_command* is the antecedent and *executed* is the consequent.

The final operator is the equality operator; again it is dyadic. It is similar to the equality operator of algebra. It is equivalent to the English phrases 'exactly when', 'only when', and 'if and only if'. Thus, if *valve_open* stands for 'the inlet valve is open', *mixer_working* stands for 'the main mixer is working', and *normal_state* stands for 'the system is in a normal state', the proposition *valve_open* ∧ *mixer_working* ⇔ *normal_state* is equivalent to the proposition

> Only when the inlet valve is open and the main mixer is working will the system be in a normal state.

It is quite easy to confuse up the meanings of implication and equality. An example will make their use clearer. The propositional expression

main_valve_open ⇒ inlet_closed

states that, when the main valve of a chemical reactor is open, the inlet to the reactor is closed i.e. you can be sure that if you examine the main valve and it is open then it is certain that the inlet is closed. What it does not say is that if you examine the inlet and find it closed, you can be sure that the valve is open. The inlet may have been closed by an event which had nothing to do with the operation of the main valve; for example, a build up of sludge may have blocked the inlet. However, the propositional expression

main_valve_open ⇔ inlet_closed

states that *only when* the main valve is opened will the inlet be closed, i.e. if you examine the main valve and find it open, you can be sure that the inlet is closed and, if you examine the inlet and find it closed, you can be sure that the main valve is open.

Except for the implication operator the order of arguments of logical operators is irrelevant, for example, *valve_closed* ∧ *system_down* is equivalent to *system_down* ∧ *valve_closed*. The names of the operators correspond to their meaning in English and large tracts of system specifications can be converted into propositional calculus form.

Example 3.1

A system specification contains the sentence

> If the mixer has been activated and the inlet valve has been opened, the reactor is working normally.

Reduce this sentence to propositional calculus.

This sentence contains three propositions which can be expressed as the propositional variables: *mixer_activated, valve_open,* and *reactor_normal.* The sentence embodies an implication and can be written as

mixer_activated $\wedge$ valve_open $\Rightarrow$ reactor_normal.

This answer assumes, of course, that there may be other conditions under which the reactor will be working normally. If there were not, the implication operator would be replaced by the equality operator $\Leftrightarrow$.

Example 3.2

Part of a system specification contains the sentences

1.1   There are only two valid commands which can be typed. They are the CHECK_TRAFFIC command and the CHECK_POPULATION command.

1.2   Only if a valid command has been typed in by an authorized user will the comand be executed normally.

1.3   If an invalid command has been typed and an authorized user has typed the command, an invalid command error is displayed.

1.4   If an unauthorized user types a command, then a warning screen (UNAUTHORIZED USER) is displayed on the master console and a violation error is written to the log file.

Reduce each sentence to propositional calculus form.

The translation of the sentences into propositional calculus is

check_traffic $\vee$ check_population $\Leftrightarrow$ valid_command
valid_command $\wedge$ authorized_user $\Leftrightarrow$ normal_execution
$\neg$valid_command $\wedge$ authorized_user $\Rightarrow$ invalid_error
$\neg$authorized_user $\Leftrightarrow$
unauthorized_screen $\wedge$ violation_error.

The first two propositions obviously involve the equality operator. The phrases 'only if' and 'only' make this clear. The fourth proposition also involves the equality operator since it is hard to see whether any other events would cause an unauthorized user screen to occur. However, in real life one would have to check the rest of the statement of requirements to ensure the correct use of the equality operator. The third proposition involves an implication operator as it is not clear from the fragment whether an invalid command error will occur when other events occur. For example, it is not quite clear whether an unauthorized user typing an invalid command will cause an invalid command error.

Note that it would have been just as correct to write the third proposition as

invalid_command $\wedge$ authorized_user $\Rightarrow$ invalid_error.

However, it would have introduced a superfluous propositional variable which would have added extra complexity to the processing of the system specification.

Exercise 3.1

Rewrite the following natural-language sentences using propositional calculus. Assume that the $\Rightarrow$ operator will normally be used rather than the $\Leftrightarrow$ operator, unless, of course, the wording of a sentence explicitly makes equivalence clear—for example, by using the pharase 'if and only if'. Also assume that the $\vee$ operator is used unless the wording makes it clear that the $\vee_e$ operator is to be used.

(i) The reactor is in either of two states. The first state is that it is functioning normally; the second state is that the reactor is shut down.

(ii) The user has typed his personal identifier and typed a group identifier.

(iii) Either the file will have been dumped to magnetic tape or it will be marked for archiving.

(iv) If the file has been marked for archiving and has not been used today then it will be archived.

   (v) If a transmission line sends a ready signal and the receiver is on-line, then the link is established and a message is sent to the master console.

  (vi) The receiver will only receive a ready message if the line is available.

 (vii) If the update program has terminated with a transaction error, then a return message is sent to the operator and the program is aborted. If any program is aborted, then a termination message is sent to the current log file and the wasted time counter is updated.

(viii) If the file sever is not on-line or the print server is not on-line, then the system will not be started.

So far the propositions which have been constructed have been relatively simple. However, when complex systems are specified, propositions will involve a number of operators and propositional variables. Typical expressions are

not_available $\land$ out_of_action $\lor$ invalid_temp $\Rightarrow$
non_functioning
$\neg$updated $\lor$ $\neg$deleted $\Rightarrow$ available $\lor$ writing $\lor$ reading.

When complex expressions are written, there is a question about the order in which they are evaluated. This is the same problem that occurs in evaluating algebraic expressions in programming languages. The solution adopted in propositional calculus is exactly the same as that adopted for programming languages: it involves specifying the precedence of operators. The rules of precedence adopted for propositional calculus are

1. Sequences of the same operator are evaluated from left to right, for example, *old_file* $\lor$ *new_file* $\lor$ *updated_file* is equivalent to ((*old_file* $\lor$ *new_file*) $\lor$ *updated_file*).

2. The order of evaluation of different, but adjacent, operators is given by the following order of precedence

$$\neg, \land, \lor, \Rightarrow, \Leftrightarrow.$$

$\neg$ has the highest order of precedence and $\Leftrightarrow$ has the lowest order.

Thus,

$$\neg\text{active} \wedge \text{monitoring}$$

is equivalent to

$$(\neg\text{active}) \wedge \text{monitoring}$$

and

$$\text{oldfile} \vee \text{newfile} \Leftrightarrow \text{read\_file} \wedge \neg\text{write\_file}$$

is equivalent to

$$(\text{oldfile} \vee \text{newfile}) \Leftrightarrow (\text{read\_file} \wedge (\neg\text{write\_file})).$$

Normally, when complex propositional expressions are written it is often necessary to make wise use of brackets in order to make the meaning of the propositions clear.

Example 3.3

For the two propositions below indicate the order of evaluation by means of brackets.

(i) $\neg\text{old\_file} \vee \text{new\_file} \Rightarrow \text{deposit\_file} \Rightarrow$
    new_event.

(ii) new $\wedge$ old $\wedge$ modified $\vee \neg$updated $\Rightarrow$
    valid_event.

(i) $(((\neg\text{old\_file}) \vee \text{new\_file}) \Rightarrow \text{deposit\_file}) \Rightarrow$
    new_event.

(ii) $(((\text{new} \wedge \text{old}) \wedge \text{modified}) \vee (\neg\text{updated})) \Rightarrow$
    valid_event.

Although the brackets are used to indicate the order of evaluation, it is usually unnecessary to write every possible set of brackets in order to make a proposition clear. For example, (i) is best written as

$$((\neg\text{old\_file} \vee \text{new\_file}) \Rightarrow \text{deposit\_file}) \Rightarrow \text{new\_event}$$

and (ii) is best written as it stands in the question.

Example 3.4

Enclose the following propositional expressions in brackets in order to make their meaning clear. Do not use superfluous brackets if you think they are not needed.

   (i) ¬read_event ∧ old_event ⇒ valid_event ⇒ global_event.
   (ii) message ∧ deposited ⇒ ¬new_message ∧ old_message.

   (i) (¬read_event ∧ old_event ⇒ valid_event) ⇒ global_event.
   (ii) Although bracketing is a personal thing, I would say that no brackets are required. The meaning is fairly clear from the propositional expression.

Exercise 3.2

Show the order of evaluation of the following expressions by using brackets.

   (i) ¬ ¬old_file_updated.
   (ii) new_reactor_on-line ∧ old_reactor_on-line ∨ error_event.
   (iii) valid_command ∧ operating ⇒ action_executed.
   (iv) transmission_started ⇒ line_open ⇒ handshake_ok.
   (v) edit_command ∨ delete_command ∨ directory_command.
   (vi) ¬edit_command ⇔ directory_command ∧ normal_command ⇒ ok_state.

Up until now the syntax of propositions has been described. An informal semantics has been given in terms of natural-language interpretations. However, the time has now arrived to give a precise meaning. This is embodied in a series of tables known as **truth tables**. Table 3.1 is a truth table for the operators

Table 3.1

A	B	¬A	A ∧ B	A ∨ B	A ⇒ B	A ⇔ B	A ∨$_e$ B
F	F	T	F	F	T	T	F
F	T	T	F	T	T	F	T
T	F	F	F	T	F	F	T
T	T	F	T	T	T	T	F

described previously. The first two columns in Table 3.1 show possible values for the propositional variables *a* and *b*. Other columns indicate values when the propositional operators are applied. Thus, when *a* is false and *b* is false, $a \Rightarrow b$ is true and $a \vee b$ is false.

Given the order of precedence of propositional operators, the value of propositional expressions can be calculated using Table 3.1. For example, the expression

$$\neg\text{valve\_open} \wedge \text{malfunction} \Rightarrow \text{error\_report} \vee \text{shut\_down}$$

has the value T when *malfunction* has the value T, *valve_open* has the value T, *error_report* has the value T, and *shut_down* has the value F. The order of evaluation is

$$\neg\text{valve\_open} \wedge \text{malfunction} \Rightarrow \text{error\_report} \vee \text{shut\_down}$$

$$\neg\text{T} \wedge \text{malfunction} \Rightarrow \text{error\_report} \vee \text{shut\_down}$$

$$\text{F} \wedge \text{T} \Rightarrow \text{error\_report} \vee \text{shut\_down}$$

$$\text{F} \Rightarrow \text{T} \vee \text{shut\_down}$$

$$\text{F} \Rightarrow \text{T} \vee \text{F}$$

$$\text{F} \Rightarrow \text{T}$$

$$\text{T.}$$

The evaluation of a fairly simple expression seems to have taken a large number of steps. However, after a large amount of practice you will find that there are a number of shortcuts. For example, when a series of conjunctions

$$C_1 \wedge C_2 \wedge C_3, \ldots, \wedge C_n$$

is encountered and one of the terms in the expression is false, then the whole expression is false. Similarly, if a series of disjunctions

$$C_1 \vee C_2 \vee C_3, \ldots, \vee C_n$$

is encountered and one of the terms is true, the whole expression is true. In evaluating an implication, if the antecedent is false, then the implication becomes true irrespective of the value of the consequent. Similarly, if the consequent of an implication is true then the implication is true irrespective of the value of the antecedent.

Exercise 3.3

What are the values of the propositional expressions shown below? Assume that the propositional variables have the values

valve_open	T	malfunction	F
valid_command	T	flow_ok	T.

(i) flow_ok ∧ valve_open ∧ malfunction.

(ii) flow_ok ∨ valve_open.

(iii) ¬flow_ok ∨ malfunction ∨ valve_open.

(iv) valid_command ∧ ¬malfunction ∨ valve_open.

(v) (valid_command ∨ ¬valve_open) ∧ (flow_ok ⇒ valve_open).

(vi) ¬ ¬flow_ok ⇒ malfunction ∨ valid_command.

(vii) valve_open ⇒ malfunction ⇒ valid_command.

(viii) ((flow_ok ⇔ ¬valve_open) ⇒ valid_command) ∧ ¬flow_ok.

(ix) (¬(malfunction ∨ flow_ok)) ⇒ malfunction.

(x) valve_open ⇔ malfunction ⇔ flow_ok ⇒ valve_open ⇔ flow_ok.

(xi) ¬ ¬ ¬(flow_ok ⇒ (malfunction ∧ valve_open)).

(xiii) ¬(flow_ok ∨$_e$ malfunction).

3.2 Contradictions and tautologies

Two important types of propositions are known as **tautologies** and **contradictions**. A tautology is true for all possible values of the variables which make up the proposition. An example of a

Table 3.2

open	malfunction	error_state	(open ∧ malfunction ∧ error_state) ⇒ (error_state ⇒ open)
T	T	T	T
T	T	F	T
T	F	T	T
T	F	F	T
F	T	T	T
F	T	F	T
F	F	T	T
F	F	F	T

trivial tautology is

$$a \lor \neg a$$

which is true for values of a of T and F. A trivial contradiction is

$$a \land \neg a$$

which is false for all values of a.

One way of discovering whether a propositional expression is a contradiction or a tautology is to evaluate it for all possible values of the variables that comprise the expression. For example, the proposition

$$(\text{open} \land \text{malfunction} \land \text{error\_state}) \Rightarrow (\text{error\_state} \Rightarrow \text{open})$$

can be demonstrated to be a tautology as shown in Table 3.2. For very large propositional expressions this method is clearly impractical. A later section will describe a more convenient way of discovering tautologies and contradictions.

3.3 Requirements analysis, system specification, and propositional calculus

When requirements analysis and specification is carried out it involves a number of activities. First, the statement of requirements should be simplified. Second, any contradictions are removed. Third, any **ambiguities** should be made precise and the system specification validated with the customer. The system specification so formed should be precise and concise.

Propositional calculus by itself is not adequate for system specification. Later sections of this book will describe other notations which use the ideas presented in this chapter and which rely on propositional calculus as their logical basis. However, in order to give an early flavour of the utility of mathematics in system specifications, this section will describe how propositional calculus can be used as a medium for the specification of relatively small and artificial systems.

First, expressing parts of a system specification in propositional calculus will always condense the specification. Simplification can be achieved by applying a series of simplication rules in the same way that algebraic simplification rules can be used to simplify an expression such as

$$a * (b + c)^2 - (ab^2 + ac^2 + abc)$$

to
$$abc.$$

Later in this chapter simplification rules for propositional calculus will be described.

Second, propositional calculus allows contradictions to be removed. For example, a system specification containing the sentence

> The system is in an alert state only when it is waiting for an intruder and is on practice alert.

can be written as

$$alert \Leftrightarrow waiting \wedge practice.$$

If a later paragraph contained the sentences

> If the system is in teaching mode and is on practice alert, then it is in an alert state.

> The system will be in teaching mode and on practice alert and not waiting for an intruder.

Then these propositions can be written as

$$teaching \wedge practice \Rightarrow alert$$
$$teaching \wedge practice \wedge \neg waiting.$$

As will be seen later in this chapter, propositional calculus allows these expressions to be manipulated in order to show that a contradiction can be formed from the first propositional expression and the second and third propositional expression and deduce that there was an error in the specification.

Now this is a simple example and could have been discovered by reading the natural-language specification. However, in real statements of requirements, contradictions are almost invariably embedded in many layers of paragraphs where connections between propositions are hidden in many levels of reference. In this case the use of a mathematical formalism is almost mandatory.

Third, propositional calculus enables ambiguities to be clarified and removed. For example, consider the sentence

> If the inlet valve is open, then the system is switched to OPEN and the outlet valve is closed if the monitoring system is functioning.

How should this be written using propositional logic? One interpretation is

$$\text{in\_valve\_open} \Rightarrow (\text{mon\_sys\_functioning} \Rightarrow$$
$$\text{open} \wedge \text{outlet\_closed}).$$

Another interpretation is

$$\text{in\_valve\_open} \Rightarrow (\text{open} \wedge (\text{mon\_sys\_functioning} \Rightarrow$$
$$\text{outlet\_closed})).$$

The fact that the analyst is forced into translating something imprecise into an exact notation enables hard questions about meaning to be posed. Such questions can be asked of the customer. The fact that the system specifier is forced to construct a mathematical document means that very close attention has to be paid to the natural-language text of the statement of requirements.

Finally, a system specification expressed in propositional calculus enables the system specifier to frame questions to the customer in order to check that his interpretation of the statement of requirements is correct. For example, a specification contained the propositions

> alert_state $\Rightarrow$ normal alert $\lor$ practice
>
> normal_alert $\land$ monitor_typed $\Rightarrow$ error1
>
> practice $\land$ monitor_typed $\Rightarrow$ error1

A developer is able to frame questions such as

> If the system is in an alert state and the operator typed a MONITOR command, would an error 1 occur?

and

> What events cause an error 1?

Again this is a very simple example. Much more complicated examples will be described later. The purpose of this chapter is to give you the tools which will enable you to carry out requirements analysis and system specification using propositional calculus and other mathematical formalisms described in later chapters.

3.3.1 Simplification

Simplification of propositional expressions is carried out in the same way that algebraic expressions are simplified. There are propositional laws similar to algebraic laws such as

$$a * 1 = a$$
$$a * (b + c) = a * b + a * c.$$

There are 12 laws. If you wish to be totally proficient at formal specification, and take full advantage of the rest of this book, you should be able to use these laws automatically with very little thought. In order to help you practice, a number of exercises are provided later in this chapter. The laws are shown below; $p1$, $p2$, and $p3$ are propositions. The names in italics are the names of the laws. These are used later in the chapter and used to justify trains of reasoning and applications of simplification. Each law is expressed as a tautology involving the equivalence operator. This means that propositional expressions which are the operands of the equivalence operator are equivalent to each other and can be substituted for each other during the simplification process.

1. Commutative laws

These laws allow the re-ordering of operands of the operators $\land$, $\lor$, and $\Leftrightarrow$. They are written as

$$(p1 \land p2) \Leftrightarrow (p2 \land p1) \qquad Comm \land$$
$$(p1 \lor p2) \Leftrightarrow (p2 \lor p1) \qquad Comm \lor$$
$$(p1 \Leftrightarrow p2) \Leftrightarrow (p2 \Leftrightarrow p1) \qquad Comm \Leftrightarrow.$$

These laws are obvious; they state the equivalence of a proposition such as

> The valve is open and the close command is typed.

to the proposition

> The close command is typed and the valve is open.

The laws state that any propositional expression constructed from the operators: $\lor$, $\land$, and $\Leftrightarrow$ can be replaced by a propositional expression formed by interchanging the operands of these operators without changing their meaning. The laws may seem obvious but there are a number of operators in discrete mathematics which do not obey commutative laws!

2. Associative laws

These laws eliminate brackets in propositional expressions when manipulating the operators $\lor$ and $\land$. They are written as

$$p1 \land (p2 \land p3) \Leftrightarrow (p1 \land p2) \land p3 \Leftrightarrow p1 \land p2 \land p3 \qquad Assoc \land$$
$$p1 \lor (p2 \lor p3) \Leftrightarrow (p1 \lor p2) \lor p3 \Leftrightarrow p1 \lor p2 \lor p3 \qquad Assoc \lor.$$

3. Distributive laws

These are used to factor out a proposition from an expression or to expand a propositional expression involving brackets and the operators $\lor$ and $\land$. They are written as

$$p1 \lor (p2 \land p3) \Leftrightarrow (p1 \lor p2) \land (p1 \lor p3) \qquad Dist \lor \land$$
$$p1 \land (p2 \lor p3) \Leftrightarrow (p1 \land p2) \lor (p1 \land p3) \qquad Dist \land \lor.$$

4. De Morgan's laws

Augustus de Morgan was a ninteenth-century English mathe-matician who was one of the major figures in the development of formal logic. His laws allow negation to be applied to the operands of the operators $\vee$ and $\wedge$. The laws are written as

$$\neg(p1 \vee p2) \Leftrightarrow \neg p1 \wedge \neg p2 \quad DeM \vee$$
$$\neg(p1 \wedge p2) \Leftrightarrow \neg p1 \vee \neg p2 \quad DeM \wedge.$$

5. The law of negation

This states that the negation of a negated proposition is the proposition itself. It is written as

$$\neg\neg p1 \Leftrightarrow p1 \quad Neg.$$

Thus, it states that a proposition such as

It is not not functioning normally.

is equivalent to

It is functioning normally.

6. The law of the excluded middle

This states that a proposition can either be true *or* false. It is written as

$$p1 \vee \neg p1 \Leftrightarrow T \quad Ex\ mid.$$

7. The law of contradiction

This states that a proposition can neither be true *and* false. It is written as

$$p1 \wedge \neg p1 \Leftrightarrow F \quad Contr.$$

8. The law of implication

This law allows implication to be removed from a proposition. It is written as

$$p1 \Rightarrow p2 \Leftrightarrow \neg p1 \vee p2 \quad Impl.$$

9. The law of equality

This law allows equality to be removed from propositions and written in terms of implication

$$(p1 \Leftrightarrow p2) \Leftrightarrow (p1 \Rightarrow p2) \wedge (p2 \Rightarrow p1) \quad Equal.$$

10. The laws of or simplication

These laws allow certain propositional expressions involving the $\vee$ operator to be transformed to a simpler form. The laws are written as

$$p1 \vee p1 \Leftrightarrow p1 \qquad \textit{or1}$$
$$p1 \vee T \Leftrightarrow T \qquad \textit{or2}$$
$$p1 \vee F \Leftrightarrow p1 \qquad \textit{or3}$$
$$p1 \vee (p1 \wedge p2) \Leftrightarrow p1 \qquad \textit{or4}$$

11. The laws of and simplification

These laws allow certain expressions which contain the $\wedge$ operator to be transformed into a simpler form. The laws are written as

$$p1 \wedge p1 \Leftrightarrow p1 \qquad \textit{and1}$$
$$p1 \wedge T \Leftrightarrow p1 \qquad \textit{and2}$$
$$p1 \wedge F \Leftrightarrow F \qquad \textit{and3}$$
$$p1 \wedge (p1 \vee p2) \Leftrightarrow p1 \qquad \textit{and4.}$$

12. The exclusive or law

This law expresses the relation between the exclusive or operator and the or operator

$$p1 \vee_e p2 \Leftrightarrow p1 \wedge \neg p2 \vee \neg p1 \wedge p2 \qquad \textit{exor.}$$

These laws hold no matter what the forms of $p1$, $p2$, or $p3$. For example, $p1$ may be the propositional variable *directory_open* and $p2$ may be the propositional variable *access_granted*, in which case the $\wedge comm$ law gives

directory_open $\wedge$ access_granted $\Leftrightarrow$

access_granted $\wedge$ directory_open.

On the other hand $p1$ may be the propositional expression

open $\Rightarrow$ directory_open $\vee$ access_denied

and $p2$ may be the propositional expression

closed $\wedge$ $\neg$access_granted $\wedge$ new_user.

Table 3.3

(open ∧ malfunction) ∨ (closed ∧ malfunction) ∨ T ∨ open	∧*comm, Dist*∧∨
(open ∧ malfunction) ∨ (closed ∧ malfunction) ∨ T	∨*comm, Or2*
(open ∧ malfunction) ∨ (closed ∨ T ∧ malfunction ∨ T)	*Comm*∨, *Dist*∨∧
(open ∧ malfunction) ∨ (T ∧ malfunction ∨ T)	*Or2*
(open ∧ malfunction) ∨ (T ∧ T)	*Or2*
(open ∧ malfunction) ∨ T	*Defn*∧
(open ∨ T) ∧ (malfunction ∨ T)	∨*comm, Dist*∨∧
(open ∨ T) ∧ T	*Or2*
T ∧ T	*Or2*
T	*Defn*∧

In this case the *impl* law would give

$$(\text{open} \Rightarrow \text{directory\_open} \lor \text{access\_denied}) \Rightarrow$$
$$(\text{closed} \land \lnot \text{access\_granted} \land \text{new\_user}) \Leftrightarrow$$
$$\lnot(\text{open} \Rightarrow \text{directory\_open} \lor \text{access\_denied}) \lor$$
$$(\text{closed} \land \lnot \text{access\_granted} \land \text{new\_user}).$$

The rules given in Table 3.3 can be used to simplify propositional expressions. As an example, consider the proposition

$$(\text{open} \lor \text{closed}) \land \text{open}.$$

This can be transformed to the proposition

$$\text{open} \land (\text{open} \lor \text{closed})$$

by means of applying the *comm*∧ law and then transformed to the proposition

$$\text{open}$$

by means of the *and4* law.

As another example, consider the simplification of the propositional expression

$$((\text{open} \lor \text{closed}) \land \text{malfunction}) \lor T \lor \text{open}.$$

In Table 3.3 each transformed version of the expression is shown on the left-hand side while the law used is written on the right-hand side in italics. Each line is annotated with the law used to achieve the simplification written in italics, or the word *defn* followed by an operator. The latter is used when patterns such as T ∨ T, F ⇒ T are replaced by their truth-table equivalents. This simplification seems long-winded. However, at this stage in the book it is probably worthwhile manipulating propositional expressions in very short steps. When you have had more practice you can skip three or four steps and need not annotate your manipulations with 'obvious' laws such as the commutative laws. In fact, this example can be quickly simplified by recognizing that the expression

$$((\text{open} \lor \text{closed}) \land \text{malfunction}) \lor T \lor \text{open}$$

is equivalent to $p1 \lor T$, where $p1$ is

$$((\text{open} \lor \text{closed}) \land \text{malfunction}) \lor \text{open}$$

and this can be directly simplified to T.

Example 3.5

Simplify the expression

$$\neg\neg(\neg((\text{open} \lor \text{closed}) \land \text{open})).$$

Name each law that you use in each simplification step.

The steps are

¬¬(¬(open ∧ open ∨ open ∧ closed))	*comm*∧ *dist* ∧ ∨
¬¬(¬(open ∨ open ∧ closed))	*and1*
¬¬(¬(open))	*or4*
¬open	*neg.*

Exercise 3.4

Simplify the following propositional expressions; state which simplification laws are used.

 (i) T ∧ open.
 (ii) T ∧ open ∧ F.
 (iii) (T ∨ open) ∧ closed.
 (iv) malfunction ∧ open ∧ closed ∧ operator_error ∧ F.
 (v) (open ∧ ¬closed) ∧ open.
 (vi) (open ∧ ¬¬closed) ∨ (open ∧ closed).
 (vii) (open ∨ open) ∧ (open ∨ closed) ∧ open.
(viii) ¬(malfunction ∨ open) ∧ malfunction.
 (ix) T ∨ (open ⇒ closed ∧ malfunction) ∨ open.
 (x) (open ∨ ¬closed) ∧ (closed ∨ ¬open).
 (xi) ¬¬¬malfunction ∧ ¬¬¬¬¬open.
 (xii) ¬¬(malfunction ∨ open).
(xiii) (open ∧ closed ∧ open) ∧ ¬(open ∧ closed).
(xiv) (open ∧ closed) ⇒ (open ∨ closed).
 (xv) (open ∨ operator_error) ∧ (T ∨ operator_error).

We have seen how the laws presented allow propositional
expressions to be simplified. You will find that system specifications and statements of requirements will contain a large number
of fragments where simplification can make the meaning of
natural-language statements clearer.

Consider this sentence taken from a system specification

> If the valve is opened, then the inlet controller is placed in a
> monitoring state, if the system is not in a startup mode.

This can be written as

$$\text{valve\_opened} \Rightarrow (\neg\text{startup} \Rightarrow \text{monitoring})$$

which can be simplified using the *impl* law to

$$\neg\text{valve\_opened} \vee (\neg\text{startup} \Rightarrow \text{monitoring}).$$

This can be further simplified by applying the *impl* law to

$$\neg\text{valve\_opened} \vee \text{startup} \vee \text{monitoring}$$

which stands for

> Either the valve is not opened or the system is in a startup
> mode or the inlet controller is in a monitoring state.

Although the implication has been removed from the 'simplified' expression it makes it clear that a disjunction of events occurs. This can be useful in examining propositions later in a system specification. For example, a later proposition may state that

> The valve is opened and the system is not in startup mode and the inlet controller is not in a monitoring state

This can be written as

$$valve\_opened \land \neg startup \land \neg monitoring.$$

But this contradicts the expression

$$\neg valve\_opened \lor startup \lor monitoring$$

derived above since there are no values which can be assigned to *valve_opened, startup,* and *monitoring* which will make both expressions true. Clearly, there is an error in the specification.

Example 3.6

Express the following statements in propositional logic and derive the relationships between the monitoring state, the test state, and the fact that the reactor is operating.

> The reactor is either in the monitoring or test state. It cannot be in both states. The reactor is functioning normally only when it is in one of these states.
>
> If a reactor is functioning normally and is not in the test state then the reactor can be regarded as being operating.

The propositional expressions derived from the statements are

$$normal \Leftrightarrow monitoring \lor_e test$$
$$normal \land \neg test \Rightarrow operating.$$

The first expression can be simplified by means of the

exor law to

normal ⇔ monitoring ∧ ¬test ∨ test ∧ ¬monitoring.

normal can then be substituted for in the second proposition giving

(monitoring ∧ ¬test ∨ test ∧ ¬monitoring)

∧ ¬test ⇒ operating)

which can be simplified to

monitoring ∧ ¬test ⇒ operating

by applying the *dist∧∨*, *and1*, and *contr* laws. This propositional expression could then be transformed into a form which doesn't involve an implication operator by applying the *impl* law. However, the form above is probably the simplest.

3.3.2 Reasoning

So far we have seen that the transformation from natural language into propositional calculus forces staff involved in specification to think more clearly and also enables them to simplify complicated statements. Another way that the transformation aids the analyst is with **reasoning**.

During the process of requirements analysis and specification development staff ask questions such as

> If the reactor is in the steady state and an update command is typed, does that mean that the reactor no longer remains in the ready state?
> If the data-base is empty and a query command is typed, does an error message get displayed?
> If a page break occurs at the same time as a chapter break, does the formatter eject a new page?

One aspect of reasoning involves the identification of a set of premises and a conclusion and then showing that the conclusion logically follows from the premises. Examples of premises which are taken from the questions above are

> reactor in a ready state,
>
> update command is typed,
>
> data-base is empty,
>
> query command is typed,
>
> page break occurs,
>
> chapter break occurs.

Examples of conclusions taken from the questions above are

> reactor is not in a ready state,
>
> error message is displayed,
>
> formatter ejects a new page.

By examining premises and attempting to deduce conclusions development staff are able to check the completeness of a specification and discover inconsistencies.

The following is a fragment of a system specification from which premises can be extracted and conclusions deduced

1. The purpose of the system is to check on the functioning of a series of chemical reactors.

2. Three commands are allowed. They are: TEMP, PRESSURE, and ERRORS.

3. The TEMP command has two parameters. The first is a temperature monitor number and the second is a chemical reactor number. When executed, this command will display the average temperature for the specified monitor in the specified reactor over a 12-hour period. If an error in a parameter occurs, then an ERROR_TEMP message is displayed on the vdu and an ERROR_TEMP log message is written to the log file.

4. The PRESSURE command has two parameters. The first is a pressure monitor number and the second is a reactor number. When executed, this command will display the average pressure for the specified monitor in the specified reactor over a 12-hour period. If an error in a parameter

occurs, then an ERROR_PRESSURE message is displayed
on the vdu and an ERROR_PRESSURE message is written
to the log file.

5. The ERRORS command has two parameters. The first is
a pressure monitor number or a temperature monitor
number. When executed, this command will display the
number of malfunctions that have occurred over the last 12
hours for a particular monitor attached to a specific reactor.
If an error in a parameter occurs, then an ERROR_
MONITOR message is displayed on the vdu and an
ERROR_MONITOR message is written to the log file.

6. Writing an error message to the log file can be inhibited
by means of the INHIBIT command. Such a command can
only be typed by a privileged user or when the system is in
test mode.

7. If the log file is not on-line, then, whenever the
PRESSURE or TEMP command is typed, an OFFLINE_
LOGFILE error is displayed. If an ERRORS command is
typed then it will be executed normally.

Given this specification a number of questions can be asked
involving premises and conclusions. A sample is shown below

If the system is in test mode **(Premise)** will the pressure
command be executed normally? **(Conclusion)**

If the log file is off-line and the system is in test mode,
(Premises) will the PRESSURE command be executed
normally? **(Conclusion)**

If the temperature command is typed with the log file
off-line and the operator mistypes both command
parameters, **(Premises)** will an error temp message be
displayed on the vdu? **(Conclusions)**

The conclusions to these premises can be shown to follow or not
follow by means of a careful reading of the system specification.
However, when such a specification occupies hundreds of pages
then a degree of mathematical formalism is invariably required.

In most mathematical texts the relationship between premises and a conclusion is written in the form

$$P_1, P_2, P_3, \ldots, P_n \vdash C$$

it states that the conclusion C logically follows from the premises $P_1, P_2, \ldots, P_n$. Thus, the fact that a conclusion *valve_open* follows from the premises: *normal_state, open_command* and ¬*test state* can be written as

normal_state, open_command, ¬test_state, ⊢valve_open.

It represents the question: would the valve be open if the reactor is in its normal state and the open command has been typed and the reactor is not in a test state? Exactly the type of question that would be asked by a system specifier in order to clarify requirements.

Premises and conclusions can be simple propositions as above or can be formed from existing propositions and the propositional operators outlined in this chapter. For example,

open ∧ normal, ¬error_state, open ⇒

test_state ∧ normal_state ⊢ open.

Given a series of premises and a conclusion, how can it be demonstrated that the conclusion follows from the premises? Two methods will be described in this section.

3.3.2.1 Reasoning using transformation to implication form
The first method involves transforming the premises and conclusion into a propositional form and simplifying by means of the laws described in this chapter. The statement

$$P_1, P_2, P_3, \ldots, P_n \vdash C$$

can be written as

$$P_1 \wedge P_2 \wedge P_3, \ldots, P_n \Rightarrow C$$

since the first statement asserts that, if P_1 and P_2 and $P_3, \ldots, P_n$ hold, then C holds. The ∧ operator replaces the comma while the implication operator replaces ⊢. Now, if it can be shown that

$$P_1 \wedge P_2 \wedge P_3, \ldots, P_n \Rightarrow C$$

is always true, i.e. is a tautology, then C has to be true (remember that if the antecedent of an implication is true and the implication is true, then the consequent is always true). The task then is to demonstrate that

$$P_1 \wedge P_2 \wedge P_3, \ldots, \Rightarrow C$$

is a tautology. This can be done by using the simplification laws described previously.

As an example consider

$$\neg closed, open \vee closed \vdash open$$

which states that, if a valve is not closed and the valve is either open or closed, then it can be deduced that the valve is open. First, the expression is transformed to

$$\neg closed \wedge (open \vee closed) \Rightarrow open.$$

This can be simplified as follows

$\neg(\neg closed \wedge (open \vee closed)) \vee open$	*impl*
$\neg\neg closed \vee \neg(open \vee closed) \vee open$	*DeM* $\wedge$
$closed \vee \neg(open \vee closed) \vee open$	*neg*
$closed \vee open \vee \neg(closed \vee open)$	*comm* $\vee$
T	*Ex mid.*

Since the expression has been reduced to a tautology, it can be deduced that *open* can be inferred from *open* $\vee$ *closed*. Note that the final step of the simplification has telescoped a number of smaller steps. The expression: *closed* $\vee$ *open* $\vee \neg(closed \vee open)$ has been identified as $p \vee \neg p$ where p is *closed* $\vee$ *open*.

The stages described seem long and painstaking. However, by this time you should be able to telescope a number of the simplification steps. The main strategy which should be adopted is to eliminate the implication operator using the *Impl* law then use a combination of the *DeM, dist, or,* and *and* laws to reduce the expression to T and hence demonstrate a tautology.

Example 3.6

Show that the conclusion ¬line_closed follows from the premises

    channel_open

    receiver_ready

    line_closed ∧ channel_open ⇒ ¬receiver_ready.

It is necessary to demonstrate that

    channel_open ∧ receiver_ready

    ∧ (line_closed ∧ channel_open ⇒ ¬receiver_ready)

    ⇒ ¬line_closed.

First, concentrate on simplifying the propositional expression to the left of the rightmost implication operator. The stages of simplification are

channel_open ∧ receiver_ready ∧ (¬(line_closed ∧ channel_open) ∨ ¬receiver_ready)	*Impl*
channel_open ∧ receiver_ready ∧ (¬channel_open ∨ ¬line_closed ∨ ¬receiver_ready)	*DeM* ∧
F ∨ channel_open ∧ receiver_ready ∧ ¬line_closed ∨ F	*Dist* ∧ ∨, *Contr*
channel_open ∧ receiver_ready ∧ ¬line_closed	*or3*

To demonstrate the tautology it is thus necessary to show that

    channel_open ∧ receiver_ready ∧

       ¬line_closed ⇒ ¬line_closed

is a tautology. The sequence of simplications is

¬(channel_open ∧ receiver_ready) ∨ line_closed ∨ ¬line_closed	*Impl DeM* ∧

¬(channel_open ∧ receiver_ready) ∨ T   *Ex mid*

T   *Or2.*

Validating a specification involves attempting to show that an assumed conclusion can be derived from a series of premises generated from 'if questions', for example,

If the reactor is closed down and the computer malfunctions. . .

If the file store is full. . .

If the user types an invalid command. . .

Almost invariably these premises alone will be inadequate to carry out the derivation. It will be necessary to use propositional expressions from the system specification in the deduction. If $P_1, P_2, \ldots, P_n$ are a series of propositions and C is a conclusion which is to be derived and $S_1, S_2, \ldots, S_m$ are a series of propositional expressions from the system specification, then it is almost always necessary to demonstrate that

$$P_1 \wedge P_2, \ldots, P_n \wedge S_1 \wedge S_2, \ldots, S_m \Rightarrow C.$$

The propositional expressions $S_1, S_2, \ldots, S_m$ are usually those which involve variables which are contained in the premises and the conclusion to be inferred from the premises. This is illustrated in Example 3.7.

Example 3.7

A system specification contains the sentences

1. If the operator types the ALARM command, then the subsidiary alarm will be activated and an alarm message written to the log file.

2. Whenever the subsidiary alarm is activated, the main valve is closed and shut-down started.

3. If the main valve is closed then the reactor can be regarded as being in a non-operational state.

Express these sentences in propositional calculus. Also show that if the alarm command is activated the reactor will be in a non-operational state.

The propositions are

$$\text{alarm} \Rightarrow \text{subsid} \land \text{alarm\_message} \qquad S_1$$
$$\text{subsid} \Rightarrow \text{valve\_closed} \land \text{shut\_down} \qquad S_2$$
$$\text{valve\_closed} \Rightarrow \text{non\_op} \qquad S_3.$$

In order to demonstrate

$$\text{alarm} \vdash \text{non\_op},$$

it is necessary to demonstrate that

$$\text{alarm} \land S_1 \land S_2 \land S_3 \Rightarrow \text{non\_op}.$$

This is shown as follows

$$\text{alarm} \land (\text{alarm} \Rightarrow \text{subsid} \land \text{alarm\_message})$$
$$\land S_2 \land S_3 \Rightarrow \text{non\_op}$$

$$\text{alarm} \land (\text{alarm} \Rightarrow \text{subsid} \land \text{alarm\_message})$$
$$\land (\text{subsid} \Rightarrow \text{valve\_closed} \land \text{shut\_down})$$
$$\land S_3 \Rightarrow \text{non\_op}$$

$(\text{alarm} \land \text{subsid} \land \text{alarm\_message})$ $\land (\text{subsid} \Rightarrow \text{valve\_closed}$ $\land \text{shut\_down}) \land S_3 \Rightarrow \text{non\_op}$	*Imp, Dist*$\land \lor$, *Contr, or3*
$\text{alarm} \land \text{subsid} \land \text{alarm\_message}$ $\land \text{valve\_closed} \land \text{shut\_down}$ $\land S_3 \Rightarrow \text{non\_op}$	*Impl, Contr* *and3, or3*

$$\text{alarm} \land \text{subsid} \land \text{alarm\_message}$$
$$\land \text{valve\_closed} \land \text{shut\_down} \land$$
$$(\text{valve\_closed} \Rightarrow \text{non\_op}) \Rightarrow \text{non\_op}$$

$\text{alarm} \land \text{subsid} \land \text{alarm\_message}$ $\land \text{shut\_down} \land \text{valve\_closed}$ $\land \text{non\_op} \Rightarrow \text{non\_op}$	*Impl, Dist*$\land \lor$ *Contr, or3*
$\neg(\text{alarm} \land \text{subsid} \land \text{alarm\_message}$ $\land \text{shut\_down} \land \text{valve\_closed}$ $\land \text{non\_op}) \lor \text{non\_op}$	*Impl*

$$\neg(\text{alarm} \wedge \text{subsid} \wedge \text{alarm\_message} \qquad DeM \wedge$$
$$\wedge \text{shut\_down} \wedge \text{valve\_closed})$$
$$\vee \neg \text{non\_op} \vee \text{non\_op}$$

$$\neg(\text{alarm} \wedge \text{subsid} \wedge \text{alarm\_message} \qquad Ex \; mid$$
$$\wedge \text{shut\_down} \wedge \text{valve\_closed}) \vee T$$

$$T \qquad\qquad\qquad or2$$

Exercise 3.5

Show that the following hold.

  (i) open, open $\vee$ steady_state $\vdash$ open.
  (ii) test, functioning $\vdash$ test $\wedge$ functioning.
  (iii) receiving, receiving $\Rightarrow$ open, open $\vdash$ receiving $\vee$ closed $\Rightarrow$ open.
  (iv) open $\wedge$ receiving $\Rightarrow \neg$closed, $\neg$open, receiving $\Rightarrow$ closed $\vdash$
        $\neg$(receiving $\wedge$ open).
  (v) $a \Rightarrow \neg b, c \Rightarrow b, c \wedge d \vdash b$.

Until now valid consequences have been shown to follow from a series of premises. Unfortunately, a system specification will always contain incomplete requirements which give rise to premises which, when manipulated, do not lead to a desired conclusion. The example which follows consists of a series of paragraphs taken from different parts of a system specification.

1. Whenever a QUERY command is typed a query confirmation message is displayed and the system goes into query mode.

14. If a query confirmation message is displayed while the system is in training mode, then the originating vdu is locked out from incoming messages.

71. If an originating vdu is locked out from incoming messages, then the system regards it as quiescent.

If the specifier wants to infer that when a query command is typed the system regards the originating vdu as quiescent, then

$$\text{query} \vdash \text{quiescent}.$$

If the propositions from the specification are S_1, S_2, and S_3 where

S_1 is   query $\Rightarrow$ confirm $\wedge$ query_mode,
S_2 is   confirm $\wedge$ training $\Rightarrow$ locked_vdu,
S_3 is   locked_vdu $\Rightarrow$ quiescent,

then it is necessary to show that

$$\text{query} \wedge S_1 \wedge S_2 \wedge S_3 \Rightarrow \text{quiescent}$$

is a tautology; however, when the expression is simplified it gives

$\neg$(query $\wedge$ confirm $\wedge$ query_mode $\wedge$ $\neg$training $\wedge$ $\neg$locked $\vee$
query $\wedge$ confirm $\wedge$ query_mode $\wedge$ $\neg$training $\wedge$ quiescent $\vee$
query $\wedge$ confirm $\wedge$ query_mode $\wedge$ locked $\wedge$ quiescent) $\vee$
quiescent

which cannot be simplified to T. Hence, *quiescent* cannot be inferred from *query* and the propositional expressions from the system specification.

3.3.2.2 *Inference using invalid argument*

The previous section described how by manipulating and simplifying propositional expressions a conclusion can be shown to be logically derived from a series of premises. This was achieved by applying the laws described in Section 3.3.1. Unfortunately, this technique can lead to a large amount of unwieldy and error-ridden manipulation, with large expressions being generated. An alternative, and quicker, technique is based on showing that an argument is invalid. It mimics the process whereby consequences are disputed in everyday discourse. If it is wished to demonstrate that

$$P_1, P_2, P_3, \ldots, P_n \vdash C$$

does not hold using a series of propositions $S_1, S_2, \ldots, S_m$ from a system specification, then all that is required is to show that when $P_1, \ldots, P_n$ and $S_1, \ldots, S_m$ have a T value then C has an F value. The way to proceed is to assume that C has an F value and that each P and S has a T value and analyse the consequence of an assignment of these values to the individual propositions that make up each *P* and *S*.

Such an analysis may lead to a contradiction; if it does, then this shows that *C* can be deduced from $P_1, P_2, \ldots, P_n$ using $S_1, S_2, \ldots, S_m$. However, if all the assumptions are satisfied and consistent, then it has been demonstrated that *C* cannot be deduced from $P_1, P_2, \ldots, P_n$ and $S_1, S_2, \ldots, S_m$.

This is an example of what is known as a **rule of inference** whereby a conclusion can be shown to follow from a series of propositional expressions. Rules of inference are vitally important in mathematics and Chapter 4 will describe a number of others. The rule of inference described in this subsection is known as **indirect proof** or **proof by contradiction** or, in older mathematics textbooks, *reductio ad absurdum*.

An example will make this rule of inference clearer. Assume that it is wished to prove that

$$\neg channel\_open \vdash sender$$

and that *channel_open* ∨ *sender* is known from the system specification. First, assume that the conclusion *sender* has the value F and that the premise ¬*channel_open* and the propositional expression *channel_open* ∨ *sender* have the values T. Now if ¬*channel_open* has the value T, then *channel_open* has the value F. If *channel_open* has the value F and *channel_open* ∨ *sender* has the value T, then, from the definition of ∨, *sender* must have the value T. This contradicts the original assumption that sender has the value F. A contradiction has been generated so it has been shown that the inference is valid.

This can be more formally described as

1	¬sender	
2	¬channel_open	
3	channel_open ∨ sender	
4	sender	{2, 3}
5	**contradiction**	{1, 4}.

Each line is a tautology. The left-hand numbers are used for reference in later sections of the proof. The numbers in curly brackets describe which lines are used to establish the proposition written on a particular line. Thus, in line 4 the fact that

sender has the value T is derived from the lines 2 and 3,
¬*channel_open* and *channel_open* ∨ *sender*.

Another more complicated example is shown below. It
involves the premises generated from the fragment of system
specification

1. Whenever the system is in startup mode, all peripherals
are closed down and, whenever the system is in functioning
mode, then all peripherals are operating normally.

2. If all the peripherals are closed down and all peripherals
are operating normally, then the system is in an inconsistent
state.

3. The system can never be in an inconsistent state.

If the conclusion to be proved is that either the system is not in
startup mode or not in functioning mode, then this can be written
as

(startup ⇒ closed) ∧ (functioning ⇒ normal), closed ∧ normal ⇒
inconsistent, ¬inconsistent ⊢ ¬startup ∨ ¬functioning.

The formal derivation of the conclusion is

1	(startup ⇒ closed) ∧ (functioning ⇒ normal)	
2	closed ∧ normal ⇒ inconsistent	
3	¬inconsistent	
4	¬(¬startup ∨ ¬functioning)	
5	startup	{4}
6	functioning	{4}
7	closed	{1, 5}
8	normal	{1, 6}
9	inconsistent	{2, 7, 8}
10	**contradiction**	{3, 9}

Example 3.8

By deriving a contradiction demonstrate that

open ⇒ normal ⊢ normal ∨ shut_down,

given the following two propositions from a system

specification

$$closed \Rightarrow shut\_down$$

$$open \lor closed.$$

1	open $\Rightarrow$ normal	
2	closed $\Rightarrow$ shut_down	
3	open $\lor$ closed	
4	$\neg$(normal $\lor$ shut_down)	
5	$\neg$normal	$\{4\}$
6	$\neg$shut_down	$\{4\}$
7	$\neg$open	$\{1, 5\}$
8	$\neg$closed	$\{2, 6\}$
9	$\neg$(open $\lor$ closed)	$\{7, 8\}$
10	**contradiction**	$\{3, 9\}$.

Example 3.9

The following extract is taken from a system specification. Express the first two paragraphs as premises and demonstrate that the third paragraph is a conclusion which follows from them.

1. If the valve is open or the monitoring computer is in a ready state, then both a recognition signal and a functioning message is sent to the controlling computer.

2. If a functioning message is sent to the controlling computer or the system is in a normal state, then operator commands will be accepted.

3. If the valve is open, then operator commands will be accepted.

What is required is a demonstration that

$$\vdash open \Rightarrow accepted$$

given the two propositional expressions

open ∨ ready ⇒ recognition ∧ functioning

functioning ∨ normal ⇒ accepted,

taken from the system specification. Thus,

1	open ∨ ready ⇒ recognition ∧ functioning	
2	functioning ∨ normal ⇒ accepted	
3	¬(open ⇒ accepted)	
4	open	{3}
5	¬accepted	{3}
6	¬(functioning ∨ normal)	{2, 5}
7	¬functioning	{6}
8	recognition ∧ functioning	{1, 4}
9	functioning	{8}
10	**contradiction**	{7, 9}.

So far indirect proof has been applied in demonstrating that a conclusion can be deduced from a set of premises in conjunction with a set of true propositional expressions taken from a system specification. However, it can also be used to demonstrate that a conclusion cannot be deduced. An example of this is the demonstration that

scheduler ⊢ ¬first_fit

does not hold when taken in conjunction with the proposition

scheduler ⇒ first_fit ∨ best_fit

taken from a system specification

1	scheduler	
2	scheduler ⇒ first_fit ∨ best_fit	
3	first_fit	
4	scheduler ∨ ¬scheduler	{2, 3}
5	**no contradiction**	{1, 4}.

Line 3 shows the assumption that *first_fit* is true. If this were so, then line 2 demonstrates that *scheduler* ⇒ *T* has the value T

which means that *scheduler* could be either T of F; this is shown
on line 4. Lines 1 and 4 are not at variance; therefore, there is no
contradiction. This means that the conclusion ¬*first_fit* does not
follow from the premise *scheduler* and the propositional
expression *scheduler* ⇒ *first_fit* ∨ *best_fit*.

Example 3.10

Demonstrate that the consequence

¬lineprinter_available

cannot follow from the premise

normal ⇒ printing

and the propositions

lineprinter_available ∨ spooler ⇒ normal ∨ on_line
¬printing

taken from a system specification.

1	lineprinter_available ∨ spooler ⇒ normal ∨ on_line	
2	normal ⇒ printing	
3	¬printing	
4	lineprinter_available	
5	¬normal	{2, 3}
6	on_line	{1, 4, 5}
7	**no contradiction**	{6}.

Exercise 3.6

Demonstrate the validity or otherwise of the following inferences using
indirect proof. In each question the inferences are written first followed
by the propositions (in bold) which are taken from a system
specification.

 (i) old ⊢ new
   old ⇒ new.
 (ii) old ⇒ next ⊢ new ⇒ next
   old ⇔ new.
 (iii) ¬normal ⊢ off_line
   on_line ∨ off_line, on_line ⇒ normal.
 (iv) directory ∨ archive ⇒ normal, ¬normal ⊢ ¬directory
   on ∨ directory.
 (v) ⊢ line_down ⇒ ready
   line_ok ∨ line_down, line_ok ⇒ message ∨ ready.
 (vi) line_ok ⇒ message, ready ⇒ normal ⊢ message ∧ normal
   line_ok ∨ ready.
 (vii) command_mode ∧ ready ⇒ ok ⊢ command_mode ⇒ ok
   command_mode, ¬ready.

3.4 The detection of inconsistencies

Related to the problem of checking validity is the problem of determining the inconsistency of a set of statements which represent the premises for an inference. For example, the two propositions

$$\text{valve\_open} \lor_e \text{monitor\_state}$$

$$\text{valve\_open} \Leftrightarrow \text{monitor\_state}$$

are inconsistent since the first premise states that a valve can be open or the system can be in a monitor state but not both but the second proposition states that if a valve is open then the system is in a monitor state and vice versa.

A series of propositional expressions are **consistent**, if and only if, there exists at least one assignment of truth values for the variables in each propositional expression such that all the expressions simultaneously receive the value T. For example, the propositional expressions

$$\text{open} \lor \text{closed}, \neg\text{closed}, \text{closed} \Rightarrow \text{open}$$

are consistent because there is one assignment to open(T) and closed(F) which leads to all the propositions having the value T.

Inconsistency is the reverse of this. A series of propositional expressions are **inconsistent**, if and only if, every assignment of

Table 3.4

open	closed	open ∧ closed	¬open ∨ ¬closed
F	F	F	T
T	F	F	T
F	T	F	T
T	T	T	F

truth values to the variables making up each propositional expression results in at least one expression receiving the value F. An example will make this clear. The propositional expressions

open ∧ closed, ¬open ∨ ¬closed

are inconsistent. This can be seen from the truth table in Table 3.4. Whatever values are assigned to *open* and *closed* one of the propositional expressions is always false.

System specifications will contain inconsistencies and it would be useful if a systematic technique existed which could be used for their detection.

Inconsistency can be detected in a way similar to that in which a conclusion can be deduced from a series of premises by the method of indirect proof. If by applying indirect proof to a series of propositional expressions we can generate a contradiction, then these statements are inconsistent. More formally, what is being attempted is a demonstration that

$$S_1, S_2, \ldots, S_n \vdash C$$

Where C is any contradiction and $S_1, \ldots, S_n$ are a series of n propositional expressions taken from a system specification. As an example consider the propositional expressions

ready ∨ processing, ¬ready ∧ ¬processing.

If it is assumed that ¬*ready* ∨ ¬*processing* is true, then *ready* must have the value F and also *processing* must have the value F. However, this contradicts the proposition *ready* ∨ *processing*, since if it is true then at least one of its variables must be true. Since a contradiction has been generated the two statements are inconsistent.

This method can be formally justified as follows. Since it is intended to demonstrate that

$$S_1, S_2, \ldots, S_n \vdash C,$$

from Section 3.3.2.1 this is equivalent to

$$S_1 \wedge S_2, \ldots, \wedge S_n \Rightarrow C.$$

Since C is a contradiction it must always have the value F. Thus, the above expression is equivalent to

$$S_1 \wedge S_2, \ldots, \wedge S_n \Rightarrow F$$

This is only true if

$$S_1 \wedge S_2, \ldots, \wedge S_n$$

is false. This conjunction will be false when at least one of its propositions is false. This corresponds to our informal definition of inconsistency.

The demonstration that a series of propositions is inconsistent can be laid out in the same way that the demonstration that a conclusion follows from a set of premises. Thus, the demonstration that the propositional expressions

$$\text{ready} \vee \text{processing}, \neg\text{ready} \wedge \neg\text{processing}$$

are inconsistent would be written as

1	ready ∨ processing	
2	¬ready ∧ ¬processing	
3	¬ready	$\{2\}$
4	¬processing	$\{2\}$
5	¬(ready ∨ processing)	$\{3, 4\}$
6	**contradiction**	$\{1, 5\}$.

The only difference between a demonstration of inconsistency and the proof that a conclusion follows from a set of premises using indirect proof is that in the latter the conclusion is assigned the value F in advance while in the former the final line is the contradiction.

A more complicated demonstration of inconsistency follows. It shows that the statements

$$\text{open} \Leftrightarrow \text{normal}, \text{normal} \Rightarrow \text{functioning}, \neg\text{functioning} \vee \text{command},$$

$$\neg\text{open} \Rightarrow \text{command}, \neg\text{command}$$

are inconsistent.

1	open ⇔ normal	
2	normal ⇒ functioning	
3	¬functioning ∨ command	
4	¬open ⇒ command	
5	¬command	
6	open	{4, 5}
7	¬functioning	{3, 5}
8	¬normal	{2, 7}
9	¬open	{1, 8}
10	**contradiction**	{6, 9}.

Example 3.11

A system specification contains the statements shown below. Determine whether they are inconsistent.

1. If the system is in update mode, then it is always functioning normally and vice versa.

2. If the system is in an update mode, then all incoming messages will be queued.

3. If all incoming messages are not queued, then they will be diverted to the overflow file.

4. If the system is not in update mode, then incoming messages will be diverted to the overflow file.

5. Incoming messages will never be diverted to the overflow file.

The sentences can be written as the series of propositional expressions

update ⇔ functioning, update ⇒ queued,

¬queued ⇒ diverted, ¬update ⇒

diverted, ¬diverted.

The attempted proof to demonstrate inconsistency follows.

1	update $\Leftrightarrow$ functioning	
2	update $\Rightarrow$ queued	
3	¬queued $\Rightarrow$ diverted	
4	¬update $\Rightarrow$ diverted	
5	¬diverted	
6	update	$\{4, 5\}$
7	queued	$\{3, 5\}$
8	functioning	$\{1, 6\}$.

No contradiction can be generated; hence the statements are consistent.

Exercise 3.7

Determine whether the following sets of statements are inconsistent.

   (i) open, ¬open ∨ ¬closed, open ∧ closed
  (ii) functioning $\Rightarrow$ normal, normal ∧ ¬functioning
 (iii) lp_on ∧ cr_on, lp_on ∨ cr_on
 (iv) monitor $\Rightarrow$ normal, normal $\Rightarrow$ steady_state, monitor ∧
        ¬steady_state
  (v) command ∧ ¬monitor ∨ normal ∧ ¬monitor, command ∨
        normal $\Rightarrow$ monitor, command ∧ normal
 (vi) normal_flow ∧ command $\Rightarrow$ steady_state, ¬normal_flow ∨
        ¬command ∨ steady_state, normal_flow ∧ command
(vii) normal_flow ∧ command $\Rightarrow$ steady_state, normal_flow ∧
        command ∧ ¬steady_state

3.5 An example of the use of propositional calculus in the specification of a coupled computer system

This chapter has described the propositional calculus and shown how proof using the invalid argument rule of inference can be constructed. This has been illustrated with small examples. This section shows the application of the propositional calculus in specifying a simple system. Each paragraph of a natural-language specification is followed by its translation into propositional calculus.

> 1. A computer system consists of two identical computers (A and B). Each computer is connected to a file store and they are both connected by a communications line. The first computer receives file commands from the user. The second computer contains an identical file store to the first; it is used when the first computer goes out of action because of a hardware malfunction.

This is just a description of the computer system. It does not express what the system is to do. The sentence starting with the words: 'The second computer contains...' implies that some form of processing is to occur. However, no details are given yet.

> 2. Each computer can be in one of two states: a ready state and a locked-out state. When one of the computers is in the ready state, then the other computer is in a ready state.

The first sentence can be expressed as the propositions

$$\text{ready}_A \lor_e \text{locked\_out}_A,$$
$$\text{ready}_B \lor_e \text{locked\_out}_B.$$

The $\lor_e$ operator is used since it is clear from the specification that a computer cannot be in both states. The second sentence can be expressed as the proposition

$$\text{ready}_A \Leftrightarrow \text{ready}_B.$$

> 3. Whenever a DELETE command is received by the first computer, the file specified in the delete command will be deleted unless there is an error in the delete command. If there is an error then a DELETE_ERROR message is displayed on the operator's console and the first computer will be locked out.

This can be translated to the propositions

$$\text{delete\_command}_A \land \neg\text{error\_delete\_command} \Rightarrow \text{file\_deleted}_A$$
$$\text{error\_delete\_command} \Rightarrow \text{delete\_error\_message} \land \text{locked\_out}_A$$

> 4. Whenever an UPDATE command is received at the first computer, the file specified in the UPDATE command will

be updated unless there was an error in the command. If an error ocurred, then an UPDATE_ERROR message is displayed on the operator's console and the first computer will be locked out.

This paragraph can be expressed as the propositions

update_command$_A$ $\wedge$ $\neg$error_update_command $\Rightarrow$ file_updated$_A$
error_update_command $\Rightarrow$ update_error_message $\wedge$ locked_out$_A$.

5. Whenever a CREATE command is received at the first computer, the file specified in the command will be created unless there was an error in the command. If an error does occur, then a CREATE_ERROR message will be displayed on the operator's console.

This can be translated to the propositions

create_command$_A$ $\wedge$ $\neg$error_create_command $\Rightarrow$ file_created$_A$
error_create_command $\Rightarrow$ create_error_message.

6. If an attempt is made to update a non-existent file on the first computer, then both computers will be locked out.

Example 3.12

Express paragraph 6 using propositional calculus.

file_updated$_A$ $\wedge$ $\neg$existing_file$_A$ $\Rightarrow$
locked_out$_A$ $\wedge$ locked_out$_B$.

---

7. If an attempt is made to delete a non-existent file on the first computer then both computers will be locked out.

The translation of this sentence is

file_deleted$_A$ $\wedge$ $\neg$existing_file$_A$ $\Rightarrow$
locked_out$_A$ $\wedge$ locked_out$_B$.

8. If an attempt is made to create a file and the file store of the first computer is full or an existing file has the same

name as the file to be created, then both computers will be locked out.

This can be expressed as

$$\text{file\_created}_A \wedge (\text{store}_A\_\text{full} \vee \text{existing\_file}_A) \Rightarrow$$
$$\text{locked\_out}_A \wedge \text{locked\_out}_B.$$

9. Whenever a file is manipulated on the first computer, the same operation is carried out on the file store of the second computer. This is achieved by sending the name of the file to be manipulated along the communications line together with a command which indicates the type of operation to be carried out. This command can have one of three values: CREATE, DELETE, or UPDATE.

There is a slight deficiency in this paragraph. It concerns the use of the word 'manipulated'. A careful reading of this paragraph indicates that it is a synonym for the collection of CREATE, DELETE, and UPDATE commands issued by the first computer. The paragraph can be converted into the propositions

$$\text{file\_updated}_A \Rightarrow \text{sent\_file\_name} \wedge \text{update\_command}_B,$$
$$\text{file\_created}_A \Rightarrow \text{sent\_file\_name} \wedge \text{create\_command}_B,$$
$$\text{file\_deleted}_A \Rightarrow \text{sent\_file\_name} \wedge \text{delete\_command}_B.$$

10. The second computer will respond to UPDATE, CREATE, and DELETE commands only when it is not locked out and a file name is sent.

Again this rule can be translated into propositions. They are

$$\text{sent\_file\_name} \wedge \text{update\_command}_B \wedge$$
$$\neg\text{locked\_out}_B \Rightarrow \text{file\_updated}_B,$$

$$\text{sent\_file\_name} \wedge \text{delete\_command}_B \wedge$$
$$\neg\text{locked\_out}_B \Rightarrow \text{file\_deleted}_B,$$

$$\text{sent\_file\_name} \wedge \text{create\_command}_B \wedge$$
$$\neg\text{locked\_out}_B \Rightarrow \text{file\_created}_B.$$

The full list of propositions is

$\text{ready}_A \vee_e \text{locked}_A$	S_1
$\text{ready}_B \vee_e \text{locked}_B$	S_2
$\text{ready}_A \Leftrightarrow \text{ready}_B$	S_3

delete_command$_A$ ∧ ¬error_delete_command ⇒	S_4
file_deleted$_A$	
error_delete_command ⇒ delete_error_message ∧	S_5
locked_out$_A$	
update_command$_A$ ∧ ¬error_update_command ⇒	S_6
file_updated$_A$	
error_update_command ⇒ update_error_message ∧	S_7
locked_out$_A$	
create_command$_A$ ∧ ¬error_create_command ⇒	S_8
file_created$_A$	
error_create_command ⇒ create_error_message	S_9
file_updated$_A$ ∧ ¬existing_file$_A$ ⇒ locked_out$_A$ ∧	S_{10}
locked_out$_B$	
file_deleted$_A$ ∧ ¬existing_file$_A$ ⇒ locked_out$_A$ ∧	S_{11}
locked_out$_B$	
file_created$_A$ ∧ (store$_A$_full ∨ existing_file$_A$)	S_{12}
⇒ locked_out$_A$ ∧ locked_out$_B$	
file_updated$_A$ ⇒ sent_file_name ∧ update_command$_B$	S_{13}
file_created$_A$ ⇒ sent_file_name ∧ create_command$_B$	S_{14}
file_deleted$_A$ ⇒ sent_file_name ∧ delete_command$_B$	S_{15}
sent_file_name ∧ update_command$_B$ ∧	S_{16}
¬locked_out$_B$ ⇒ file_updated$_B$	
sent_file_name ∧ delete_command$_B$ ∧	S_{17}
¬locked_out$_B$ ⇒ file_deleted$_B$	
sent_file_name ∧ create_command$_B$ ∧	S_{18}
¬locked_out$_B$ ⇒ file_created$_B$	

It is possible to explore some questions which can be asked of the specification. For example, when computer A is locked is computer B locked? This entails demonstrating that

$$\text{locked}_A \vdash \text{locked}_B.$$

This demonstration uses indirect proof and uses the propositional expressions: S_1, S_2, and S_3 taken from the system specification.

1	locked$_A$	
2	ready$_A$ ∨$_e$ locked$_A$	
3	ready$_B$ ∨$_e$ locked$_B$	
4	ready$_A$ ⇔ ready$_B$	
5	¬locked$_B$	
6	ready$_B$	{3, 5}

7	$\neg$ready$_A$	$\{1, 2\}$
8	**contradiction**	$\{4, 6, 7\}$.

Another set of questions that can be asked is: if a file is correctly deleted on the first computer will it mean that the corresponding file on the second computer will be deleted?

Example 3.13

What propositions from the specification would you use to demonstrate that when a correct deletion operation has been carried out on the first computer on an existing file, then the corresponding file on the second computer is deleted?

It is necessary to demonstrate that

$\neg$error_delete_command, delete_command$_A$,

existing_file$_A$ $\vdash$ file_deleted$_B$.

Possible propositions required from the specification are those concerned with deletion operations. They are

$$S_4, S_5, S_{11}, S_{15}, S_{17}.$$

An attempted proof that *file_delete$_B$* can be deduced from the premises in Example 3.13 follows.

1	$\neg$error_delete_command
2	delete_comand$_A$
3	existing_file$_A$
4	delete_command$_A$ $\wedge$ $\neg$error_delete_command $\Rightarrow$ file_deleted$_A$
5	error_delete_command $\Rightarrow$ delete_error_message $\wedge$ locked_out$_A$
6	file_deleted$_A$ $\wedge$ $\neg$existing_file$_A$ $\Rightarrow$ locked_out$_A$ $\wedge$ locked_out$_B$
7	file_deleted$_A$ $\Rightarrow$ sent_file_name $\wedge$ delete_command$_B$

8	sent_file_name $\wedge$	
	delete_command$_B$ $\wedge$	
	$\neg$locked_out$_B$ $\Rightarrow$ file_deleted$_B$	
9	$\neg$file_deleted$_B$	
10	file_deleted$_A$	$\{1, 2, 4\}$
11	sent_file_name	$\{7, 10\}$
12	delete_command$_B$	$\{7, 10\}$
13	locked_out$_B$	$\{8, 9, 11, 12\}$.
14	**no contradiction**	

No contradiction is capable of being generated; so what has happened? The problem has arisen in line 8. The file on the second computer will only be deleted if a file name has been sent along the communications line together with a delete command *and* the second computer has not been locked out. Therefore, an added additional proposition $\neg$*locked_out$_B$* has to be added to the list of premises. This would then contradict the proposition on line 13 and hence the conclusion would follow. This is an example where natural language and, admittedly, some degree of carelessness might have seduced us into believing that, if a valid delete command had been typed and an existing file were to be deleted on the first computer, then the corresponding file on the second computer would have been deleted. The two examples of reasoning presented were artificial. the specification processed was still very small and an extremely careful reading of the English could possibly have sufficed. However, the examples of reasoning are typical of those carried out on much larger specifications.

3.6 Summary

This chapter has described a mathematical notation known as the **propositional calculus** and shown how complicated fragments of natural language found in statements of requirements and system specifications can be represented in a concise and unambiguous manner, and in a form which facilitates reasoning. The reasoning was described with reference to an example of a rule of interence based on invalid argument and mirrors a proof process found in mathematics. It enabled consequences to be deduced from premises and inconsistencies to be discovered in a series of propositions.

Unfortunately, propositional calculus is not adequate as a formalism in itself for requirements analysis and specification. It has to be supplemented with other notations which will be described in later chapters. However, this chapter should have given you an idea of the utility of mathematics for system specification.

4 Predicate calculus

In the previous chapter propositional calculus was described. System specifications and statements of requirements were used as concrete examples of its utility. It was stressed that the examples used were artificial in the sense that they were small. However, the examples were artificial in another respect. They were carefully chosen so that they could be expressed in propositional calculus. Unfortunately, the propositional calculus alone is an inadequate medium for expressing many system specifications. As an example consider the two propositions

> All the monitoring computers will be ready.
> X12 is a monitoring computer.

Using propositional calculus it is not possible to prove that

> X12 will be ready.

And from the propositions

> If a thermocouple registers a temperature
> outside the range 10°C to 100°C then the
> thermocouple is malfunctioning.
>
> ThermocoupleA is reading 112°C.

it is not possible to prove that

> ThermocoupleA is malfunctioning.

These examples demonstrate that propositional calculus has two weaknesses. The first example demonstrates that it is not possible to reason about classes of objects. Thus, sentences such as

> At least one user is logged on.
>
> All thermocouples will either be functioning
> normally or malfunctioning.

> If all the valves are open, then at least one
> monitoring computer will be on-line.

cannot be adequately expressed. The second example demonstrates that propositional calculus manipulates objects which are not fine-grained enough to reason adequately about. For example, the sentence

> If one of the line voltages lies outside the
> range 110°C to 200°C, then the line is
> malfunctioning

could be represented as the propositional expression

$$\text{Line\_volts\_110\_200} \Rightarrow \text{malfunction,}$$

but such a proposition is inadequate to reason with if, for example, later sentences referred to temperature values. What is required is a means of splitting up propositions such as *line_volts_110_200* into its constituent parts.

4.1 Propositions as predicates

In order to overcome some of the disadvantages of propositional calculus the idea of a proposition will be generalized in two ways. The first generalization is that a proposition can be replaced by any expression which can be evaluated to either T or F. This chapter will limit these expressions to contain: identifiers which have integer values, integer constants, relational operators applied to integer variables and constants, and arithmetic operators applied to integers.

Such expressions will be written in the same way that they would be written in a computer program with the occasional use of brackets to make their meaning clear. Thus,

$$\text{newtemp} > 10$$

$$(\text{oldtemp} * 10 + \text{newtemp}) > \text{max\_limit}$$

$$\text{old\_monitor} > 10 \Rightarrow \text{new\_monitor} > 10$$

are all examples of expressions which can replace propositions.

Propositions, as described in this book, can also include a construct which describes the relationship between two objects which can be variables or constants. These objects can be of any type; for example, they may be computers, users, files, or monitoring instruments. Relationships are written in the form

name(*variable or constant, variable or constant*).

At this stage of the book such a construct can be regarded as being similar to a boolean function which has two parameters of an arbitrary type. An example in the use of the construct is

is_connected(computer1, computer7)

which will return a truth value T when *computer1* is connected to *computer7* and F otherwise, and

file_state(file1, deleted)

returns a value T when the file *file1* has been deleted and F otherwise. The objects that can replace propositions in the propositional calculus are known as **predicates**. The combined use of predicates and the operators of propositional calculus gives rise to the **predicate calculus**.

Some examples of statements taken from system specifications together with their predicate calculus equivalents follow.

The reactor temperature lies between 0 and 10°C	$\text{temp} \geq 0 \wedge \text{temp} \leq 10$
Operator commands will always consist of three letters	command_length(command, 3)
If the line voltage is active, then the line is malfunctioning	line_voltage(line, active) $\Rightarrow$ line_state(line, malfunctioning)
If a line is malfunctioning, then the line is disconnected	line_state(line, malfunctioning) $\Rightarrow$ connection(line, disconnected)
Whenever the computer is brought off-line, the communications line is set to a high value of 5 volts	computer_state(computer, off_line) $\Rightarrow$ com_volt = 5

If the temperature of the main reactor is over 1000°C, then the monitoring computer is placed in an alarm state	temp(main_reactor, main_reac_temp) $\wedge$ main_reac_temp $> 1000 \Rightarrow$ comp_state(monitoring_comp, alarm)

The use of *main_reac_temp* in the last predicate often gives some trouble to the reader. This states that if the temperature of the main reactor is *main_reac_temp* and if its value is over 1000°C, then. . . .

Example 4.1

Convert the following extract from a natural-language specification into predicate calculus form.

> Only when the main computer is in a monitoring state will the subsidiary computer be in a monitoring state.

The predicate employs the $\Leftrightarrow$ operator as it is clear that the only time that the subsidiary computer is in the monitoring state is when the main computer is in a monitoring state. The predicate will then be

comp_state(main, monitoring) $\Leftrightarrow$
    comp_state(subsid, monitoring).

Exercise 4.1

Convert the following sentences into predicate calculus form.

  (i) A transaction is invalid if its amount is greater than £500.

 (ii) A transaction is valid if the account number is greater than 1000 and the transaction amount lies between £10 and £200.

(iii) Whenever a sensor malfunctions then the master console is activated and the sensor voltage is grounded at 0 volts.

(iv) There will never be more than seven reactors on-line.
 (v) If more than six vdus are currently active, and provided that the second processor is on-line, then a first-fit algorithm will be used for storage allocation.
(vi) If more than three-quarters of memory is occupied by programs then no more than 12 interactive users will be allowed on the system at one time.
(vii) A transaction will never contain more than five parameters and never have more than 20 trailing blocks and be greater than 150 characters in length.
(viii) If the length of the address field is more than 10 characters, then the transaction can be regarded as rejected.
(ix) If the /A option forms part of the command then the system is placed in training mode.

Exercise 4.2

Translate the following statements expressed in predicate calculus into English.

   (i) comp_state(main_comp, down) $\Rightarrow$ line_volts $= 0$.
  (ii) no_users $< 10 \wedge$ no_terminals < 15.
 (iii) no_users $< 5 \Leftrightarrow$ no_processors < 10.
  (iv) ambient_temp $> 50 \vee \neg$ambient_pressure $> 100 \Rightarrow$ line_volts $= 40$.
   (v) periph_state(lprinter, busy) $\vee$ periph_state(lprinter, down) $\Rightarrow$ $\neg$connected(lprinter, printbus).
  (vi) $\neg$(no_users $\geq 10 \wedge$ no_files ≤ 100).
 (vii) malfunctioning_sensors $>$ sensor_numbers $* 2 \Rightarrow$ state(main_computer, idle).
(viii) $\neg$periph_state(transducer, malfunctioning) $\Rightarrow$ comp_state(main, idle) $\vee$ is_connected(main, subsid).

Exercise 4.3

The following is an extract from the specification of a financial transaction system. Convert it into predicate calculus.

1. The system is to process a number of transactions stored in an update file. There will never be more than 100 transactions in the file.

2. There are two types of transactions: account transactions and report transactions. The account transaction will never contain more than five fields unless the first field contains the integer 1; in this case the transaction will contain between five and 10 fields. The report transaction will contain either two or three fields.

3. If the update file contains more than 80 account transactions, then a warning1 message should be sent to the operator's vdu. If the update file contains more than 90 transactions, then a warning2 message should be sent to the operator's vdu.

4. If a transaction contains more than the allowable number of fields, then a warning3 message is sent to the operator's vdu.

4.2 Quantifiers as predicates

Propositional calculus is unable to adequately express statements about the properties of classes of objects and to reason about them. For example, given the propositions

If one of the sensors is malfunctioning, then a zero reading is received at the communications terminal.

Whenever a zero reading is received at the communications terminal, a process is allocated to deal with the malfunction providing that the process is in the ready state,

we are unable to deduce that, if SE11 is a sensor and is malfunctioning, then the malfunction will be dealt with by allocating a ready process.

What is required is a mathematical shorthand for expressing propositions that hold for a class of objects. The mathematical shorthand involves two operators known as the **existential quantifier** and the **universal quantifier**. The former is written as a mirror-image of the capital letter E ($\exists$). The latter is written as an inverted capital A ($\forall$).

4.2.1 Existential quantification

The existential operator asserts tht at least one object in a collection of objects has a particular property. Two examples of the use of the existential quantifier are

$$\exists i: 1..10 \cdot i^2 = 64,$$

$$\exists \text{proc: processors} \cdot \text{processor\_state(proc, active)}.$$

The first example asserts that there is a value of i in $1, 2, 3, 4, \ldots, 10$ which has its square equal to 64. The second example asserts that there is a processor which is currently active. The general form for existential quantification is

$$\exists \text{identifier/class list} \cdot \text{predicate}$$

where *identifier/class* is a series of identifiers separated by commas followed by a colon and a class. Each identifier/class is separated by semicolons.

Class represents a class or set of objects over which the quantification holds. At this stage of the book *class* will be restricted to a range expression consisting of two integers separated by two periods; for example,

$$7..26$$

is the set of numbers $7, 8, 9, \ldots, 26$, the natural numbers $\mathbf{N}\{0, 1, 2, \ldots\}$ the integers $\mathbf{Z}\{-\infty.. -1, 0, +1, \ldots, \infty\}$ and sets of objects such as *processors, transaction_types,* or *monitors.* Examples of the use of $\exists$ follow

$$\exists i: \mathbf{N} \cdot i > 10 \wedge \text{monitor\_temp} = i \tag{1}$$

$$\exists \text{mon: allocated\_monitors} \cdot \text{monitor\_state(mon, ready)} \tag{2}$$

$$\exists \text{transaction: transactions} \cdot \text{transaction\_state(valid)} \tag{3}$$

$$\exists i: 1..100; \text{mon: allocated\_monitors} \cdot$$
$$\text{activity(mon, functioning)} \wedge \text{ambient\_temperature} = i \tag{4}$$

$$\exists \text{reactor: current\_reactors; monitor: allocated\_}$$
$$\text{monitors} \cdot \text{mon\_state(monitor, functioning)} \wedge$$
$$\text{connected(reactor, monitor)} \tag{5}$$

$$\exists \text{vdu: allocated\_vdus} \cdot \text{vdu\_status(vdu, on)} \Rightarrow$$
$$\text{global\_status(vdu, active)} \tag{6}$$

(1) is a long-winded way of saying that *monitor_temp* is greater than 10. (2) states that out of all allocated monitors at least one is ready. (3) states that out of all transactions at least one is valid. (4) states that out of all allocated monitors there will be at least

one which is functioning when the ambient temperature is between 1 and 100°C. (5) states that there is at least one functioning monitor which is connected to a reactor. (6) states that there is at least one allocated vdu which, when it is in the on state, will be regarded as active.

Example 4.2

Convert the following sentences into predicate calculus form.

One of the actuators will be functioning provided that the system ambient temperature is within safety limits and the main reactor is not in a warm up state. The current safety limits are 10 to 100°C.

Assume that the system ambient temperature is represented by the integer variable *ambient_temp*.

---

ambient_temp $\geq$ 10 $\wedge$ ambient_temp $\leq$ 100 $\wedge$
$\neg$reactor_state (main, warm_up) $\Rightarrow$
$\exists$ act: actuators $\cdot$ actuator_state (act, functioning).

Example 4.3

Convert the following sentences into predicate calculus form.

(i) The queueing system handles the processing of retrieval messages from remote systems. There will be a maximum of 25 queues.

(ii) One of the queues will always be in an active state.

(iii) At least one queue will be in an active state and awaiting messages from priority users.

(iv) No queue will ever be in an active state, awaiting messages from priority users and in a ready state.

Assume that the number of queues is represented by the integer variable *no_queues*; *queue_status.* (,) is a predicate which gives the status of a queue; and *wait_status* (,) is a predicate which describes whether a queue is waiting for messages from remote users. *available_queues* contains the name of the queues.

---

no_queues ≤ 25

∃queue: available_queues · queue_status(queue, active)

∃queue: available_queues · queue_status(queue, active)
∧ wait_status(queue, waiting)

¬∃queue: available_queues ·
queue_status(queue, active) ∧
wait_status(queue, waiting) ∧
queue_status(queue, ready).

Exercise 4.4

Convert the following sentences to predicate calculus form.

   (i) At least one command line will be active.

  (ii) No files in the file store will be marked for archiving and marked for deletion.

 (iii) At least one transaction will be a delete transaction provided that the transaction file is in a ready state.

 (iv) No directories in the file store will be open or no file in the file store will be closed.

  (v) At least one vdu will be connected to the peripheral processor.

 (vi) If the main valve is open and one of the exhaust valves is open, then the control signal will be in a ready state providing that the ambient reactor pressure lies between 0 and 100 mm.

 (vii) Either at least one communication line will be active or at least one response line will be active.

(viii) If at least one communication line is down, then the system is switched to a warning state.

(ix) If at least one transaction is a delete transaction or an update transaction, then at least one update record will be modified.

There are a number of important features of quantifiers. First, an expression which is quantified is itself a predicate and thus can be used in conjunction with other predicates. Thus, predicates such as

$\neg\exists$program: file_store $\cdot$ name(program, tracker) $\lor$

$\exists$file: filestore $\cdot$ $\neg$file_state(file, deleted) $\lor$

$\exists$arch: archive_store $\cdot$ $\neg$archive_state(arch, deleted)

can be formed from quantifiers and the standard propositional operators such as $\land$, $\lor$, and $\neg$. Second, since quantified expressions are predicates, they can have a value T or F. For example,

$$\exists i: 1..10 \cdot i^2 = 144$$

is patently false since there is no number between 1 and 10 which has a square of 144, while

$$\exists j: 1..100 \cdot j \geq 3 \land j \leq 8 \land j^2 = 49$$

is true ($j = 7$). Third, quantification involves a different use of variables from that found in propositional calculus. As an example consider the predicate

$$\exists j: 1..50 \cdot j = \text{min\_temp}.$$

This is equivalent to the predicate

$$\text{min\_temp} \geq 1 \land \text{min\_temp} \leq 50.$$

Now in the first predicate j takes no part. Obviously, identifier j takes a different role from that of *min_temp*.

Identifier *min_temp* is known as a *free variable* while j is known as a *bound variable*. Bound variables use scoping rules similar to those used in languages such as Pascal and Ada. Any bound variables are recognized as such within the predicate which is quantified; an identifier identical to a bound variable, but used outside a quantification is regarded as a free variable.

Thus, in

comp_state(monitor, active) ∨

∃monitor: working_monitors · comp_state(monitor, ready),

the first occurrence of *monitor* is an example of it being used as a free variable; the second occurrence is an example of it being used as a bound variable.

4.2.2 *Universal quantification*

So far this section has shown how statements which assert the existence of *one* object can be written using existential quan-tification. There is also a need to express the fact that *all* objects in a certain class have a particular property. Typical expressions of this taken from system specifications and statements of requirements are shown below.

Unless the exhaust valve is closed, all the inlet valves will be open and all the transfer valves will be closed.

All operator commands will be received from either the master console or, in the case of an emergency, from the subsidiary console.

A program in main memory will either be suspended, ready, or active.

The first two statements are obviously connected with asserting a property of a class of objects. The first concerns the class of inlet valves and transfer valves; the second concerns the class of operator commands. The third statement asserts a property of objects in a class, but not obviously so. If the statement is written in the form: 'Every program in main memory . . . , it is much clearer.

To handle such statements a second quantifier is used. It is known as the **universal quantifier** and is written as an inverted capital a (∀). It has the same form as the existential quantifier. Some examples of its uses are

$\forall i: 1..10 · i^3 \le 1000,$

$\forall$valves: exhaust_valves ·

valve_status(valve, open) $\vee_e$ valve_status(valve, closed),

∀prog: in_memory_progs ·

    prog_status(prog, suspended) ∧ ¬prog_status(prog, active).

The first example states that all the integers between 1 and 10 have their cubes less than or equal to 1000. The second example states that all the exhaust valves are either open or closed. The third states that all programs resident in main memory are suspended and not active.

Example 4.4

Convert the following extract of a system specification into predicate calculus.

If the main computer is in a quiescent state, then all processes are suspended and all critical devices will be down.

comp_state(main, quiescent) ⇒
∀proc: processes · proc_state
(proc, suspended) ∧ ∀dev: critical_devs ·
dev_state(dev, down).

Example 4.5

Translate the following predicate into natural language

∀prog: progs_in_memory · prog_state(prog, suspended)
⇒ ∀proc: processors · processor_state(proc, idle).

The translation is

    If all the programs resident in memory are
    suspended, then all the processors are idle.

Exercise 4.5

Express the following predicates in natural language.

(i) ∀device: active_devices · comm_status(device, transfer).

(ii) ∀monitor: attached_monitors · mon_state(monitor, on) ⇒
test_state(monitor, dummy_test).

(iii) (∀monitor: attached_monitors · mon_state(monitor, on)) ∧
ambient_temp < 120.

(iv) ∀device: active_devices · device_state(device, on) ⇒
comp_state(satelite_computer, on).

(v) ∀device: active_devices · device_state(device, on) ⇒
∀process: device_processes · process_state(process, running).

(vi) ∀trans: trans_files · file_category(file, trans) ∨
file_category(file, update) ∨ file_category(file, modify).

(vii) ∀file: filestore; user: users · owns(user, file) ⇒
user_status(user, known).

(viii) ∀tfile: trans_files; mast: master_file · refers(tfile, mast) ∨
error(tfile, error1).

(ix) ∀user: users; seg: memory_segments ·
user-status(user, current) ⇒ has_access(user, seg).

(x) ∀user: users; file: filestore · user_status(user, super_user) ⇒
access(file, read) ∧ access(file, write).

Exercise 4.6

Convert the following extracts from a system specification into predicate
calculus form.

(i) All the files in the file store will either be active or passive but
not both.

(ii) A reactor in the monitoring system will always be on-line if it
is marked as functioning in the reactor table.

(iii) Each user has read or write access to the monitor file but not
both.

(iv) If a file in the main file store is marked for archiving, then it is
also marked for deletion and for logging.

(v) Every process in every active queue is attached to the master
table header.

(vi) A system contains thre types of processes: active processes; suspended processes; and ready processes. If a process is active, then all devices attached to that process are regarded as not available. If a process is suspended, then all the devices attached to that process are regarded as available. If a process is ready, no devices should be attached to the process.

(vii) If all the transactions have the first field blank, then the update file should be opened for overnight processing.

(viii) A computer system serves a number of users. Each user can be categorized as being a normal user or a super user but not both.

(ix) A system contains two types of processes: active processes and suspended processes. All suspended processes will be attached to the monitor queue.

(x) A monitoring system consists of a series of reactors. Attached to a reactor will be a series of thermocouples. If the monitor line for a reactor on the monitoring screen is not flashing, then all the thermocouples attached to the reactor are functioning normally.

A statement involving universal quantification is, like a statement involving existential quantification, a predicate. For example, if a monitor attached to a chemical reactor is malfunctioning and is generating a ready signal and it is asserted that

$\forall$mon: monitors $\cdot$ monitor_state(mon, malfunctioning) $\wedge$ signal(mon, ready),

then it is obvious that the assertion is false.

Example 4.6

The following is an extract from a system specification. It is followed by a series of assertions written in predicate calculus. Indicate the truth or otherwise of each assertion.

Users of a computer system are either normal users or privileged users. Files in the computer system can either be read-protected or write-protected. A normal user only has access to read-protected files while the privileged user has access to both types of file.

∀user: users ·

user_type(user, normal) ∧ user_type(user, privileged),

∀user: users; file: files ·

file_status(file, read_protected) ⇒ access(user, file),

∀user: users; file: files ·

user_type(user, privileged) ⇒ access(user, file).

The first assertion is false since it states that all users are both normal users and privileged users. The second assertion is true since it states that all users have access to all read-protected files. The third assertion is true as it states that all privileged users have access to all files.

Exercise 4.7

The following is an extract from a system specification. It is followed by five assertions in predicate calculus. Indicate the truth or otherwise of these assertions.

There are three types of transactions which are to be processed by the system. They are: query transactions, update transactions, and verification transactions. Two sorts of programs are allowed to issue transactions. They are: privileged programs and normal programs. Privileged programs are allowed to issue all types of transaction while normal programs are allowed to issue only query transactions. A program can be executed by any of the processors currently allocated to the system. However, if the processor is an Ia33 processor or an Ia22 processor, only update transactions are allowed.

(i) ∀prog: programs ·
    prog_status(prog, privileged) ∨ prog_status(prog, normal).

(ii) ∀prog: programs ·
prog_status(prog, privileged) ⇒ issue(prog, update) ∨
issue(prog, verify) ∨ issue(prog, query).

(iii) ∀prog: programs ·
(running(prog, Ia33) ∨ running(prog, Ia22)) ∧
(prog_status(prog, normal) ⇒ issue(prog, update)).

(iv) ∀prog: programs ·
¬running(prog, Ia33) ⇒ issue(prog, query).

(v) ∀prog: programs ·
¬running(prog, Ia33) ∧ ¬running(prog, Ia22) ∧
prog_status(prog, privileged) ⇒ issue(prog, update).

There is a relationship between universal and existential quantification. Universal quantification expresses a property of *all* objects in a class while existential quantification asserts *at least one* object in a class has a property.

An assertion that not all objects in a class have a particular property is also an assertion that at least one object in the class does not have the property. Formally, this means that

$$\neg\forall \ldots \cdot \text{property} \Leftrightarrow \exists \ldots \cdot \neg\text{property}.$$

Similarly, an assertion that there doesn't exist an object which has a property is equivalent to an assertion that all the objects do not have the property. Formally, this means that

$$\neg\exists \ldots \cdot \text{property} \Leftrightarrow \forall \ldots \cdot \neg\text{property}.$$

Some examples of these equivalences follow. They are expressed as tautologies

$$\neg\forall\text{proc: processes} \cdot \text{process\_state(proc, active)} \Leftrightarrow$$
$$\exists\text{proc: processes} \cdot \neg\text{process\_state(proc, active)},$$

$$\neg\exists i: \mathbf{N} \cdot i^2 = 100 \Leftrightarrow \forall i: \mathbf{N} \cdot \neg i^2 = 100,$$

¬∃reac: reactors · reactor_state(reac, active) ∧
line_status(reac, on-line) ⇔
∀reac: reactors · ¬reactor_state(reac, active) ∨
¬line_status(reac, on-line).

The first example states that, if not all processors are active, it is equivalent to saying at least one process is not active. The second example states that, if there isn't a natural number j whose square is equal to hundred, this is equivalent to asserting that all the natural numbers do not have their square equal to a hundred. Although both these statements are patently false, they are still equivalent. The final example states that, if it is not true that there is a reactor which is both active and on-line, then it is equivalent to saying that all reactors are not on-line or not active. These statements are the same since

$$\neg(\text{reactor\_state}(\text{reac}, \text{active}) \wedge \text{line\_status}(\text{reac}, \text{on-line}))$$

is equivalent to

$$\neg\text{reactor\_state}(\text{reac}, \text{active}) \vee \neg\text{line\_status}(\text{reac}, \text{on-line})$$

by the DeM $\wedge$ law.

Intuition convinces us that the equivalences between universal and existential quantification hold. However, a proof is not difficult. The proof can be established by considering the meaning of both universal and existential quantification. When quantification is written as

$$\forall \ldots \cdot P$$

where P is a predicate, what is being asserted is that P is true for all combinations of the bound variables in the signature. Thus,

$$\forall \ldots \cdot P \Leftrightarrow P_1 \wedge P_2 \wedge P_3 \wedge P_4, \ldots, P_n$$

where n is the number of different combinations of bound variables and P_i is the predicate formed by substituting each combination of bound variable. For example, if there are two reactors, *reactora* and *reactorb,* and two monitors, *monitora* and *monitorb,* then

$$\forall\text{mon: monitors; react: reactors} \cdot \text{attached}(\text{mon}, \text{react})$$

is equivalent to

$$\text{attached}(\text{reactora}, \text{monitora}) \wedge \text{attached}(\text{reactorb}, \text{monitora})$$

$$\wedge\, \text{attached}(\text{reactora}, \text{monitorb}) \wedge \text{attached}(\text{reactorb}, \text{monitorb})$$

Similarly, existential quantification is equivalent to asserting a series of predicates separated by or operators

$$\exists \ldots \cdot P \Leftrightarrow P_1 \vee P_2 \vee P_3, \ldots, P_n$$

where n is the number of different combinations of bound variables in the signature of the quantifier. For example if there are three communication lines, *comm1, comm2,* and *comm3,* and two multiplexors, *mul1* and *mul2.* The predicate

∃comm: communication_lines · line_state(comm, active)

is equivalent to

line_state(comm1, active) ∨ line_state(comm2, active) ∨
    line_state(comm3, active)

and

∃comm: communication_lines; multi: multiplexors ·
    line_state(comm, active) ∧ connected(comm, multi)

is equivalent to

(line_state(comm1, active) ∧ connected(comm1, mul1)) ∨
(line_state(comm1, active) ∧ connected(comm1, mul2)) ∨ . . . ∨
(line_state(comm3, active) ∧ connected(comm3, mul2)).

Given that

$$\forall \ldots \cdot P \Leftrightarrow P_1 \wedge P_2 \wedge P_3, \ldots, P_n$$

and

$$\exists \ldots \cdot P \Leftrightarrow P_1 \vee P_2 \vee P_3, \ldots, P_n,$$

it is now possible to demonstrate the equivalences.

If $\forall \ldots \cdot P \Leftrightarrow P_1 \wedge P_2 \wedge P_3, \ldots, P_n$, then
$\neg(\forall \ldots \cdot P) \Leftrightarrow \neg(P_1 \wedge P_2 \wedge P_3, \ldots, P_n)$.
Now $\neg(P_1 \wedge P_2, \ldots, P_n) \Leftrightarrow \neg P_1 \vee \neg P_2 \vee \ldots \neg P_n$ by the DeM ∧ law
but $\neg P_1 \vee \neg P_2 \vee \neg P_3 \ldots \neg P_n \Leftrightarrow \exists \ldots \cdot \neg P$. Thus,

$$\neg \forall \ldots \cdot P \Leftrightarrow \exists \ldots \cdot \neg P.$$

Example 4.7

Demonstrate that $\neg\exists \ldots \cdot P \Leftrightarrow \forall \ldots \cdot \neg P$.

$$\exists \ldots \cdot P \Leftrightarrow P_1 \vee P_2 \vee P_3, \ldots, \vee P_n.$$

This means that

$$\neg\exists \ldots \cdot P \Leftrightarrow \neg(P_1 \vee P_2 \vee P_3, \ldots, \vee P_n).$$

However,

$$\neg(P_1 \vee P_2 \vee P_3, \ldots, \vee P_n) \Leftrightarrow$$

$(\neg P_1 \wedge \neg P_2 \wedge P_3, \ldots, \wedge \neg P_n)$ by the DeM $\vee$ law,

$$(\neg P_1 \wedge \neg P_2 \wedge \neg P_3, \ldots, \wedge \neg P_n) \Leftrightarrow \forall \ldots \cdot \neg P.$$

Hence,

$\neg\exists \ldots \cdot P$ is equivalent to $\forall \ldots \cdot \neg P$.

Until now universal and existential quantification have appeared singly in predicates. However, there is no reason why they cannot be mixed. For example, the predicate

$\exists$prog: programs $\cdot$ $\forall$us: users $\cdot$ has_access(us, prog)

states that there is at least one program to which all users have access. Predicates with both universal and existential quantifiers tend to be a little difficult to read. Exercise 4.8 gives you practice in understanding predicates. You would be well advised to complete it before proceeding further.

Exercise 4.8

Translate the following predicates into natural language.

    (i) $\forall$us: users $\cdot$ $\exists$prog: programs $\cdot$ has_access(us, prog)
    (ii) $\forall i$: $1..100 \cdot \exists j$: $1..100 \cdot i^2 = j$
    (iii) $\forall i$: $1..50 \cdot \exists j$: $1..10 \cdot i + j = 3$
    (iv) $\exists$mon: monitors $\cdot$ $\forall$line: comms_lines $\cdot$ is_attached(mon, line)

(v) $\exists j: 1..1000 \cdot \forall i: 1..100 \cdot j = i$

(vi) $\exists$file: filestore $\cdot$ $\forall$us: users $\cdot$
    read_access(us, file) $\wedge$ write_access(us, file)

(vii) $\exists$file: filestore $\cdot$ $\forall$us: users; dir: directories $\cdot$
    has_access(file, us) $\wedge$ can_be_copied(file, dir)

(viii) $\exists i: 1..10 \cdot \forall j: 1..10 \cdot \exists k: 1..200 \cdot j^2 + i = k$

(ix) $\forall k: 1..10 \cdot \exists p: 1..5 \cdot \forall j: 1..3 \cdot k * p > j$

4.3 Proof and deduction

Chapter 3 demonstrated how, starting with some premises, it was possible to deduce and prove a conclusion using a rule of inference. The method used was indirect proof, also known as proof by contradiction or *reductio ad absurdum* proof. This section examines proof in more detail and describes a number of rules of inference which can be used in the proof process.

The proof process starts with a series of predicates known as **premises** or **hypotheses** which are assumed to be true and a statement (predicate) known as a **conclusion** which needs to be demonstrated to be true. For example, if, using the propositional calculus, we wish to demonstrate that

walking, walking $\vee$ running $\Rightarrow$ travelling $\vdash$ travelling,

the proof would start with the premises

walking

walking $\vee$ running $\Rightarrow$ travelling

and demonstrate the conclusion

travelling.

Between the premises and the conclusion are intermediate predicates which can be deduced from a premise or from a predicate which precedes the intermediate predicate. This is shown below in the indirect proof of

walking, walking $\vee$ running $\Rightarrow$ travelling $\vdash$ travelling.

1   walking

2   walking $\vee$ running $\Rightarrow$ travelling

3 ¬travelling

4 ¬(walking ∨ running)   {2, 3}

5 ¬walking   {1, 4}

6 **contradiction**   {1, 5}.

The two premises are written on lines 1 and 2, line 3 is the denial of the conclusion, line 4 is derivable from lines 2 and 3, and, finally, line 5 is the contradictory predicate derivable from lines 1 and 4. Each line consists of a predicate which is either a premise or a predicate which can be derived from a previous predicate.

Each intermediate statement can be derived from examination of the truth table for the relevant propositional operator. For example, predicate 4 may be derived from the fact that, since *¬travelling* is true and *walking ∨ running ⇒ travelling* is true, then *¬(walking ∨ running)* is true.

Since the derivation of intermediate statements is a vital and frequent activity, it is rather inconvenient to examine truth tables continually. The practising mathematician remembers a number of patterns of statements where, if one type of statement is true and another type of statement is true, then another statement is true. A selection of some of these patterns is shown in Table 4.1. P, Q, R, P_1, P_2, ..., P_n are all predicates and C is a contradiction.

The patterns in Table 4.1 are all examples of **rules of inference**. The sixth rule of inference—that, if $\neg P$ implies C, then P must be true—is a re-formulation of the indirect proof rule of inference used in Chapter 3. The truth of the predicate in the right-hand column can be inferred from the truth of the predicate(s) in the left-hand column. In many books you will find such rules written in the form

$$\frac{\text{predicate(s) in left-hand column}}{\text{predicate in right-hand column}}.$$

Thus, if the rule of inference—that if P were true and $P \wedge Q$ were true, then it can be inferred that Q is true—would be written as

$$\frac{P, P \wedge Q}{Q}.$$

Table 4.1

If these are true	Then this must be true
P	$P \lor Q$
$P \land Q$	$P \lor Q$
$P, P \land Q$	Q
$P \lor Q, \neg P$	Q
$P, P \Rightarrow Q$	Q
$(\neg P) \Rightarrow C$	P
$P \Rightarrow Q, Q \Rightarrow R$	$P \Rightarrow R$
$P \Rightarrow Q, Q \Rightarrow P$	$P \Leftrightarrow Q$
$P, \neg Q \Rightarrow \neg P$	Q
$P_1, P_2, P_3, \ldots, P_n$	$P_1 \land P_2 \land P_3, \ldots, P_n$
$P_1, P_2, P_3, \ldots, P_n$	Q
$P_1 \lor P_2 \land P_3, \ldots, P_n \Rightarrow Q$	

Patterns can be verified by examining the truth tables of the predicates involved. For example, the fact that, if P implies Q and if Q implies P, then P is equivalent to Q is demonstrated in Table 4.2. It shows that, whenever $P \Rightarrow Q$ is true and $Q \Rightarrow P$ is true, then $P \Leftrightarrow Q$ is true.

A proof thus consists of a series of premises expressed as predicates which are tautologies, a conclusion expressed as a tautology, and a series of intermediate statements expressed as tautologies. Intermediate predicates and the conclusion can be deduced from preceding predicates by means of rules of inference.

Such rules of inference are important because they telescope a number of lines of a proof. They are well worth memorizing.

Table 4.2

P	Q	$P \Rightarrow Q$	$Q \Rightarrow P$	$P \Leftrightarrow Q$
F	F	T	T	T
F	T	T	F	F
T	F	F	T	F
T	T	T	T	T

Table 4.3

If these statements are true	then this must be true
$\forall x\colon S \cdot P(x)$, $\forall x\colon S \cdot Q(x)$	$\forall x\colon S \cdot P(x) \wedge Q(x)$
$\forall x\colon S \cdot P(x)$	$\exists x\colon S \cdot P(x)$
$\forall x\colon S \cdot P(x)$	$P(a)(a$ is in $S)$
$P(a)(a$ is in $S)$	$\exists x\colon S \cdot P(x)$
$\neg\forall x\colon S \cdot P(x)$	$\exists x\colon S \cdot \neg P(x)$
$\neg\exists x\colon S \cdot P(x)$	$\forall x\colon S \cdot \neg P(x)$

They not only hold for simple variables but for any predicate. Thus, the rule of inference: if P implies Q and also Q implies P, then P is equivalent to Q, can be used to show that if $\neg(old \wedge new)$ implies *replacement* and if *replacement* implies $\neg(old \wedge new)$ then $\neg(old \wedge new)$ is equivalent to *replacement*, where P has been replaced by the complex predicate $\neg(old \wedge new)$ and Q has been replaced by the predicate *replacement*. A number of rules of inference involving both universal and existential quantification can be constructed. Some important ones are shown in Table 4.3 where P and Q are predicates, S is a class of objects, for example, **N** or 1..100, a is an object in S and x is a bound variable which can be assigned values in S. Typical examples of the use of these patterns in proof are

$$\vdots$$

8   $\forall$mon: monitors $\cdot$ m_state(mon, active)
9   $\forall$mon: monitors $\cdot$ m_state(mon, on)
10 $\forall$mon: monitors $\cdot$ m_state(mon, active) $\wedge$
    m_state(mon, on) $\{8, 9\}$

$$\vdots$$

23 $\forall$th: thermocouples $\cdot$ th_state(th, off) $\vee$
    th_state(th, malfunctioning)
24 $\exists$th: thermocouples $\cdot$ th_state(th, off) $\vee$
    th_state(th, malfunctioning) $\{23\}$

$$\vdots$$

35 $\forall$th: ready_thermocouples $\cdot$ th_state(th, functioning)

36 th_state(th12, functioning)
(th12 is in ready_thermocouples)   {35}

⋮

44 th_state(reactor1, off) ∨
th_state(reactor1, functioning)
(reactor1 is in reactors)
45 ∃react: reactors ·
th_state(react, off) ∨ th_state(react, functioning).   {44}

Example 4.8

Demonstrate that

∀mon: monitors · monitor_state(mon, on)

⊢ processor_state(z2, active)

(z2 is in processors)

given the following predicates taken from a system specification

∃mon: monitors · monitor_state(mon, on) ⇒
∀chan: channels · channel_state(chan, ok) ∧
channel_state(chan, functioning)

∀chan: channels · channel_state(chan, ok) ⇒
∀prog: programs · program_state(prog, running)

∃prog: programs · program_state(prog, running) ⇒
∃proc: processors · processor_state(proc, active).

---

1 ∀mon: monitors · monitor_state(mon, on)
2 ∃mon: monitors · monitor_state(mon, on) ⇒
∀chan: channels · channel_state(chan, ok) ∧
channel_state(chan, functioning)
3 ∀chan: channels · channel_state(chan, ok) ⇒
∀prog: programs · program_state(prog, running)
4 ∃prog: programs · program_state(prog, running) ⇒
∃proc: processors · processor_state(proc, active)
5 ∃mon: monitors · monitor_state(mon, on) ⇒   {2}

∀chan: channels · channel_state(chan, ok) ∧
∀chan: channels · channel_state(chan, functioning)
6   ∃mon: monitors · monitor_state(mon, on) ⇒   {5}
∀chan: channels · channel_state(chan, ok)
7   ∃mon: monitors · monitor_state(mon, on) ⇒   {5}
∀chan: channels · channel_state(chan, functioning)
8   ∃mon: monitors · monitor_state(mon, on)   {1}
9   ∀prog: programs · program_state(prog, running) {3, 6, 8}
10 ∃prog: programs · program_state(prog, running)   {9}
11 ∃proc: processors · processor_state(proc, active) {4, 10}
12 processor_state($z2$, active) ($z2$ is in processors).   {11}

Exercise 4.9

Demonstrate whether the following hold.

(i) process_state(idle_process, active) (idle_process is in process)
⊢ on_line(Wilkins) (Wilkins is in operators).

given the following predicates taken from a system specification

(∃proc: processes · process_state(proc, active) ∨
process_state(proc, ready)) ⇒ ∃vdu: vdus · vdu_state(vdu, on)

and
¬∀vdu: vdus · ¬process-state(proc, ready) ⇒
∃op: operators · operator_condition(op, on_line).

(ii) ∀prog: programs · program_state(prog, running),
∃prog: programs · program_state(prog, running) ∨
program_state(prog, ready) ⇒ ok(system),
⊢ screen_potential(screen1, displ) ∨
screen_potential(screen2, displ) (screen1, screen2 in screens)

given the following predicate taken from a system specification

system_state(system, ok) ⇒ ∀screen: screen ·
screen_state(screen, displ).

(iii) ∀react: reactors · reactor_state(react, on_line) ⇒
reactor_condition(react, ok),
reactor_message(cat_cracker, signal) (cat-cracker is in reactors)
⊢ ∃mon: monitors · connected(cat_cracker, mon)

given the following predicates taken from a system specification

∀react: reactors · reactor_message(react, signal) ⇒
reactor_state(react, on_line)

and

∀react: reactors · ∃mon: monitors · reactor_state(react, ok) ∧
connected(react, mon).

4.4 Reasoning about natural numbers

The remainder of this book will assume that you are relatively proficient in reasoning about natural numbers and integers. There will be no specific teaching on the properties of these objects. Thus, lines, of proof, such as

$$14 \quad (x > y) \wedge (y > 10)$$
$$15 \quad x > 10 \qquad \{15\}$$

and

$$23 \quad x > 15 \Rightarrow y > 22$$
$$24 \quad x = 27$$
$$25 \quad y > 22 \qquad \{23, 24\},$$

will be written without comment. If you feel that your knowledge of the natural numbers and integers is inadequate, then [Stew77] provides a good introduction. In order to help you discover whether your knowledge is sufficient for productively reading the remainder of this book two exercises are reproduced below. If you can complete them with little trouble then you can continue with the book without recourse to revision.

Exercise 4.10

Which of the following statements are true and which are false; assume that x, y, and z are all natural numbers.

(i) $7 > 3$.
(ii) $7 > 3 \vee 3 = 4$.

(iii) $\neg 7 > 3 \wedge \neg 8 = 8.$
(iv) $(x = y \wedge y = z) \Rightarrow x = z.$
(v) $(x > 0 \wedge y > 0) \Rightarrow x * y > 0.$
(vi) $(x > 0 \wedge y < 0) \Rightarrow x + y > 0.$
(vii) $x * y = 10 \wedge x = 2 \vee x = 5 \Rightarrow y = 5 \vee y = 2.$
(viii) $\forall x: \mathbf{N} \cdot x \geq 0.$
(ix) $\forall x: \mathbf{N} \cdot x = 2.$
(x) $\forall x, y, z: \mathbf{N} \cdot x < y \wedge y < z \Rightarrow x < z.$
(xi) $\forall x: \mathbf{N} \cdot \exists y: \mathbf{N} \cdot x^2 = y.$
(xii) $\forall x: \mathbf{N} \cdot \exists y: \mathbf{N} \cdot y = x - 2.$
(xiii) $\exists y: \mathbf{N} \cdot \forall x: 1..100 \cdot y > x + 5.$
(xiv) $\forall z: \mathbf{N} \cdot \exists y: \mathbf{N} \cdot y * z = 7.$
(xv) $(x^2 + y^2 = 25) \wedge (x = 3 \Rightarrow y = 4).$
(xvi) $\forall y: 1..10 \cdot \exists x: 1..100 \cdot \forall z: 1..10 \cdot y + x = z.$

Exercise 4.11

Complete the following lines of proof.

(i) 8 $x = 120$
     9   $x > 14 \Rightarrow y > 8$
     10 $y > 6 \Rightarrow z = 4$
         ?
(ii) 11 temp > 500
     12 ambient > 100
     13 temp $*$ ambient $> 10000 \Rightarrow$ system_state(sys1, alarm)
         ?
(iii) 6 $\forall$mon: monitors $\cdot$ monitor_state(mon, on) $\Rightarrow$
         monitor_condition(mon, functioning)
      7 $\forall$mon: monitors $\cdot$ monitor_condition(mon, functioning)
         $\wedge$ ambient $> 500 \Rightarrow$ system_state(sys1, alarm)
      8 ambient $= 702$
      9 $\forall$mon: monitors $\cdot$ monitor_state(mon, on)
         ?
(iv) 4   pressure $= 100$
     5   temperature $= 50$
     6   (temperature $> 70 \vee$ pressure $> 80) \Rightarrow \forall$mon: monitors $\cdot$
         monitor_state(mon, on)
     7   ?   (mon22 in mon)
(v) 14 width $= 17$

15   (width < 20 ∨ width > 35) $\Rightarrow$ (temp > 12 ∧ temp < 20)
16   temp $> 10 \Rightarrow$ sub-sys_state(subsys1, on)
17   ?

(vi)   37   width < 20 ∨ width > 30
      38   width $< 18 \Rightarrow$ roller_contact(roller, on)
      39   width $\geq 18 \Rightarrow$ roller_contact(roller, off)
      40   temp $> 42 \Rightarrow$ width $= 18$
      41   pressure $> 17 \Rightarrow$ temp > 50
      42   pressure $= 18$
      43   ?

4.5   Predicate calculus and design specification

Enough mathematics has been described for a practical application to be described. Such an application is the specification of program units using predicate calculus. During system design a functional specification is transformed into a system design. Such a design will consist of a series of discrete units. In turn these units will consist of modules which contain procedures and functions which are related by virtue of the tasks they perform. For example, in a system design for controlling a chemical plant there may be a module which is concerned with those processing functions associated with the thermocouples attached to the reactor. This module may contain procedures and functions which: read a temperature from a thermocouple; check on the functioning of a thermocouple; and sense and decode malfunctions which may arise in a thermocouple.

The normal way to specify the function of such procedure and functions is to use natural language. A typical example is

> The procedure *summupout* has two parameters. The first parameter is an integer array *vals* which has a range 1..10. The second parameter is a boolean variable *outrange*. This is set true if any value in *vals* is less than or greater than 2000.

Given such a description a programmer can construct a program which satisfies the specification. The same drawbacks of using natural language in system specifications are true for design specifications. Fortunately, predicate calculus, augmented by a few extra facilities, can be used as an exact notation for describing the function of program units.

The first extra facility is a predicate formed from the existential quantifier which asserts that only one object in a class holds. This quantifier is known as the **singular existential quantifier**, and it is written in the same form as the existential quantifier except for the fact that an exclamation mark precedes the ∃. Thus,

$$!\exists x: \mathbf{N} \cdot x = 5$$

asserts that there is only one natural number which equals 5. It is important to recognize that this singular existential quantifier is different from the existential quantifier which you are already familiar with. For example,

$$!\exists \text{mon: monitors} \cdot \text{monitor\_state(mon, off)}$$

asserts that there is *exactly one* monitor which is off while

$$\exists \text{mon: monitors} \cdot \text{monitor\_state(mon, off)}$$

asserts that there is *at least one* monitor that is off. For example, if there were 100 monitors, there could be anything from one to 100 monitors that are in the off state.

The second extra facility is provided by a quantifier known as the **counting quantifier**. Again it is written in the same way as the existential and universal quantifiers. The counting quantifier is not a predicate. It does not deliver a true or false value but an integer. This integer represents the number of objects in a class which have a certain property. The quantifier is written as Ω. Some examples of its use are

$$\Omega x: 1..20 \cdot x^2 < 17.$$
$$\Omega \text{mon: monitors} \cdot \text{monitor\_state(mon, off)} \vee$$
$$\text{monitor\_state(mon, functioning)}$$
$$\Omega \text{lines: line} \cdot \text{connected(line, reactor12)},$$
$$\Omega x: 1..100 \cdot \exists y: 1..50 \cdot x + y < 10.$$

The first example counts the number of values of x which lie between 1 and 20 whose squares are less than 17. There are in fact four $(1, 2, 3, 4)$. The second example gives the number of monitors which are either off or functioning. The third example gives the number of communication lines which are connected to *reactor12*. The final example gives the number of integers which lie between 1 and 100 which, when added to a number between 1 and 50, give a sum less than 10. The value of this will be eight since there are eight values of x which satisfy the predicate. They are $1, 2, 3, \ldots, 8$.

The final extra facility is the summation operator Σ. This returns the value of the sum of all objects in a class. The operator is written in the same way as the quantifiers previously described. Some examples of its use are

$$\Sigma i: 1..10 \cdot i$$

$$\Sigma i: 1..100 \cdot i^2$$

The first example gives the sum of the first 10 natural numbers while the second example gives the sum of the squares of the first 100 natural numbers.

Equipped with this slightly augmented form of the predicate calculus, it is relatively straightforward to construct precise specifications of the function of program units. Such specifications will consist of two predicates. The first is called a **pre-condition**. It relates the values of global variables and parameters *before* a program unit is executed. The second predicate is called a **post-condition**. It relates the values of global variables and parameters *after* a program unit has been executed. As an example, consider the translation of the following specification into post-condition and pre-condition form.

> The function of the update procedure is to update the value of the global variable *system_state*. The procedure has one integer parameter *temp*. If *temp* is greater or equal to 200, then *systemstate* is set to zero; otherwise *system_state* is set to a value of one. *system_state* will have a value ranging between zero and five. *temp* will range from zero to 1000. *temp* will be unaffected by the procedure.

This predicate for the pre-condition can be written as

$\text{temp} \geq 0 \wedge \text{temp} \leq 1000 \wedge \text{system\_state} \geq 0 \wedge \text{system\_state} \leq 5.$

The post-condition should state that, if *temp* is greater than or equal to 200, then *system-state* is set to zero; otherwise *system-state* is set to one. This can be written as

$\text{temp}' = \text{temp} \wedge (\text{temp} \geq 200 \Rightarrow \text{system\_state}' = 0) \wedge$

$(\text{temp} < 200 \Rightarrow \text{system\_state}' = 1).$

The primes over a variable indicate the value of the variable *after* a program unit has been executed. Thus, the post-condition above indicate that *temp* remains unchanged and that *system_state* is given a value which is dependent on the value of *temp*.

Normally predicates such as *temp' = temp* are omitted in post-conditions. The fact that a variable such as *temp'* is omitted in a predicate is sufficient to indicate that its value remains unchanged. However, if it is really necessary to make explicit that a variable value remains unchanged after execution of a program unit, then such equalities will be used.

Example 4.9

A procedure *update* has two integer parameters. The function of the procedure is to examine its first parameter *flag* and set its second parameter *value*. If *flag* lies between zero and 10 then *value* is set to zero. However, if *flag* does not lie between zero and 10, then *value* is unchanged.

Write the corresponding post and pre-conditions.

The question says nothing about the values of the parameters *flag* and *value* on entry to *update*. Therefore, no pre-condition can be constructed. The post-condition is

$$(\text{flag} \geq 0 \wedge \text{flag} \leq 10) \Rightarrow \text{value}' = 0.$$

If the fact that *value* was unchanged if flag lay outside the range zero to 10 were specified, then the predicate

$$(\text{flag} < 0 \vee \text{flag} > 10) \Rightarrow \text{value}' = \text{value}$$

would be conjoined to the above predicate.

Exercise 4.13

Write post- and pre-conditions for the following design specifications.

(i) The function of the procedure *examine* is to examine its first integer parameter *val* and update its second integer parameter *newval*. If *val* is greater than zero, then it is added to *newval*; otherwise it is subtracted from *newval*. *Val* will always have a value between −100 and 100.

(ii) The procedure *select* has three parameters. The first parameter *flag* is boolean; the second and third parameters *add* and *val* are integers. If the first parameter is true, then the second parameter is set to the modulus of the third parameter.

(iii) The procedure *quotandrem* has four parameters: *x, y, q, r*. They are all integers. The third parameter *q* will be set to the quotient of the first two parameters *x* and *y* while the fourth parameter *r* will be set to the remainder upon dividing the first parameter by the second parameter. The first two parameters will be positive.

(iv) The procedure *newval* has one integer parameter *val*. The function of *newval* is to increment the parameter by 1.

Quantification can be used in both pre- and post-conditions. Indeed, if the properties of arrays need to be specified, then the use of quantification is the only way to achieve succinctness. For example, assume that a post-condition required that all the elements of an array *A[1..100]* be zero. This would be written as

$$\forall i: 1..100 \cdot A[i] = 0$$

rather than

$$A[1] = 0 \wedge A[2] = 0, \ldots \wedge A[100] = 0.$$

As an example of the use of quantifiers used in a design specification, consider the following natural-language description of the function of a procedure *addup*.

The procedure *addup* has three parameters *arr1*, *arr2* and *arr3*. All the parameters are integer arrays with range 1..50. The function of *addup* is to add corresponding elements of *arr1* and *arr2* and place their sum in the corresponding element of *arr3*. On entry to *addup* all the elements of *arr3* will be zero.

The pre-condition will be

$$\forall i: 1..50 \cdot \text{arr3}[i] = 0.$$

The post-condition will be

$$\forall i: 1..50 \cdot \text{arr3}[i] = \text{arr2}[i] + \text{arr1}[i].$$

A more complicated example in the use of quantification occurs in connection with a sorting procedure *sort* whose natural-language specification is

> The procedure *sort* has one parameter A. This is an integer array with a range 1..40. The function of *sort* is to place the elements of A in ascending order. All the values contained in A will be less than 100 and greater than or equal to 0.

A first attempt at writing post- and pre-conditions is

Pre-condition $\forall i: 1..40 \cdot A[i] \geq 0 \wedge A[i] < 100$

Post-condition $\forall i: 1..39 \cdot A'[i] < A'[i+1].$

The pre-condition is correct but what about the post-condition? Certainly it states that the elements of A after *sort* has been executed will be in ascending order. However, there is an important component of the post-condition missing. This is the fact that the elements of A' after sorting match the elements of A, although they may not be in the same position in the array. One way of writing this might be

$$\forall i: 1..40 \cdot \exists j: 1..100 \cdot A'[j] = A[i].$$

This states that for every element in A there is an element in A' that matches it. The post-condition can then be written as

$$\forall i: 1..39 \cdot A'[i] < A'[i+1] \wedge \forall i: 1..40 \cdot \exists j: 1..100 \cdot A'[j] = A[i].$$

Is this correct? Unfortunately not. If A just contained ones and A' had a one in its first element and two in the rest of its elements the postcondition would hold since for each of the elements in A there exists an element in A' that matches it but A' does not represent the sorted version of A. If A contained distinct elements, i.e. there was no duplication, then the post-condition above would be adequate. However, the pre-condition does not state this. This is an excellent example of the use of mathematics to clarify and question a specification.

An adequate post-condition would have to include a predicate which asserts that A' is a permutation of A, i.e. the number of occurrences of an integer in A matches the number of occurrences in A'. A predicate which asserts this is

$$\forall j: 0..99 \cdot ((\Omega i: 1..40 \cdot A'[i] = j) = (\Omega k: 1..40 \cdot A[k] = j)).$$

This gives the correct post-condition

$$\forall i: 1..39 \cdot A'[i] < A'[i+1] \wedge$$
$$\forall j: 0..99 \cdot ((\Omega i: 1..40 \cdot A'[i] = j) = (\Omega k: 1..40 \cdot A[k] = j)).$$

Example 4.10

If the pre-condition for the sorting example presented above had to indicate that, at most, A contained only one occurrence of an integer, how would you write the pre-condition?

The pre-condition would still have to state that all the elements of A ranged between zero and 100. However, this would have to be augmented with the fact that A contained only one occurrence of an integer. Since the range of A is 1..40 and the integers lie between 1 and 100, some integers will not occur at all. The pre-condition will hence be

$$\forall i: 1..40 \cdot A[i] < 100 \wedge A[i] \geq 0 \wedge$$
$$\forall k: 0..99 \cdot (\Omega i: 1..40 \cdot A[i] = k) \leq 1.$$

Example 4.11

A procedure *search* has three parameters: *vals*, *searchfor*, and *found*. *vals* is an integer array with a range of 1..200. *searchfor* is an integer parameter, and *found* is an integer parameter. If *searchfor* occurs in *vals* then *found* is set to one; otherwise it is set to two. Write down the post- and pre-conditions.

Unfortunately, the natural-language specification does not say anything about the values that the parameters have on entry to search. Hence a pre-condition cannot be written. The post-condition is

$$(\exists i: 1..200 \cdot \text{vals}[i] = \text{searchfor} \Rightarrow \text{found}' = 1) \wedge$$
$$(\neg \exists i: 1..200 \cdot \text{vals}[i] = \text{searchfor} \Rightarrow \text{found}' = 2).$$

Exercise 4.14

Write down pre- and post-conditions for the following design specifications expressed in natural language.

(i) The procedure *examine* has four parameters. The first parameter is an integer array *vals* which has a range 1..20. The other parameters: *searchfor_range*, *obj*, and *flag* are integers. *Examine* looks at the first *searchfor_range* elements of *vals* and sets *flag* to one if at least one element is equal to *obj*.

(ii) The procedure *descend* has two parameters. The first is *valarr* which is an integer array with range 1..50. The second is an integer *flagset*. If *valarr* is in descending order than *flagset* will be set to zero; otherwise it remains unchanged.

(iii) The procedure *clear* has three parameters. The first parameter *exam* is an integer array with a range 1..50. The second parameter *to_be_cleared* is an integer array with a range 1..75. The third parameter is an integer *obj* which lies between 0 and 200. If *obj* is contained in exam, then all the elements of *to_be_cleared* are set to zero; otherwise it remains unchanged.

(iv) The procedure *sametime* has three parameters: *op1,op2*, and *clear*. These are all integer arrays with a range 1..100. *Op1* and *op2* all contain positive integers less than or equal to 500. The function of *sametime* is to examine *op1* and *op2* and, if they are identical, to set all the elements of *clear* to zero; otherwise it remains the same.

(v) The procedure *plateau* has two parameters. The first parameter *vals* is an integer array which has a range 1..500. The second parameter *flag* is an integer. If *vals* contains a sequence of equal integers the length of which is greater than one, then *flag* is set to one; otherwise *flag* remains unchanged. *vals* contains positive integers less than or equal to 100.

(vi) The procedure *checkup* has four parameters. The first parameter is an integer array *first* which has a range 1..100. The second and third parameters, *second* and *third,* are integer arrays with a range 1..75. The fourth parameter *flag* is an integer. The function of *checkup* is to examine the arrays and set *flag* to 1 if those integer values in *first* that are not in *second* are in *third*; otherwise *flag* remains unchanged. *Flag* will be a positive integer less than four.

4.6 Requirements analysis and specification as the construction of informal theory

One of the major concepts in pure mathematics is that of an **axiomatic theory**. Such a theory consists of a number of **primitive terms** and a set of statements which are true within that theory. An example of such a theory is Euclid's elements upon which much of school geometry was based. The primitive terms are objects such as lines and points; typical statements which are true within this theory are: 'the sum of the angles of a triangle is equal to 180°' and 'the square of the hypotenuse of a right-angled triangle is equal to the sum of the squares of the other two sides'. In presenting a theory a system of logic is used; if this system is presupposed as already known, then the theory is known as an **informal theory**.

Statements of a theory are categorized into two sets. The first set are those statements which are assumed to be true: they are known as **axioms**; the second set are those statements which can be derived from axioms by means of rules of inference: they are known as **theorems** or **laws**.

A proof in a theory is a finite sequence $S_1, S_2, S_3, \ldots, S_n$ of statements in the theory such that each S is an axiom, or can be derived from any of the preceding statements by applying a rule of inference. A theorem then is the last statement of a proof. Mathematicians regard axioms as theorems with only a single item in their proof sequence; thus, axioms are a subset of theorems.

If T is a finite set of statements in an axiomatic theory then the fact that C is deducible from T is symbolized by

$$T \vdash C$$

if and only if there is a sequence $S_1, S_2, S_3, \ldots, S_m$ of statements where each S is either an axiom, a statement in T, or a statement derivable from previous Ss by a rule of inference. The sequence $S_1, S_2, S_3, \ldots, S_m$ and $C = S_m$ is known as a **formal deduction** of C from T. The statements in T are known as **premises** or **hypotheses**. In the case where T is empty the formal deduction is written as

$$\vdash C$$

and symbolizes the proof of a theorem.

Propositional calculus can be regarded as an axiomatic theory. It consists of the axioms

$$A \vee A \Rightarrow A$$
$$A \Rightarrow (A \vee B)$$
$$A \vee B \Rightarrow B \vee A$$
$$(A \Rightarrow B) \Rightarrow (C \vee A \Rightarrow C \vee B)$$

together with the following abbreviations for certain propositional expressions

$$A \Rightarrow B \quad \text{for} \quad \neg A \vee B$$
$$A \wedge B \quad \text{for} \quad \neg(\neg A \vee \neg B)$$
$$A \Leftrightarrow B \quad \text{for} \quad (A \Rightarrow B) \wedge (B \Rightarrow A).$$

From these axioms all the theorems or laws of propositional calculus can be derived. As an example, the demonstration that

$$\vdash \neg A \Rightarrow \neg A$$

is

1	$A \vee A \Rightarrow A$	
2	$(A \vee A \Rightarrow A) \Rightarrow (\neg A \vee (A \vee A) \Rightarrow \neg A \vee A)$	
3	$\neg A \vee (A \vee A) \Rightarrow \neg A \vee A$	$\{1, 2\}$
4	$(A \Rightarrow A \vee A) \Rightarrow (A \Rightarrow A)$	$\{3\}$
5	$A \Rightarrow A \vee A$	

6    $A \Rightarrow A$ {4, 5}

7    $\neg A \vee A$ {6}

8    $\neg A \vee A \Rightarrow A \vee \neg A$

9    $A \vee \neg A$ {7, 8}.

Line 1 is axiom 1 and line 2 is axiom 4 with A replaced by $A \vee A$, B replaced by A, and C replaced by $\neg A$, respectively. Line 3 follows from lines 1 and 2 using the rule of inference that, if A is true and $A \Rightarrow B$ is true, then B must be true. Line 4 is just a restatement of line 3 in terms of $\vee$ and $\neg$. Line 5 is axiom 2 with B replaced by A. Line 6 follows from lines 4 and 5 using the rule of inference that, if A is true and $A \Rightarrow B$ is true, then B must be true. Line 7 is just a restatement of line 6 with $\Rightarrow$ replaced by $\vee$ and $\neg$. Line 8 is just axiom 3 with A replaced by $\neg A$ and B replaced by A. Finally, line 9 follows from lines 7 and 8 using the rule of inference that, if A is true and $A \Rightarrow B$ is true, then B must be true. Line 9 is just a restatement of $\neg A \Rightarrow \neg A$.

What has occurred is a formal proof which consists of a sequence of statements 1, 2, 3, . . . , 9 each of which is an axiom or can be derived by means of a rule of inference from previous statements.

This derivation of a theorem may seem rather long-winded. Establishing theorems initially in any axiomatic system is usually a tedious affair. However, once a number of theorems have been established the derivation of further theorems usually follows quite easily.

Requirements analysis and system specification is an example of the construction of informal theories. A statement of requirements is translated into a set of axioms. This then comprises the system specification. The specification is validated by checking the axioms for consistency. Next, the system specification is validated for completeness. This can be done in two ways. The first involves the analyst constructing a set of theorems representing known properties of the system and attempting to prove each theorem from the axioms. If the theorems about known properties of the system can be proved, then a high degree of confidence in the system specification can be achieved. The second involves the analyst stating premises about the system, asking the user to produce a statement about the assumed behaviour of the system, based on these premises and then attempting to demonstrate that the statement can be deduced from the premises using axioms and known theorems about the system.

The theory which this book uses for specification is concerned with collections of objects. It is known as set theory and is described in full detail in Chapter 5.

5 Set theory

The previous sections of this book have concentrated on using propositional or predicate calculus for describing the functionality of a software system. For example, you have now been given the mathematical tools to express the essence of the paragraph

> If all the monitoring valves are functioning normally and at least one computer is on-line, then, provided the system is in a functioning state, the header line will be displayed on all the vdus attached to the system.

However, the mathematical tool-kit is not yet complete. Consider the paragraphs

> There are two types of file: user files and system files. A file cannot be both a user file and a system file.
>
> All the files which are user files cannot be deleted.
>
> If a file is an archive file, then it cannot be either an user or system file.

It is possible to express these paragraphs using predicates such as *owner*. For example, the first paragraph can be expressed in predicate calculus as

$$\forall \text{file}: \text{files} \cdot \neg(\text{file\_type}(\text{file}, \text{user}) \land \text{file\_type}(\text{file}, \text{system})).$$

However, the concept of a class and the concept of membership crop up time and time again in specifications. Consequently, it is worth introducing symbols, operators, and laws to cater for this. This is the role of **set theory**.

5.1 Sets and subsets

A set is a collection of objects. The objects may be natural numbers, names of files, locations of monitoring instruments, user names, or whatever objects are of interest to the specifier. The sets and the objects in a set are of a certain type in the sense that variables in a programming language such as Pascal are of a certain type. As will be seen later, this means that, as in modern programming languages, certain operators are only valid when their operands are of the same type.

A set can be specified as a collection of objects surrounded by curly brackets. Thus

$$\{21, 7, 14, 3\}$$

is an example of a set of objects which are natural numbers and

$$\{\text{archiver, sorter, editor, finder}\}$$

is a set of utility programs. The important property of a set is that **duplicates are not allowed**. Thus

$$\{1, 3, 4, 1, 9, 3\}$$

is not an example of a set.

A set cannot only contain single-element objects but can also contain aggregates of objects. For example,

$$\{(1, 2), (3, 4), (4, 5)\}$$

is a set of pairs of natural numbers and

$$\{(\text{mon1, mon2, mon3}), (\text{mon2, mon4, mon5}),$$
$$(\text{mon3, mon7, mon8})\}$$

is a set of triples which contain monitor names.
A set can be **finite** or can be **infinite**.

$$\{1, 3, 5\}$$

is an example of a finite set while the set of all natural numbers is an example of an infinite set.

The objects which make up a set are known as **members**. The fact that an object is a member of a set is written as

$$x \in S.$$

If x does not belong in a set, then this is written as

$$x \notin S.$$

Thus,

$$3 \in \{3, 4, 7\},$$
$$5 \in \{17, 230, 46, 5\},$$
$$\text{update} \in \{\text{update, write, read}\}$$

are examples of predicates which are true and

$$1 \notin \{2, 5, 7\},$$
$$\text{vdu1} \notin \{\text{vdu3, vdu8, vdu9}\}$$

are examples of predicates which are also true.

Example 5.1

The following is an example of an extract from a natural-language specification. Convert it into predicate calculus using the $\in$ and $\notin$ operators.

> If the file is a read_access file or not an update_access file then the system manager will regard the file as a non_archivable file.

file $\in$ read_access_files $\lor$ file $\notin$ update_access_files $\Rightarrow$ file $\in$ non_archivable_files.

This illustrates the fact that set operators can be used in predicates and also that an object can be a member of a number of sets.

Exercise 5.1

Convert the following paragraphs of natural-language specification into predicate calculus. Use the operators $\in$ and $\notin$ where necessary.

(i) All the files in the system will be read_access files or write_access files.

(ii) No file in the system will be an active file and a passive file, provided the monitoring subsystem is in a normal condition status.

(iii) There is only one file which is a modify_file and an update_file.

(iv) There will be five system files in the system.

(v) The password2 file will contain the passwords of those users who are system users.

5.1.1 Set specification

How is it possible to specify members of a set? Already one method has been described where the elements of a set were explicitly listed. For example,

$$\{1, 3, 5\}$$

is an explicit listing of the set containing those odd numbers less than 6. Unfortunately, listing a set this way has a number of disadvantages. The first disadvantage is that, for large finite sets, explicit listing is tedious and, for infinite sets, impossible. The second disadvantage is that such a listing does not make the relationship between the elements of a set clear. For example, does the set

$$\{1, 3, 5\}$$

represent the odd numbers less than six or the positive square root of the elements of the set

$$\{1, 9, 25\}?$$

In order to cope with these disadvantages mathematicians have developed a notation which enables a set to be succinctly and unambiguously defined. An example of this is

$$\{n : \mathbf{N} \mid n^2 < 25 \cdot n\}.$$

It defines a set of natural numbers whose squares are less than 25, i.e. it specifies the set

$$\{0, 1, 2, 3, 4\}.$$

This way of defining a set is known as a **comprehensive**

specification. Its general form is

{ ↑ | ↑ · ↖ }.

| Signature | Predicate | Term |

Thus, the comprehensive specification

$$\{n: \mathbf{N} \mid n < 20 \wedge n > 10 \cdot n\}$$

denotes the set of natural numbers which lie between 10 and 20, $n: \mathbf{N}$ is the signature, $n < 20 \wedge n > 10$ is the predicate, and n is the term.

A signature consists of a series of identifiers together with the sets to which they belong. Thus,

$$n: \mathbf{N}$$

states that n is a natural number and

$$a, b, c: \mathbf{N}$$

states that a, b and c are all natural numbers. There is no restriction on the number and type of each identifier; for example,

$$x, y, z: \mathbf{N}; \text{file1: system\_files; file2: user\_files}$$

is a signature which introduces three identifiers x, y, and z which belong to the set of natural numbers, *file1* which belongs to the set *system_files*, and *file2* which belongs to the set *user_files*.

The predicate part of a comprehensive set specification defines the properties of the members of the set which is specified. Thus,

$$\{n: \mathbf{N} \mid n^3 > 10 \cdot n\}$$

specifies the set of natural numbers which have the property that their cubes are greater than 10.

The term part of a comprehensive set specification defines the form of the members of the set. A term consists of an expression which, when evaluated, will deliver a value which is of the same type as the set. For example,

$$\{n: \mathbf{N} \mid n > 20 \wedge n < 100 \cdot n\}$$

states that a set will contain single natural numbers which satisfy the predicate $n > 20 \wedge n < 100$, while

$$\{x, y \colon \mathbf{N} \mid x + y = 100 \cdot (x, y)\}$$

specifies the set of pairs which are natural numbers whose sum is 100. i.e. $\{(0, 100), (1, 99), (2, 98), \ldots, (100, 0)\}$. Thus, the term in this example defines the fact that elements of the set are pairs. Some more examples of comprehensive set specifications with their natural-language equivalents are now given.

$$\{x \colon \mathbf{N} \mid x = 3 \cdot x\}$$

is the set of all natural numbers whose elements are equal to 3. This specifies the set $\{3\}$.

$$\{x, y \colon \mathbf{N} \mid x + y = 5 \cdot x^2 + y^2\}$$

is the set of natural numbers of the form $x^2 + y^2$ where $x + y$ equals 5. This specifies the set $\{13, 17, 25\}$.

$$\{x, y \colon \mathbf{N} \mid x + y = 5 \cdot (x, y)\}$$

specifies the set of pairs of natural numbers whose sum is 5. It represents the set $\{(0, 5), (1, 4), (2, 3), (3, 2), (4, 1), (5, 0)\}$.

$$\{\text{mon} \colon \text{monitors} \mid \text{monitor\_state(mon, on)} \cdot \text{mon}\}$$

specifies the set of monitors which are on.

$$\{\text{file} \colon \text{system\_files} \mid \text{file} \in \text{deleted\_files} \wedge \text{file} \in \text{archived\_files} \cdot \text{file}\}$$

specifies the set of system files which are both deleted files and archived files.

If a term involves simple elements such as a, (a, b), or (a, b, c), then the term is normally omitted. For example, the set specification

$$\{n \colon \mathbf{N} \mid n < 10 \wedge n > 5 \cdot n\}$$

would normally be written as

$$\{n \colon \mathbf{N} \mid n < 10 \wedge n > 5\}$$

and the set specification,

$$\{a, b \colon \mathbf{N} \mid a < 10 \wedge b < a \cdot (a, b)\},$$

would normally be written as

$$\{a, b \colon \mathbf{N} \mid a < 10 \wedge b < a\}.$$

Example 5.2

The set *oddten* is

$$\{1, 3, 5, 7, 9\}.$$

Write down the comprehensive set specification of a set which is formed by extracting those members of *oddten* which are in the range 3 to 7.

The set that is asked for is that whose members (x) are in *oddten* and which satisfy the predicate $x \geq 3 \wedge x \leq 7$. The full specification is

$$\{x: \text{oddten} \mid x \geq 3 \wedge x \leq 7\}.$$

Example 5.3

Write down the comprehensive specification of the set of pairs for which the first element is a natural number greater than 10 and the second element is the square of the first element.

The specification is

$$\{n: \mathbf{N} \mid n > 10 \cdot (n, n^2)\}.$$

Exercise 5.2

Define the following sets using a comprehensive specification omitting the term if necessary.

    (i) The set of natural numbers less than 10.
    (ii) The set of pairs of natural numbers whose sum of squares is less than 200.

(iii) The set of natural numbers which are between 10 and 53.

(iv) The set of pairs of the form (x, x^2) where x is greater than 100.

(v) The set of files which are both system files and user files.

(vi) The set of files which are user files and are owned by Thomas.

(vii) The set of files which are user files and are accessed by more than 10 users.

(viii) The set of files which are not user files and not system files and which are in the directory *ControlIX*.

Exercise 5.3

If *system_files* is the set

{scheduler, file_handler, command_handler, peripheral_handler}

and *master_files* is the set

{scheduler, file_handler, us_file1, us_file2, us_file3},

which of the following predicates are true and which are false?

(i) scheduler ∈ system_files.

(ii) scheduler ∈ system_files ∧ scheduler ∉ master_files.

(iii) scheduler ∈ {file: files | file ∈ system_files ∧ file ∉ master_files · file}.

(iv) scheduler ∈ {file: files | file ∈ system_files ∧ file ∈ master_files · file}.

(v) peripheral_handler ∈ {file: files | file ∈ system_files ∧ file ∈ master_files}.

5.1.2 The empty set

Consider the comprehensive specification

$$\{n: \mathbf{N} \mid n > 10 \land n < 3\}.$$

This is the set of all natural numbers which are greater than 10 and less than 3. How many elements would this set contain? Unfortunately, there is no natural number which satisfies the predicate of the specification. Thus, there are no elements in the set. This set is known as the **empty set**. In this book it will be written as { }. In some mathematics books it is written as $\emptyset$.

5.1.3 Subsets and the power set

Within any given set A there exist other sets which can be obtained by removing some of the elements of A. These are called **subsets** of the set A. For example, if A is

$$\{1, 3, 9, 14, 200\},$$

then both $\{1, 3, 9\}$ and $\{1, 9, 14\}$ are subsets of A. The fact that a set is a subset of another set is expressed by the operators: $\subset$ and $\subseteq$. The predicate

$$A \subseteq B$$

is true if A is a subset of B including being equal to B. Thus,

$$\{1, 2\} \subseteq \{1, 2, 3, 4\}$$
$$\{1\} \subseteq \{1, 2, 3, 4\}$$
$$\{1, 2, 3, 4\} \subseteq \{1, 2, 3, 4\}$$

are all true. The predicate

$$A \subset B$$

is true when A is a **proper subset** of B, that is, A is a subset of B but not equal to B. Thus, the predicates

$$\{1, 2\} \subset \{1, 2, 3, 4\}$$
$$\{4\} \subset \{1, 2, 3, 4\}$$
$$\{1, 4\} \subset \{1, 2, 3, 4\}$$

are all true, while

$$\{1, 2, 3, 4\} \subset \{1, 2, 3, 4\}$$

is false.

One curious result involving subsets and the empty set which confuses many students who start studying pure mathematics is that the empty set is a subset of *every* set. The formal proof of this is

1	X is any set	
2	$\neg((\{\ \}) \subset X)$	
3	$\exists x: \{\ \} \cdot x \notin X$	$\{2\}$
4	$a \notin X \wedge a \in \{\ \}$	$\{3\}$
5	$a \in \{\ \}$	$\{4\}$
6	**contradiction**	$\{5\}$.

This is a proof by contradiction. First, it is assumed that $\{\ \}$ is not a subset of any set X (line 2). This means that there is an element of $\{\ \}$ which is not in X (line 3). This implies that there is an element a contained in $\{\ \}$ which is not in X (line 4). This implies that there is an element a which is in $\{\ \}$ (Line 5). This is a contradiction since $\{\ \}$ is the empty set and hence has no elements. Consequently, the assumption (Line 2) is false and the empty set is a subset of every set.

Exercise 5.4

Which of the following predicates are true and which are false?

   (i) $\{file1, file2\} \subset \{file1, file2, file3\}$.
  (ii) $\{n: \mathbf{N} \mid n < 4\} \subset \{n: \mathbf{N} \mid n < 7\}$.
 (iii) $\{\ \} \subset \{file: files \mid file\_state(file, on) \wedge file\_state(file, normal)\}$.
  (iv) $\{a, b: \mathbf{N} \mid a + b = 4 \cdot a^2 + b^2\} \subset \{n: \mathbf{N} \mid n > 10\}$.
   (v) $\{n: \mathbf{N} \mid n > 10\} \subset \{n: \mathbf{N} \mid n < 10\}$.
  (vi) $\{n: \mathbf{N} \mid n^2 \leq 100\} \subset \{n: \mathbf{N} \mid n \leq 10\}$.
 (vii) $\{3, 4\} \subset \{7, 8, 9\} \Rightarrow \{2, 4\} \subset \{2, 3, 4\}$.
(viii) $\{3\} \subset \{n: \mathbf{N} \mid n > 2 \cdot n\} \vee \{3\} \subset \{4, 5, 6\}$.
  (ix) $\{file1, file2\} \subset \{file2, file3\} \wedge \{file1, file2\} \subset \{file1, file3\}$.

The set of all possible subsets of a set A is known as the **power set** of A. The concept of a power set occurs time and again in mathematics and in system specifications. Because of this it is given a special symbol $\mathbb{P}$. The power set of A is written $\mathbb{P}A$. The power set of any set A is defined formally by means of the predicate

$$a \in \mathbb{P}A \Leftrightarrow a \subseteq A.$$

Thus, $\mathbb{P}\{1, 2, 3\}$ is

$$\{\{\,\}, \{1\}, \{2\}, \{3\}, \{1, 2\}, \{1, 3\}, \{2, 3\}, \{1, 2, 3\}\},$$

remembering, of course, that the empty set is a subset of *any* set.

Example 5.4

Write down $\mathbb{P}X$ where X is $\{\text{file1}, \text{file2}\}$.

Since the power set of a set is the set of all combinations of the members of that set plus the empty set, the answer is

$$\{\{\,\}, \{\text{file1}\}, \{\text{file2}\}, \{\text{file1}, \text{file2}\}\}.$$

5.2 Set operators

The previous section introduced the concept of a set as a collection of distinct objects or elements which have a certain type. To manipulate such sets requires a series of operators. Already, the operators $\subset$, $\subseteq$, $\in$, $\notin$, and $\mathbb{P}$ have been described. The operator $\in$ can be regarded as a primitive as all other set operators can be defined in terms of it using predicate calculus.

5.2.1 Set equality

A new operator which has been used informally in the previous section is the equality operator. This is written as $=$. Its operands must be of the same type. If A and B are two sets of the same type, then $A = B$ is true when each set contains the same elements. Thus,

$$\{1, 2, 4, 5\} = \{1, 2, 5, 4\}$$
$$\{9, 8, 7, 6, 5\} = \{7, 8, 6, 9, 5\}$$

are true while

$$\{1, 3, 5\} = \{1, 3, 7, 11\},$$
$$\{1, 3, 5\} = \{1, 3, 5, 9, 11\}$$

are false. Again = can be defined in terms of $\in$ and predicate calculus.

$$A = B \Leftrightarrow \forall a: A \cdot a \in B \wedge \forall b: B \cdot b \in A.$$

Given this definition of =, it is possible to define the $\subset$ operator as

$$A \subset B \Leftrightarrow \forall a: A \cdot a \in B \wedge \neg(A = B)$$

which just states that A is a proper subset of B when every element of A occurs in B and A is not equal to B.

5.2.2   *Set union and set intersection*

System specifications often contain sentences such as

> Those monitors which are in the on state and are also attached to a critical reactor will be defined in this document as critical monitors.

> The collection of files which are in the system directory and which are accessible by users with a level 2 status are known as low-level files.

> Communication lines which are quiescent or which are active will be referred to as current communication lines.

Such sentences define new sets by combining previously defined sets. There is hence a need for set operators which form new sets from existing sets. The two most important operators which perform this function are $\cap$ and $\cup$. $\cup$ is the **union operator**. Both its two arguments are sets. It forms the set whose elements are in *either* of its arguments. Thus,

$$\{1, 2, 3\} \cup \{3, 4, 5, 6\}$$

is

$$\{1, 2, 3, 4, 5, 6\}.$$

$\cap$ is the **intersection operator**. Again this operator has two arguments. It forms the set whose elements occur in *both* of its arguments. Thus,

$$\{3, 4, 7, 9, 11\} \cap \{7, 11, 13, 15\}$$

is

$$\{7, 11\}.$$

Both the union and intersection operators take as operands sets which are of the same type, i.e. they contain objects of the same type. Thus, it is not legal to write

$$\{1, 2, 3\} \cup \{\text{monitor1}, \text{monitor2}\}.$$

The union operator can be formally defined using $\in$ and predicate calculus as

$$A \cup B = \{X: T \mid X \in A \vee X \in B\}$$

Where T is the type of the objects which make up the set, for example, the set **N** or the set of all functioning monitors.

Example 5.5

Formally define the intersection operator $\cap$.

The intersection operator forms a set whose elements are in both of its arguments

$$A \cap B = \{x: T \mid x \in A \wedge x \in B\}.$$

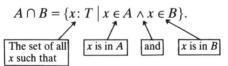

| The set of all x such that | x is in A | and | x is in B |

Exercise 5.5

Which of the following predicates are true and which are false?

(i) $\{3, 4, 5\} \cup \{\} = \{\}$.
(ii) $\{3, 4, 5\} \cap \{\} = \{\}$.

(iii) $\{n: \mathbf{N} \mid n^2 < 20\} \cap \{1, 2, 3\} = \{2, 3\}$.
(iv) $\{n: \mathbf{N} \mid n > 5 \wedge n < 10\} \cup \{n: \mathbf{N} \mid n \le 5\} = \{n: \mathbf{N} \mid n < 10\}$.
(v) $\{\text{mon1}\} \subset \{\text{mon2}, \text{mon3}\} \cap \{\text{mon1}, \text{mon2}, \text{mon3}\}$.
(vi) $\{\text{mon2}, \text{mon3}\} \subset \{\text{mon2}, \text{mon3}\} \cup \{\text{mon1}, \text{mon2}, \text{mon3}\}$.
(vii) $\{\text{mon2}, \text{mon3}\} \subset \{\text{mon2}, \text{mon3}\} \cap \{\text{mon1}, \text{mon2}, \text{mon3}\}$.
(viii) $\{\text{mon: monitors} \mid \text{on(mon)}\} \cap \{\text{mon: monitors} \mid \text{off(mon)}\} =$
$\{\text{mon: monitors} \mid \text{off(mon)} \wedge \text{on(mon)}\}$.
(ix) $\{\text{line: comms\_lines} \mid \text{high(line)}\} \subset$
$\{\text{line: comms\_lines} \mid \text{high(line)} \vee \text{off(line)}\}$.

5.2.3 *Set difference*

Often in a system specification there will be sentences which describe the fact that a set of objects are like one set of objects but not like another set. For example,

> Global files are those system files which are not secure files.
> Working lines are those communication lines which are not quiescent.

The set operator which is used to model these statements is the **set difference operator** $-$. It has two arguments both of the same type. It forms the set which is its first argument with elements of the second argument removed. Thus,

$$\{1, 2, 4, 8, 9\} - \{1, 2, 3\} = \{4, 8, 9\}$$
$$\{1, 2, 3\} - \{1, 2, 3\} = \{\ \}.$$

5.2.4 *The cross-product*

The cross-product of two sets A and B is denoted by

$$A \times B.$$

The operator forms the set of pairs where the first element of each pair is drawn from A and the second element is drawn from B. Thus,

$$\{1, 2, 3\} \times \{4, 5\} = \{(1, 4), (1, 5), (2, 4), (2, 5), (3, 4), (3, 5)\}$$

and

{line1, line2) × {10, 12, 3} = {(line1, 10), (line1, 12), (line1, 3), (line2, 10), (line2, 12), (line2,3))}.

Formally, the cross-product is defined as

$$A \times B = \{a: A; b: B \cdot (a, b)\}.$$

The notion of a cross-product can be generalized for any number of operands

$A_1 \times A_2 \times A_3, \ldots, \times A_n$
$$= \{a_1: A_1; a_2: A_2; a_3: A_3; \ldots, a_n: A_n \cdot (a_1, a_2, a_3, \ldots, a_n)\}.$$

Thus,

$$\{1, 2\} \times \{3, 4\} \times \{line1, line2\}$$

is

{(1, 3, line1), (1, 3, line2), (1, 4, line1), (1, 4, line2), (2, 3, line1), (2, 3, line2), (2, 4, line1), (2, 4, line2)}.

5.2.5 Set cardinality

The **cardinality** of a set is the number of elements in the set. For example, the cardinality of the set

{tax, update, oldupdate}

is 3. In set theory the operator $^\#$ is the cardinality operator. When applied to a set it gives the number of elements in the set. For example,

$$^\#\{old, new, medium, fast, slow\} = 5$$

and

$$^\#\{n: \mathbf{N} \mid n < 4\} = 4$$

are both true predicates.

5.3 Reasoning and proof in set theory

In the same way that it is possible to reason and derive theorems in predicate calculus, it is possible to reason and derive theorems in set theory using rules of inference. Some rules of inference and a number of set theorems are now shown.

A, B, and C are sets of the same type while x is an object of the same type as the objects contained in A, B, and C.

If these are true	**then this must be true**
$x \in A, x \in B$	$x \in A \cap B$
$x \in A$	$x \in A \cup B$
$x \in A, A \subset B$	$\{x\} \subset B$
$A = B, B = C$	$A = C$
$A \subset B, B \subset C$	$A \subset C$

$$\vdash A \cup A = A$$
$$\vdash A \cup \{\} = A$$
$$\vdash A \cup B = B \cup A$$
$$\vdash (A \cup B) \cup C = A \cup (B \cup C)$$
$$\vdash A \cap \{\} = \{\}$$
$$\vdash A \cap B = B \cap A$$
$$\vdash A \cap A = A$$
$$\vdash (A \cap B) \cap C = A \cap (B \cap C)$$
$$\vdash A \cup (B \cap C) = (A \cup B) \cap (A \cup C)$$
$$\vdash A \cap (B \cup C) = (A \cap B) \cup (A \cap C)$$

These theorems can all be proved by recourse to the formal definition of operators such as $\cup$ and $\cap$. For example,

$$\vdash A \cup A = A$$

can be demonstrated by the proof

1	$A \cup A = \{t : T \mid t \in A \vee t \in A\}$	
2	$\{t : T \mid t \in A \vee t \in A\} = \{t : T \mid t \in A\}$	$\{1\}$
3	$\{t : T \mid t \in A\} = A$	
4	$\{t : T \mid t \in A \vee t \in A\} = A$	$\{2, 3\}$
5	$A \cup A = A$	$\{1, 4\}$.

This proof assumes that the set A consists of objects of type T.

Line 1 is just the formal definition of union. Line 2 simplifies the constructive specification on line 1. Line 3 is a restatement of the definition of the set A. Finally, line 4 uses lines 2 and 3 to derive the theorem using the rule of inference that if $A = B$ and $B = C$, then $A = C$. Line 5 uses the same rule of inference.

Example 5.6

Write down the full proof that

$$A \cup B = B \cup A.$$

---

1    $A \cup B = \{t: T \mid t \in A \lor t \in B\}$

2    $\{t: T \mid t \in A \lor t \in B\} = \{t: T \mid t \in B \lor t \in A\}$

3    $\{t: T \mid t \in B \lor t \in A\} = B \cup A$

4    $\{t: T \mid t \in A \lor t \in B\} = B \cup A$ $\{2, 3\}$

5    $A \cup B = B \cup A$ $\{1, 4\}$.

Line 1 of the proof is the definition of $\cup$. Line 2 uses the fact that $\lor$ is commutative. Line 3 is just the definition of $\cup$ and, finally, line 4 is obtained by using the rule of inference that if $A = B$ and $B = C$, then $A = C$. Line 5 is the theorem and is obtained in a similar way to line 4. This proof is a little tedious; at this stage in the book you will probably have the confidence to telescope lines of proof.

Exercise 5.5

Prove set theorems 5, 7, 8, and 9 above.

5.4 Modelling a filing system

To conclude this chapter an example of using set theory and predicate calculus for system specification is presented. It shows that a relatively realistic example can be easily modelled with the limited mathematical tool-kit which this book has so far presented. Each paragraph of the system specification is written in natural language; it is followed by the mathematical equivalent in terms of sets, set operators, and predicates. The prime notation introduced in the previous chapter is used to describe the effect of events on the mathematical structures used to model the system. The whole specification is based on the following informal statement of requirements.

> The purpose of the filing system, is to keep and maintain a series of files belonging to a number of users of a computer system. There will be two types of user; normal users and system users. The latter will have extra privileges such as the ability to access user files and introduce new users into the system.

The specification is written as a series of paragraphs.

> 1. There will be two different types of users: normal users and system users. The latter will have extra privileges.

Assume first that there is a set of all possible user names *all_user_names*. Also there will be a set *users* which will contain all the user names of current users of the system. Furthermore, there will be two sets of names *normal_users* and *system_users*. These will hold each category of user. Assuming that there are no other types of user and that a user cannot be simultaneously a normal user and a system user, then this paragraph can be written as

$$\text{users} \subseteq \text{all\_user\_names} \land$$
$$\text{normal\_users} \cup \text{system\_users} = \text{users} \land$$
$$\text{normal\_users} \cap \text{system\_users} = \{\ \}$$

> 2. Each user is allowed to own a number of files. These are stored in the file store of the computer. Each normal user can own up to 50 files while a system user can own up to 100 files.

This paragraph opens up a number of questions concerning how to model the file store of the computer. One possible solution is to represent it as a set of file names. Unfortunately, there are two major drawbacks to this. First, there is a high probability that two users will give the same name to two different files. Since a set only contains distinct elements, there would be no way of modelling these files as sets. Second, there is no way to relate each file in the file store to the owner of that file.

A better solution is to model the file store as a set of pairs. Each pair consists of the name of a user and the name of the file owned by that user. If *all_file_names* is the set of all possible valid file names, then the file store can be written as

$$\text{file\_store} \in \mathbb{P}(\text{all\_user\_names} \times \text{all\_file\_names}).$$

The restriction about the number of files which each user can own can then be written as

$\forall us: \text{normal\_users}.$

$$ ^{\#}\{\text{file: all\_file\_names} \mid (us, \text{file}) \in \text{file\_store}\} \le 50 $$

$\forall us: \text{system\_users}.$

$$ ^{\#}\{\text{file: all\_file\_names} \mid (us, \text{file}) \in \text{file\_store}\} \le 100. $$

3. Each file can be in two states: public or private. A public file can be read by all users and a private file can only be read by the user that owns it. A file which a user wants to be stored on magnetic tape is known as an archive file.

Assuming that a file cannot simultaneously be a private file and a public file, then the paragraph can be written as

$$\text{archive\_files} \subseteq \text{file\_store}$$
$$\text{private\_files} \cap \text{public\_files} = \{\ \}$$
$$\text{private\_files} \cup \text{public\_files} = \text{file\_store}.$$

4. Users of the filing system can perform any of the following operations

CREATE	Creates a new file,
DELETE	Deletes an existing file,
SET_PUBLIC	Places a file in a public state,
SET_PRIVATE	Places a file in a private state,
ARCHIVE	Marks a file for archiving,
DE_ARCHIVE	Reverses the effect of the ARCHIVE command,
CREATE_USER	Introducers a new user into the system.

Each command will normally refer to a file or a user.

During the operation of the file store a number of events will occur which leave all the elements of the file store unchanged. For example, a user mistyping a command will not affect the file store. In order to describe this a predicate *unchanged* is used which is defined as

$$\text{unchanged} \Leftrightarrow (\text{normal\_users}' = \text{normal\_users} \wedge$$
$$\text{system\_users}' = \text{system\_users} \wedge$$
$$\text{file\_store}' = \text{file\_store} \wedge$$
$$\text{public\_files}' = \text{public\_files} \wedge$$
$$\text{private\_files}' = \text{private\_files} \wedge$$
$$\text{archive\_files}' = \text{archive\_files}).$$

5. The CREATE command creates a new file in the filestore. This command can be used both by normal users *and* system users. The effect of the command is to add a file to the filestore. This file will be owned by the user who issued the command. The file so created will have private status.

In order to specify the effect of this command it will be necessary to denote the user who types the command as *user* and the file to be created as *file_name*. The effect of the CREATE command is

$$\text{command} = \text{CREATE} \Rightarrow$$
$$(\text{file\_store}' = \text{file\_store} \cup \{(\text{user, file\_name})\}$$
$$\wedge \ \text{private\_files}' = \text{private\_files} \cup \{(\text{user, file\_name})\}$$
$$\wedge \ \text{normal\_users}' = \text{normal\_users}$$
$$\wedge \ \text{system\_users}' = \text{system\_users}$$
$$\wedge \ \text{public\_files}' = \text{public\_files}$$
$$\wedge \ \text{archive\_files}' = \text{archive\_files}.)$$

There are two important points to notice about this predicate. First, primes are used to indicate the value of an object *after* a command has been executed. In the case of the CREATE command above, the sets *private_files* and *file_store* are modified by the CREATE command and hence appear with primes. Second, the sets *normal_users* and *system_users* are unaffected by the correct operation of the CREATE command.

6. The DELETE command removes an existing file from the filestore. The command can be used by both normal and system users. If a system user types the command, then any file can be deleted from the file store. If a normal user types the command, then only a file owned by the user can be deleted from the file store.

There is a slight complication when this command is typed in by a system user. In order to identify uniquely a file not only must the file name be provided but also the name of the user whose file is to be deleted. No clue can be gained about the way that this name is communicated to the filing system. The specification shall assume that a user name *usname* is provided by the system user. The effect of the DELETE command is

$$
\begin{aligned}
\text{command} = \text{DELETE} \Rightarrow (\text{user} \in \text{system\_users} \\
\Rightarrow (\text{file\_store}' = \text{file\_store} \\
- \{(\text{usname}, \text{file\_name})\}) \\
\wedge\ \text{user} \in \text{normal\_users} \Rightarrow (\text{file\_store}' = \text{file\_store} \\
- \{(\text{user}, \text{file\_name})\}) \\
\wedge\ \text{normal\_users}' = \text{normal\_users} \\
\wedge\ \text{system\_users}' = \text{system\_users} \\
\wedge\ \text{private\_files}' = \text{private\_files} \\
\wedge\ \text{public\_files}' = \text{public\_files} \\
\wedge\ \text{archive\_files}' = \text{archive\_files}).
\end{aligned}
$$

7. The SET_PUBLIC command sets the state of an existing file to be public. The command can be employed by both normal and system users. If a system user types the command, then any file can be marked public. If a normal user types the command, then only a file owned by that user can be made public.

The effect of the SET_PUBLIC is

$$
\begin{aligned}
\text{command} = \text{SET\_PUBLIC} \Rightarrow \\
(\text{user} \in \text{normal\_users} \Rightarrow \\
(\text{private\_files}' = \text{private\_files} - \{(\text{user}, \text{file\_name})\} \\
\wedge\ \text{public\_files}' = \text{public\_files} \cup \{(\text{user}, \text{file\_name})\}) \\
\wedge\ \text{user} \in \text{system\_users} \Rightarrow \\
(\text{private\_files}' = \text{private\_files} - \{(\text{usname}, \text{file\_name})\} \\
\wedge\ \text{public\_files}' = \text{public\_files} \cup \{(\text{usname}, \text{file\_name})\})
\end{aligned}
$$

$\wedge$ normal_users' = normal_users
$\wedge$ system_users' = system_users
$\wedge$ file_store' = file_store
$\wedge$ archive_files' = archive_files).

8. The SET_PRIVATE command sets the state of an existing file to be PRIVATE. The command can be used by both normal and system users. If a system user types the command, then any file can be marked private. If a normal user types the command, then only a file owned by that user can be made private.

The effect of the SET_PRIVATE command can now be specified

command = SET_PRIVATE $\Rightarrow$
 (user $\in$ normal_users $\Rightarrow$ (public_files' =
 public_files $-$ {(user, file_name)}
$\wedge$ private_files' = private_files $\cup$ {(user, file_name)})
$\wedge$ user $\in$ system_users $\Rightarrow$ (public_files' =
 public_files $-$ {(usname, file_name)}
$\wedge$ private_files' = private_files $\cup$ {(usname, file_name)})
$\wedge$ normal_users' = normal_users
$\wedge$ system_users' = system_users
$\wedge$ file_store' = file_store
$\wedge$ archive_files' = archive_files)

9. The ARCHIVE command marks a file for archiving. At certain times of the working week a program known as an archiver is executed. The archiver removes files which are marked for archiving from the file_store and writes them to magnetic tape. This command can only be used by a system user.

The effect of the ARCHIVE command can now be specified

command = ARCHIVE $\Rightarrow$
(archive_files' = archive_files $\cup$ {(usname, file_name)}
$\wedge$ normal_users' = normal_users
$\wedge$ system_users' = system_users
$\wedge$ private_files' = private_files
$\wedge$ public_files' = public_files).

10. The DE_ARCHIVE command unmarks a file which has already been marked for archiving.

The effect of the DE_ARCHIVE command is

command = DE_ARCHIVE $\Rightarrow$
(archive_files' = archive_files − {(usname, file_name)}
$\wedge$ normal_users' = normal_users
$\wedge$ system_users' = system_users
$\wedge$ private_files' = private_files
$\wedge$ public_files' = public_files.)

Example 5.7

During the operation of the filing system a number of users asked for extra commands. One popular request was for a command which displayed the status of a file, i.e. whether it was private or public. The specification for this command was

> The STATUS command displays the status of a file in the file system. It can be used by both system users and by normal users. Any file can be examined by this command.

Write a specification which gives the effect of this command, do not worry about errors. Assume the existence of a predicate *display_status(user_device, file_name)* which is true when the status of *file_name* is displayed on a user device.

The specification which describes the effect of this command is

command = STATUS_DISPLAY $\Rightarrow$
(display_status(user_device, file_name)
$\wedge$ unchanged.)

Notice that the user has to specify a *usname* since any file in the file store can be examined.

Postscript

The example in 5.4 is relatively realistic. To be totally realistic it would have to include details about directory structure and access rules for public and private files. Nevertheless, it contains a substantial part of the functionality expected in a filing system.

6 Relations and relational operators

6.1 Relations as sets of ordered pairs

A **relation** is one of the most important concepts in pure mathematics. It is a set of ordered pairs. An **ordered pair** is a pair of items which have the property

$$((x, y) = (u, v)) \Leftrightarrow ((x = u) \wedge (y = v)),$$

i.e. two ordered pairs are equal *only when* their first elements are equal and their second elements are equal. The formal definition of a relation is

$$\{a: A; b: B \mid p(a, b) \cdot (a, b)\}$$

where p is a predicate which relates a and b and defines members of the relation. For example, the set

$$\{a, b: \mathbf{N} \mid a + b = 4 \cdot (a, b)\}$$

defines the relation

$$\{(0, 4), (1, 3), (2, 2), (3, 1), (4, 0)\}.$$

Note that since ordered pairs are only equal if their corresponding elements are equal the relation contains both $(0, 4)$, $(1, 3)$, and $(4, 0)$, $(3, 1)$.

A relation is used to express the fact that there is a connection between the elements that make up an ordered pair. In the constructive specification of a relation it is the predicate which defines this connection. For example, the predicate $a + b = 4$ used in the constructive specification above expresses the fact that the elements of each ordered pair that make up the relation always add up to 4.

Relations are normally named. Naming a relation is equivalent to naming the set of pairs which make up the relation. Thus, the relation *eqless*

$$\{x, y \colon \mathbf{N} \mid x = y \wedge x < 4\}$$

can be written as either the constructive specification

$$\text{eqless} = \{x, y \colon \mathbf{N} \mid x = y \wedge x < 4\}$$

or by enumeration

$$\text{eqless} = \{(0, 0), (1, 1), (2, 2), (3, 3)\}.$$

The fact that an ordered pair (x, y) is contained in a relation R can be written as $(x, y) \in R$ or $R(x, y)$. However, it is customary to write this predicate as xRy. When the ordered pairs that make up a relation are obtained from two sets A and B it is usual to refer to the relation as being over A and B or as being on A and B or as being over $A \times B$. This book will adopt the latter description. Thus, the relation *eqless* above is over $\mathbf{N} \times \mathbf{N}$.

Relations are not quite a new topic in this book. In Chapter 4 predicates such as *connected* and *uses* were employed to express the fact that there was a relation between two objects. It can now be seen that this was just another way of writing relations.

Example 6.1

Write down the elements of the relation

$$\text{peoplen} = \{p \colon \text{person}; n \colon \mathbf{N} \mid n < 3 \cdot (p, n)\}$$

where person = {Roberts, Jones, Monroe}. Which of the following predicates then hold?

(i) (Timms, 2) $\in$ peoplen.
(ii) (Williams, 2) $\notin$ peoplen.
(iii) Roberts peoplen 3.
(iv) Jones peoplen 2.
(v) Jones peoplen 4.

The relation *peoplen* is the set of all ordered pairs whose first element is taken from *person* and whose second element is taken from $\mathbf{N}$. The second element will always be less than 3, the contents of the relation will be

> {(Roberts, 0), (Roberts, 1), (Roberts, 2),
>
> (Jones, 0), (Jones, 1), (Jones, 2),
>
> (Monroe, 0), (Monroe, 1), (Monroe, 2)}.

Hence (ii) and (iv) are true and (i), (iii), and (v) are all false.

Exercise 6.1

If files = {archive, dir, newlog} and sys = {archive, dir}, write down the elements of the following relations.

(i) $\{n: \mathbf{N}; \text{fil: files} \mid 2 * n < 9 \cdot (n, \text{fil})\}$.
(ii) $\{n: \mathbf{N}; \text{fil: files} \mid \text{file} \in \text{sys} \wedge n < 4 \cdot (n, \text{fil})\}$.
(iii) $\{n: \mathbf{N}; \text{fil: files} \mid \text{fil} \in \text{sys} \wedge n = 2 \cdot (\text{fil}, n)\}$.
(iv) $\{n: \mathbf{N}; \text{fil: files} \mid n < 0 \cdot (n, \text{fil})\}$.
(v) $\{\text{fil: files}; n: \mathbf{N} \mid n > 2 \wedge n < 5 \cdot (n^2, \text{fil})\}$.
(vi) $\{\text{fil: files}; n: \mathbf{N} \mid n = 3 \wedge \text{fil} = \text{dir} \cdot (n^3, \text{fil})\}$.

You will already be familiar with relations from numerical mathematics. For example, the less than relation, $<$, for natural numbers can be written as

$$\{a, b: \mathbf{N} \mid \exists k: \mathbf{N}_1 \cdot a + k = b\}$$

where $\mathbf{N}_1$ is the set of natural numbers excluding zero. The elements of this infinite set are

$$\{(0, 1), (0, 2), (0, 3), \ldots, (1, 2), (1, 3), (1, 4), \ldots,$$
$$(2, 3), (2, 4), (2, 5), \ldots, \}.$$

Example 6.2

Why is $\mathbf{N}_1$ used in the definition of $<$?

The definition of $<$ states that two elements are related if there is a natural number in $\mathbf{N}_1$ which, when added to the first element of the pair, gives the second element of the pair. If $\mathbf{N}$ were used, then elements such as $(2, 2)$ and $(19, 19)$ would be part of the relation $<$ since 0 added to the first element would give the second element. To exclude these possibilities $\mathbf{N}_1$ has to be used.

Relations, as their name suggests, describe a relationship between their elements. You have already seen an example of a relation in Section 5.4 where the file store of a computer was modelled as a relation over file names and user names where the predicate which described the relation was the fact that a user owned a file. It is this property of relations that make them useful for modelling computer systems.

Some examples of fragments of specifications which imply that a relation exists between two objects are shown below.

Privileged users are those users who have a priority of 7 or more.

Each stock item will be associated with the number in stock and the minimum level below which the item must not fall before a back order is placed.

The stock data-base system should contain information which allows a query clerk to discover which division has ordered a particular shipment of parts.

Each computer is connected to a number of monitors.

The first fragment expresses the fact that there will be a relation over customers and priorities. The second fragment embodies two relations: the first is over stock items and natural numbers and expresses the connection between a stock item and the number in stock; the second is over stock items and natural numbers and expresses the connection between a stock item and the minimum re-order level. The third fragment embodies a relation over divisions and orders, and, finally, the fourth fragment describes a relation over computers and monitors.

The elements of a relation can be ordered pairs whose

elements are sets. For example, if

files = {new, old, archive, summary, tax}

and

users = {Jones, Roberts, Wilson},

the relation *can_access*

{(Jones, {new, old}), (Roberts, {new, old, summary}),

(Wilson, {tax})}

is an example of a relation over *users* × $\mathbb{P}$*files,* which may describe those files which a particular user can access.

A number of operators are defined for relations. The domain operator *dom* has one operand; its value is the set whose members are the left-hand elements of the pairs in a relation. Thus, if *owns* is a relation over *users* × *files* and its current value is

{(Jones, tax), (Jones, new), (Roberts, summary),

(Wilson, archive)},

then *dom owns* is

{Jones, Roberts, Wilson}.

Formally, *dom* is defined as

$$\text{dom } A = \{t_1 \colon T_1 \mid \exists t_2 \colon T_2 \cdot t_1 A t_2\}$$

where *A* is a relation over $T_1 \times T_2$.

The range operator *rng* is similar to *dom.* It returns the set of the right-hand elements in a relation. Thus, if *uses_computer* is a relation over *user* × *computers* where

computers = {VAX780, DEC2060, ICL2960}

and the current value of *uses_computer* is

{(Jones, VAX780), (Roberts, DEC2060), (Wilson, VAX780)},

then *rng uses_machine* is

{VAX780, DEC2060}.

Example 6.3

Formally define the *rng* operator.

$$\mathrm{rng}\, A = \{t_2\colon T_2 \mid \exists t_1\colon T_1 \cdot t_1 A t_2\}$$

where the relation A over $T_1 \times T_2$ where T_1 and T_2 are any types. All the definition states is that the range of a relation is the set of t_2s which are related to a t_1 in A.

Exercise 6.2

Suppose *owns* and *can_read* are relations over *user* × *files* and their current values are

owns = {(Roberts, archive), (Wilson, tax),
             (Roberts, summary), (Jones, old)},

can_read = {(Roberts, archive), (Wilson, archive), (Wilson, tax),
                  (Jones, tax), (Roberts, summary), (Jones, old),
                  (Jones, archive)}.

Indicate which of the following predicates are true and which are false.

    (i) Roberts owns archive.
   (ii) ¬(Roberts owns summary).
  (iii) (Jones, tax) ∈ owns ∧ (Roberts, archive) ∈ can_read.
  (iv) owns ⊂ can_read.
   (v) $^{\#}$owns = 7.
  (vi) dom owns = dom can_read.
 (vii) Thomas ∈ owns ∨ Ince ∈ dom can_read.
(viii) dom owns ∩ dom can_read ≠ {Wilson, Timms}.
  (ix) dom owns ∩ {Timms} = { }.
   (x) dom owns ∩ {Timms} ≠ {Wilson, Timms}.
  (xi) $^{\#}$can_read > 7.
 (xii) {(Roberts, archive)} ∪ {(Wilson, tax))} ⊂ can_read.
(xiii) Roberts owns archive ∧ Roberts can_read archive.
(xiv) Roberts owns archive ∧ (Roberts, archive) ∈ can_read.

A further useful operator is the **inverse** operator. It has one operand which is a relation. It reverses the elements of the pairs of the relation it operates on. The operator is written by writing -1 as a superscript above the relation whose inverse is to be expressed. Thus, if *owns* is a relation over *users* × *computers* and is currently

$\quad$ {(Wilson, DEC2060), (Jones, VAX70), (Timms, ICL2960)},

then $owns^{-1} =$

$\quad$ {(DEC2060, Wilson), (VAX780, Jones), (ICL2960, Timms)}.

Example 6.4

Formally define the inverse operator.

The inverse operator takes each ordered pair in a relation and reverses the elements. This can be expressed as

$$R^{-1} = \{t_1: T_1; t_2: T_2 \mid (t_1, t_2) \in R \cdot (t_2, t_1)\}$$

where R is a relation over any two arbitrary types T_1 and T_2.

Exercise 6.3

size is a relation over *file_names* × N. Its current value is

$\quad$ {(archive, 273), (tax, 123), (lister, 459), (newark, 450)}.

Which of the following predicates are true and which are false?

$\quad$ (i) dom $size^{-1} = \{\text{archive, tax, lister, newark}\}$.
$\quad$ (ii) dom $size^{-1} = \{273, 123, 459, 450\}$.
$\quad$ (iii) $^\#$rng size $= 4$.
$\quad$ (iv) $^\#$rng size $= {}^\#$dom size.
$\quad$ (v) dom {fil: file_names; n: **N** $\mid$ fil size $n \wedge n < 400 \cdot (\text{fil}, n)\} =$
$\qquad$ {lister}.

(vi) $\{$fil: file_names; n: $\mathbf{N}$ $|$ fil size $n \wedge n < 400 \cdot$ (file, n)$\}^{-1} =$
        $\{(273, \text{archive}), (123, \text{tax})\}$.

(vii) $(\text{size}^{-1})^{-1} = \text{size}$.

(viii) dom$\{$fil: file_names; n: $\mathbf{N}$ $|$ fil size $n \wedge n > 500 \cdot$ (file, n)$\} = \{\ \}$.

6.2 Relation composition

Relations can be combined by an operation known as **composition**. As an example of this consider the two relations: *has_queue* and *contains_trans*. The first relation is over *computers* $\times$ *queues* while the second is over *queues* $\times$ *transactions*. *has_queue* describes the fact that a particular computer has a series of queues associated with it; *contains_trans* describes the fact that a particular queue contains a transaction which is to be processed. Given these relations, it may be necessary to construct a relation *has_trans* over *computers* $\times$ *transactions* which describes the fact that a computer is waiting to process a series of transactions. Thus, if the current value of *has_queues* is

$\{$(VAX780A, q1), (VAX780B, q2), (DEC2060A, q3),

(DEC2060B, q4)$\}$

and the current value of *contains_trans* is

$\{$(q1, upd1), (q1, upd3), (q3, read1), (q4, read2),

(q3, read2), (q2, read4), (q2, read5), (q1, tranup)$\}$,

then the relation *has_trans* would be

$\{$(VAX780A, upd1), (VAX780A, upd3), (VAX780A, tranup),

(VAX780B, read4), (VAX780B, read5), (DEC2060A, read1),

(DEC2060A, read2), (DEC2060B, read2)$\}$.

has_trans has been formed by taking the first elements of the ordered pairs in *has_queue* and combining them with the second elements of *contains_trans* whose first elements match the second elements of *has_queue*. The operator used to indicate composition is a semicolon. Thus, in the example above, the composition of *contains_trans* and *has_queue* is written as

$$\text{has\_trans} = \text{has\_queue}; \text{contains\_trans}.$$

It is important to realize that in the expression

$$\text{relation1}; \text{relation2}$$

the type of the range of *relation1* must match the type of the domain of *relation2*. Thus,

$$\{(1,17),(2,15),(3,8)\}; \{(\text{file1},\text{Jones}),(\text{file3},\text{Wilson}),(\text{upd},\text{trans})\}$$

is not defined since the range of the first relation contains the natural numbers while the domain of the second relation contains files. The formal definition of relation composition follows. It is defined for a relation R_1 over $T_1 \times T_2$ and R_2 over $T_2 \times T_3$ where T_1, T_2, and T_3 are any arbitrary type

$$R_1; R_2 = \{t_1: T_1, t_3: T_3 \mid \exists t_2: T_2 \cdot (t_1, t_2) \in R_1 \wedge (t_2, t_3) \in R_2\}.$$

It states that the composition of two relations is formed by first finding any two pairs such that the second element of the first pair matches the first element of the second pair; a pair is then formed from the first element of the first pair and the second element of the second pair.

Exercise 6.4

computers is a set of computers whose current value is

$$\{\text{VAX780}, \text{DEC2060}, \text{ICL2960}\},$$

lines is a set of communication lines whose current value is

$$\{\text{comm1}, \text{comm3}, \text{comm5}\},$$

and *conn* is a relation over *computers* × *lines* which models the fact that a computer is connected to a communication line. Its current value is

$$\{(\text{VAX780}, \text{comm1}), (\text{DEC2060}, \text{comm3})\}.$$

Write down the values of the following expressions.

(i) (computers × lines); {(comm1, on), (comm3, off)}.
(ii) conn; conn.
(iii) conn; conn^{-1}.

(iv) conn^{-1}; conn.
(v) (computers $\times$ lines)$^{-1}$.
(vi) conn^{-1}; (computer $\times$ lines).
(vii) conn $\subseteq$ computers $\times$ lines.
(viii) {(VAX780, comm2)} $\subset$ conn.

Some mathematical texts use the symbol $\circ$ for relation composition; it can be defined as

$$R_1 \circ R_2 = R_2 ; R_1.$$

In this book ; will be preferred to $\circ$ for relation composition.

A relation can be composed with itself. As an example of this consider the relation *receives_data* which models the fact that one monitor receives data from another and is over *monitors $\times$ monitors*. If its current value is

{(mon1, mon3), (mon3, mon2), (mon4, mon2), (mon2, mon1)},

then the composition of *receives_data* with itself

receives_data; receives_data

is

{(mon1, mon2), (mon3, mon1), (mon4, mon1), (mon2, mon3)}.

The new relation *receives_data*; *receives_data* so formed describes the fact that a monitor can receive data from another monitor via another; thus,

(mon1, mon2) $\in$ (receives_data; receives_data)

asserts the fact that *mon2* receives data from *mon1* via another monitor (*mon3*).

It is important to stress that a relation can only be composed with itself if the type of its domain is the same as the type of its range. Such relations are called **homogeneous**.

In general, a relation can be composed with itself any number of times. Thus, one can write

is_connected; is_connected

for a twofold composition, and

is_connected; is_connected; is_connected

for a threefold composition. For an n-fold composition it is customary to use a power notation involving superscripts. For example, the fourfold composition of *is_connected* would be written as

$$\text{is\_connected}^4.$$

6.3 The identity relation

An important relation used in specifications is the **identity relation**. It is formally defined as

$$\text{id } A = \{x: A \cdot (x, x)\}$$

where A is any set whose elements are of an arbitrary type. Thus, $\text{id}\{1, 3, 5, 9\}$ is

$$\{(1, 1), (3, 3), (5, 5), (9, 9)\}$$

and $\text{id}\{\text{Wilson, Wallis}\}$ is:

$$\{(\text{Wilson, Wilson}), (\text{Wallis, Wallis})\}.$$

Example 6.5

The relation *owns_file* is over *users* $\times$ *filenames*. Its current value is

$$\{(\text{Jones, upd}), (\text{Wilson, tax1}),$$
$$(\text{Jones, newupd}), (\text{Harris, newloc})\}.$$

What is the value of the expression

$$(\text{id}\{\text{Jones, Wilson}\}); \text{owns\_file}$$

Can you express the relationship between this expression and *owns_file* in natural language?

The value of this expression is

$$\{(\text{Jones, Jones}), (\text{Wilson, Wilson})\};$$
$$\{(\text{Jones, upd}), (\text{Wilson, tax1}),$$
$$(\text{Jones, newupd}), (\text{Harris, newloc})\}$$

which gives

{(Jones, upd), (Wilson, tax1), (Jones, newupd)}.

The effect of the operations is to form the relation between Jones or Wilson and the files which are owned by them.

Exercise 6.5

The operation of a chemical plant computer system can be modelled using the sets: *reactors, monitors,* and *computers* where

reactors = {cracker1, cracker2, cracker3, distill1, distill2},

monitors = (mon1, mon2, mon3, mon4, mon7, mon8, mon9},

computers = {VAX780A, VAX780B}.

The fact that a monitor is connected to a reactor is recorded in the relation *reactor_connected_to* which is over *reactors* × *monitors*. The fact that a computer is connected to a monitor is recorded in the relation *computer_connected_to* which is over *computers* × *monitors*. If the current value of *reactor_connected_to* is

{(cracker1, mon1), (cracker2, mon2), (cracker2, mon3),

(cracker3, mon1), (cracker3, mon2), (distill1, mon7),

(distill2, mon8), (distill2, mon9)}

and the current value of *computer_connected_to* is

{(VAX780A, mon1), (VAX780A, mon2), (VAX780B, mon2),

(VAX780B, mon3), (VAX780B, mon7), (VAX780B, mon8),

(VAX780B, mon9)},

then what is the value of

    (i) id reactors.
    (ii) id(reactors^{-1}).
    (iii) (id reactors)$^{-1}$.
    (iv) (id computers); computer_connected_to.
    (v) (id{VAX780A}); computer_connected_to.
    (vi) rng((id{VAX780A}); computer_connected_to).

   (vii) id({cracker1, cracker2}); reactor_connected_to.
 (viii) rng(id({cracker3})); reactor_connected_to).
   (ix) id dom(reactor_connected_to).
    (x) id(dom(reactor_connected_to) − {cracker1, cracker2}).
   (xi) rng(id({VAX780A}); computer_connected_to) −
       {mon1, mon2, mon9}.

Example 6.6

The relation *updates* is a relation over *units* × *variables,* it describes the fact that a program unit (procedure or function) updates a particular global variable. Write down the relation *same_update* over *units* × *units* which describes the fact that two units are related if they update the same variable. The relation should be expressed in terms of *updates* using relational composition.

The relation *same_update* can be expressed as

   same_update = (updates; updates^{-1}) − id updates.

The identity function is required since *updates*; *updates*$^{-1}$ will contain pairs containing identical elements made up of the first elements of the pairs in *updates*.

6.4 Relation restriction

In system specifications there is a need for relations to be restricted over their domain or range. For example, the specification extract

> The effect of the TEMP command is to display the current temperature of the monitors connected to the reactors which are specified in the command.

implies that if the connection between monitors and reactors is modelled by a relation, then the part of the specification for this command involves restricting the relation only to include those pairs which reference the reactors specified in the command.

Since restriction occurs time and time again in specifications, a number of operators can be defined which describe various forms of this restriction. The first operator ◁ restricts the domain. It has two operands: the first operand is a set; the second operand is a relation. It forms a subset of the second operand which only contains pairs whose first elements are contained in the first operand. For example, if *is_connected* is a relation over *reactors × monitors* and has a current value of

{(reactor1, mon1), (reactor2, mon2), (cracker1, mon2),

(cracker2, mon1), (cracker2, mon3), (cracker3, mon4),

(distill1, mon4), (distill1, mon1), (distill2, mon1)},

then

{reactor1, reactor2} ◁ is_connected

is

{(reactor1, mon1), (reactor2, mon2)}

and

{distill3} ◁ is_connected

is

{ }.

A similar operator is ▷ which restricts the range of a relation. For example, the value of

is_connected ▷ {mon1, mon4}

is

{(reactor1, mon1), (cracker2, mon1), (cracker3, mon4),

(distill1, mon4), (distill1, mon1), (distill2, mon1)}.

Both these restriction operators can be defined in terms of the operators previously introduced

$$S \triangleleft R = (\text{id } S); R$$
$$R \triangleright T = R; (\text{id } T)$$

where R is a relation over two arbitrary types T_1 and T_2, S is a subset of T_1, and T is a subset of T_2.

Two further restriction operators can be defined. The operator $\trianglelefteq$ is similar to $\triangleleft$ except that the subset over which the restriction is to hold includes those elements not specified as the first operand. In order to illustrate the use of this operator consider the relation *access_file* over *users* × *files* which models the fact that a user can access a number of files where

$$users = \{\text{Williams, Thomas, Jones, Ross, Timms}\}$$
$$files = \{\text{upd3, upd4, upd5, tax1, tax2, tax3}\}$$

and where the current value of *access_file* is

{(Williams, upd3), (Thomas, upd4), (Jones, upd4), (Ross, tax1),

(Ross, tax2), (Timms, upd3), (Timms, tax3)}.

Then the value of {Williams, Jones} $\trianglelefteq$ access_files is

{(Thomas, upd4), (Ross, tax1), (Ross, tax2),

(Timms, upd3), (Timms, tax3)}.

The operator $\trianglerighteq$ is similar to $\triangleright$ in its action. It restricts the range of its first operand to those elements which are not contained in its second operand. For example, the value of access_files $\trianglerighteq$ {upd3, tax3} is

{(Thomas, upd4), (Jones, upd4), (Ross, tax1), (Ross, tax2)}.

Again these operators can be defined in terms of previously defined operators

$$S \trianglelefteq R = (T_1 - S) \triangleleft R,$$
$$R \trianglerighteq T = R \triangleright (T_2 - T)$$

where R is a relation over $T_1 \times T_2$, S is a subset of T_1 and T is a subset of T_2.

One operator which is related to the restriction operators is the relational **override** operator $\oplus$. This is often used in specifications where a number of relations are used and where one relation is very much like another except for some pairs. Typical example of this which occur in specifications are

> The effect of the POOL operation is to change those files in the file store which are specified in the command so that they are owned by the system manager.
>
> The effect of the UPDATE command is to replace existing accounts by new accounts. These new accounts may have the same account number as those accounts which are replaced but will have a different account holder.

The formal definition of $\oplus$ is

$$R \oplus S = (\text{dom } S \lhd R) \cup S$$

where R and S are relations over two arbitrary types T_1 and T_2. The effect of the $\oplus$ operator is to replace those pairs in R whose first elements are in the domain of S by the elements of S. Thus,

$$\{(1, \text{file1}), (3, \text{upd}), (5, \text{tax}), (7, \text{new}), (8, \text{upd})\} \oplus$$
$$\{(1, \text{newtax}), (7, \text{oldtax})\}$$

is equal to

$$\{(1, \text{newtax}), (3, \text{upd}), (5, \text{tax}), (7, \text{oldtax}), (8, \text{upd})\}.$$

A typical application of $\oplus$ might occur in a data-base application for banking where the fact that an account holder has a numbered account is modelled by the relation *has_account* which is over $N \times names$. At times during the day a new account has to be added to *has_account* and, occasionally, a new account is assigned to an existing account holder. If these are held in the relation *update* which is over $N \times names$ then the effect of updating *has_account* is

$$\text{has\_account}' = \text{has\_account} \oplus \text{update}.$$

Note that this operation, as well as introducing new accounts, re-assigns new account holders to existing accounts. For example, if the current value of *has_account* is

$$\{(1173, \text{Jones}), (1148, \text{Thomas}), (1176, \text{Jones}), (493, \text{Wilson})\}$$

and *update* is

$$\{(1148, \text{Timms}), (1922, \text{Roberts}), (1111, \text{Wilson})\},$$

then the new value of *has_account* would be

$\{(1173, \text{Jones}), (1148, \text{Timms}), (1176, \text{Jones}),$

$(493, \text{Wilson}), (1922, \text{Roberts}), (1111, \text{Wilson})\}.$

Another useful operator is the **set image** operator. The image of a set S through a relation R is the set of elements which are second elements of pairs contained in R whose first elements are in S. Formally, the set image operator $[\![\ ]\!]$ is defined as

$$R[\![S]\!] = \{t_2 \colon T_2 \mid \exists t_1 \colon S \cdot t_1 R t_2\}$$

where R is over $T_1 \times T_2$ and S is a subset of T_1.
  For example, if the set *has_access* is

$\{(\text{Jones}, \text{tax2}), (\text{Roberts}, \text{tax3}), (\text{Roberts}, \text{upd}),$

$(\text{Thomas}, \text{newupd}), (\text{Thomas}, \text{tax2}), (\text{Wilson}, \text{tax3}),$

$(\text{Timms}, \text{trans})\}$

and if the set *file_query* was

$\{\text{Jones}, \text{Roberts}\},$

then has_access$[\![$file_query$]\!]$ would be

$\{\text{tax2}, \text{tax3}, \text{upd}\}.$

  If *file_query* was

$\{\text{Jones}, \text{Thomas}\},$

then has_access$[\![$file_query$]\!]$ would be

$\{\text{tax2}, \text{newupd}\}$

and has_access$[\![\{\text{Wilkinson}\}]\!]$ would be the empty set $\{\ \}$.

Exercise 6.6

A data-base application for a wholesaler can be modelled by means of the relations *price, in_stock,* and *supplies*. *Price* is a relation over *products* $\times$ 1..20 which models the association between prices and stock items. *In_stock* is a relation over *products* $\times$ *N* which models the association between stock items and the current number in stock of a product. *Supplies* is a relation over *suppliers* × *products* which models the relation between a supplier and the product that is delivered by that supplier. If the current value of these relations is

price = {(nut, 3), (bolt, 5), (screw, 1), (board, 17), (fastener, 12)},

in_stock = {(nut, 500), (bolt, 2100), (screw, 45), (board, 0),

(fastener, 500)},

supplies = {(Thomas, nut), (Thomas, bolt), (Wilks, bolt),

(Wilks, screw), (Wilks, board), (Wilks, fastener),

(Rogers, board), (Rogers, fastener)},

then what is the value of the following expressions? Also express in natural language the relations described by each expression.

    (i) id price.
    (ii) {nut, bolt} ◁ price.
    (iii) dom(price ▷ 1..5).
    (iv) dom(price ▷ 1..5).
    (v) rng(price ▷ 1..10).
    (vi) in_stock ▷ {0}.
    (vii) dom(supplies; (in_stock ▷ {0})).
    (viii) price ⊕ {(bolt, 6)}.
    (ix) price ⊕ {(hanger, 2), (screw, 2)}.
    (x) dom(supplies; (price ▷ 5..20)).
    (xi) supplies⟦{Robinson}⟧.
    (xii) supplies⟦{Rogers, Wilson}⟧.
    (xiii) ((supplies; price) ▷ 1..10)⟦{Robinson, Rogers}⟧.
    (xiv) supplies − ({Thomas} ◁ supplies).
    (xv) {Thomas} ◁ supplies.
    (xvi) (in_stock ▷ {0})⟦{nut, bolt}⟧.
    (xvii) #dom(supplies⟦{bolt}⟧).

Exercise 6.7

The file store of a small computer is modelled by the relations: *owns, size, has_user_status*, and *has_file_status*. *Owns* is a relation over *users* × *files* which models the fact that the user of a computer owns a particular file. *Size* is a relation over *files* × *file_sizes* which relates a file to its size in kbytes. *Has_user_status* is a relation over *users* × *user_status* which relates a user to his status in the computer system and *has_file_status* is a relation over *files × file_status* which relates a file to its status, where

$$\text{file\_sizes} = 1..100,$$

$$\text{user\_status} = \{\text{normal, super user}\},$$

$$\text{file\_status} = \{\text{read, write, delete}\}.$$

Write down expressions that are equivalent to the following natural-language extracts taken from the system specification for the file access system. Use the relational operators described in this chapter.

(i) At most only three super users are allowed at one time.
(ii) The total number of users who own files should never exceed 15.
(iii) No user is allowed to own a file which has delete status and which is over 8 kbytes in size.
(iv) When the file name and name have been typed the file size is increased by 1 kbyte.
(v) ... those files which do not belong to a normal user and which are under 6 kybtes long.
(vi) ... those files which do not belong to a super user and which have write status.
(viii) ... those users who own files greater or equal to 7 kybtes in size.

6.5 The transitive closure of a relation

An important relational operator is known as the **transitive closure** operator. However, before defining what exactly is meant by this, it is first necessary to define formally an operator which is used in its definition and which was defined informally earlier in this section. The *n*th iterate of a homogeneous relation is its *n*-fold composition with itself. It is written with a superscript over the relation. For example,

$$\text{is\_in\_sys}^4$$

is the fourfold composition of *is_in_sys*, i.e.

$$\text{is\_in\_sys; is\_in\_sys; is\_in\_sys; is\_in\_sys.}$$

The formal definition of the operator is shown below. If *R* is a homogeneous relation on $T \times T$ where T is any type, then

$$R^0 = \text{id } T$$

and

$$R^n = R; R^{n-1}$$

Thus, if the relation *lower_address* on *programs* $\times$ *programs* has a value

{(us1, us2x), (us2x, us3x), (us3x, us9b), (us9b, us7y)}

where *programs* is

{us1, us2x, us3x, us9b, us7y, us11x, us14r},

then *lower_address*[3] will, from the definition of composition, be

{(us1, us2x), (us2x, us3x), (us3x, us9b), (us9b, us7y)};
lower_address[2].

This can be further expanded to

{(us1, us2x), (us2x, us3x), (us3x, us9b), (us9b, us7y)};
{(us1, us2x), (us2x, us3x), (us3x, us9b), (us9b, us7y)};
lower_address.

This can be further simplified using the definition of ; to

{(us1, us3x), (us2x, us9b), (us3x, us7y)}; lower_address

which can then be rewritten as

{(us1, us3x), (us2x, us9b), (us3x, us7y)};
{(us1, us2x), (us2x, us3x), (us3x, us9b), (us9b, us7y)}

which, when simplified, is

{(us1, us9b), (us2x, us7y)}.

Given this definition of composition the transitive closure of a relation can be defined. There are in fact two transitive closures: the **reflexive transitive closure** and the **non-reflexive transitive closure**.

The reflexive transitive closure of a homogeneous relation is the union of all its iterates; its non-reflexive closure is the union of all its iterates except for its zeroth. The reflexive transitive closure of a relation R, written R^*, is therefore

$$R^0 \cup R^1 \cup R^2 \cup R^3 \ldots R^n.$$

The non-reflexive transitive closure of a homogeneous relation R, written R^+, is therefore

$$R^1 \cup R^2 \cup R^3 \ldots R^n.$$

Example 6.7

If *peripherals* is the set

$$\{\text{reader1, reader2, lpl, lp2, lp3}\}$$

and *is_alternative* is a homogeneous relation over *peripherals* $\times$ *peripherals* whose current value is

$$\{(\text{reader1, reader2}), (\text{lp1, lp2}), (\text{lp2, lp3}), (\text{lp3, lp1})\},$$

then what is the value of *is_alternative*$^+$?

---

is_alternative is

$$\{(\text{reader1, reader2}), (\text{lp1, lp2}), (\text{lp2, lp3}), (\text{lp3, lp1})\}.$$

is_alternative^2 is

$$\{(\text{lp1, lp3}), (\text{lp2, lp1}), (\text{lp3, lp2})\}.$$

is_alternative^4, *is*

$$\{(\text{lp1, lp2}), (\text{lp2, lp3}), (\text{lp3, lp1})\},$$

is_alternative^5 = *is_alternative*^{2} and
is_alternative^6 = *is_alternative*^{3}

Therefore, *is_alternative*$^+$ is

$$\{(\text{reader1, reader2}), (\text{lp1, lp2}), (\text{lp2, lp3}),$$
$$(\text{lp3, lp1}), (\text{lp1, lp3}), (\text{lp2, lp1}), (\text{lp3, lp2}),$$
$$(\text{lp1, lp1}), (\text{lp2, lp2}), (\text{lp3, lp3})\}.$$

As an example of the use of transitive closures consider a programming language such as Ada or Modula2 which supports modules. A large software developer will construct a system using these languages as a series of modules which are separately compiled. Each module will consist of a set of facilities such as procedures and functions and will use facilities supplied by other modules.

A module consists of a specification part which provides details of the facilities offered by the module and an implementation part which is the program code that implements the facilities. If the specification part of a module is changed, then all the modules which use that changed module will need to be re-compiled.

If a module needs another module for its processing then this can be modelled by the homogeneous relation *needs_module* over *modules* × *module*. Thus, if *modulea* requires facilities provided by *moduleb* then

modulea needs_module moduleb

is true.

If, as part of a language support system, a facility were provided which would enable a user to type in a series of modules and display which modules are needed for these typed modules, however indirectly, then the specification for this command would involve the non-reflexive transitive closure of *needs_module*. Thus, *needs_module*$^+$ is a relation which describes the dependencies (direct and indirect) between the developed modules in a software system. If it were required to discover those modules which are needed by a set of modules *module_set* then this would be given by

needs_module$^+$[module_set].

Example 6.8

The relation *next_to* is over *programs* × *programs*. It expresses the fact that programs in a computer system are located next to each other in main memory. Thus,

programA next_to programB

is true when *programA* is next to *programB* with

programB occupying a higher address. The relation *higher_address* is over *programs* × *programs* and expresses the fact that one program occupies a higher address than another program. Express *higher_address* in terms of *next_to*.

The relation will be the non-reflexive transitive closure of *next_to*

$$higher\_address = next\_to^+.$$

6.6 Theorems involving relations

In the same way that theorems can be developed and proved in set theory and predicate calculus, a number of theorems can be derived and proved concerning relations.

If R is a relation over $T_1 \times T_2$, then

$$R[\![\text{dom } R]\!] = \text{rng } R,$$
$$R^{-1}[\![\text{rng } R]\!] = \text{dom } R.$$

If R is a relation over $T_1 \times T_2$ and S_1 and S_2 are sets of objects of type T_1, then

$$R[\![S_1 \cup S_2]\!] = R[\![S_1]\!] \cup R[\![S_2]\!],$$
$$R[\![S_1 \cap S_2]\!] \subseteq R[\![S_1]\!] \cap R[\![S_2]\!],$$
$$S_1 \cap S_2 \Rightarrow R[\![S_1]\!] \cap R[\![S_2]\!].$$

If R_1 and R_2 are relations over $T_1 \times T_2$ and $T_2 \times T_3$ then

$$(R_1; R_2)^{-1} = R_2^{-1}; R_1^{-1}.$$

If R_1 is a relation over $T_1 \times T_2$, R_2 a relation over $T_2 \times T_3$, and R_3 a relation over $T_3 \times T_4$, then

$$R_1; (R_2; R_3) = (R_1; R_2); R_3.$$

If R is any relation over $T_1 \times T_2$, then

$$R; (\text{id } T_2) = R$$
$$(\text{id } T_1); R = R.$$

If R_1 and R_2 are relations over $T_1 \times T_2$ and R_3 a relation over $T_2 \times T_3$, then

$$(R_1 \cup R_2); R_3 = (R_1; R_3) \cup (R_2; R_3),$$
$$R_1 \subseteq R_2 \Rightarrow (R_1; R_3) \subseteq (R_2; R_3).$$

If R_1, R_2, and R_3 are relations over $T_1 \times T_2$, then

$$(R_1 \cup R_2)^{-1} = R_1^{-1} \cup R_2^{-1},$$
$$(R_1 - R_2)^{-1} = R_1^{-1} - R_2^{-1},$$
$$R_1 \oplus (R_2 \oplus R_3) = (R_1 \oplus R_2) \oplus R_3,$$
$$(R \oplus \{\,\}) = R,$$
$$(\{\,\} \oplus R) = R.$$

All these theorems can be derived from the definitions of the relational operators presented in this chapter together with theorems from predicate calculus and set theory. For example, the proof of the theorem

$$R[\![\text{dom } R]\!] = \text{rng } R$$

1 $R[\![\text{dom } R]\!] = R[\![\{t_1\colon T_1 \mid \exists t_2\colon T_2 \cdot t_1 R t_2\}]\!]$
2 $R[\![\{t_1\colon T_1 \mid \exists t_2\colon T_2 \cdot t_1 R t_2\}]\!] =$
   $\{t_e\colon T_2 \mid \exists t_f\colon \{t_1\colon T_1 \mid \exists t_2\colon T_2 \cdot t_1 R t_2\} \cdot t_f R t_e\}$
3 $\{t_e\colon T_2 \mid \exists t_f\colon \{t_1\colon T_1 \mid \exists t_2\colon T_2 \cdot t_1 R t_2\} \cdot t_f R t_e\} =$
   $\{t_e\colon T_2 \mid \exists t_f\colon T_1 \cdot t_f R t_e\}$
4 $\{t_e\colon T_2 \mid \exists t_f\colon T_1 \cdot t_f R t_e\} = \text{rng } R$
5 $R[\![\text{dom } R]\!] = \text{rng } R.$ $\{1, 2, 3, 4\}.$

The crucial line of the proof is line 3 where

$$\exists t_f\colon \{t_1\colon T_1 \mid \exists t_2\colon T_2 \cdot t_1 R t_2\} \cdot t_f R t_e$$

is replaced by

$$\exists t_f\colon T_1 \cdot t_f R t_e.$$

This replacement can be carried out because

$$\{t_1\colon T_1 \mid \exists t_2\colon T_2 \cdot t_1 R t_2\}$$

is a subset of T_1.

The theorem

$$(R_1 \cup R_2)^{-1} = R_1^{-1} \cup R_2^{-1}$$

can be similarly proved by recourse to the definition of a relational operator, in this case $^{-1}$

1   $R_1^{-1} \cup R_2^{-1} = \{v_1: T_1; v_2: T_2 \mid (v_1, v_2) \in R_1^{-1} \vee (v_1, v_2) \in R_2^{-1}\}$

2   $\{v_1: T_1; v_2: T_2 \mid (v_1, v_2) \in R_1^{-1} \vee (v_1, v_2) \in R_2^{-1}\} =$
    $\{v_1: T_1; v_2: T_2 \mid (v_2, v_1) \in R_1 \vee (v_2, v_1) \in R_2\}$

3   $\{v_1: T_1; v_2: T_2 \mid (v_2, v_1) \in R_1 \vee (v_2, v_1) \in R_2\} =$
    $\{v_1: T_1; v_2: T_2 \mid (v_2, v_1) \in (R_1 \cup R_2)\}$

4   $\{v_1: T_1; v_2: T_2 \mid (v_2, v_1) \in (R_1 \cup R_2)\} =$
    $\{v_1: T_1; v_2: T_2 \mid (v_1, v_2) \in (R_1 \cup R_2)^{-1}\}$

5   $\{v_1: T_1; v_2: T_2 \mid (v_1, v_2) \in (R_1 \cup R_2)^{-1}\} = (R_1 \cup R_2)^{-1}$

6   $R_1^{-1} \cup R_2^{-1} = (R_1 \cup R_2)^{-1}$ $\hspace{2cm} \{1, 2, 3, 4, 5\}.$

7 Functions and sequences

7.1 Functions

A **function** is an important type of relation. It has the property that each element of its domain is associated with just *one* element of its range. Thus,

$$\{(1, \text{file2}), (3, \text{file4}), (7, \text{file2}), (6, \text{filetax}), (9, \text{fileupd})\}$$

is an example of a function while

$$\{(1, \text{file2}), (3, \text{file5}), (7, \text{file3}), (1, \text{file5}), (2, \text{file4})\}$$

is not an example since 1 is associated with both the files *file2* and *file5*. When a pair of elements occurs in a function it is said that the function **maps** the first element to the second element. Thus, in the function above 1 is mapped to *file2* and 6 is mapped to *filetax*.

A **partial function** is a function whose domain is a proper subset of the set from which the first elements of its pairs is taken. Thus, the function

$$\{(1, 3), (4, 9), (8, 3)\}$$

over $\mathbf{N} \times \mathbf{N}$ is a partial function because its domain: $\{1, 4, 8\}$ is a proper subset of the natural numbers. Examples of partial functions abound in system specifications. For example,

The main salesman file will hold data on the current performance of salesmen; this data will be retrieved by typing a unique salesman identity number.

Each file in the file store will have a unique name. This is formed by concatenating the user name and the directory name. A file will be held in a non-overlapping area of the file store.

Each entry in the process table consists of a process name

and its location in store and corresponds to a currently functioning process. There will be no duplicate entries in the table.

The first paragraph describes a partial function whose domain is a subset of salesman numbers. Its range is a subset of performance data. The second paragraph describes a function whose domain is a subset of all user names concatenated with directory names; its range is a subset of possible addresses. Last, the third paragraph describes a function whose domain is a subset of possible process names and whose range is a subset of the natural numbers.

Example 7.1

Identify any functions in the system specification extract shown below.

> Each input device will have an entry in the peripheral table; the contents of the table entry represents the state of the device. The system will also store in the activity file each input device together with the names of those program(s) which currently have the input device allocated to them.

First, there is a function which models the association between an input device and its state. The association between programs and devices which are allocated to them can either be modelled by a relation over *input devices* × *programs* or a function over *input devices* × $\mathbb{P}$ *programs*.

A relation R over $T_1 \times T_2$ is a partial function if and only if

$$\forall t_1\colon T_1; t_2, t_3\colon T_2 \cdot (t_1 R t_2 \wedge t_1 R t_3) \Rightarrow t_2 = t_3.$$

This states that in a partial function t_1 is mapped to both t_2 and t_3 only when both t_2 and t_3 are equal.

An important type of function is a **total function**. This is a function whose domain is equal to the set from which the first elements of its pairs is taken. For example, if the set *sysprogs* is

{archiver, editor, compilerA, compilerB, filer}

and *location* is a function over *sysprogs* × **N**

{(archiver, 12), (editor, 480), (compilerA, 903),
(compilerB, 202), (filer, 17)},

then *location* is a total function because its domain

{archiver, editor, compilerA, compilerB, filer}

is equal to *sysprogs*.

Formally, a function R over $T_1 \times T_2$ is total if

$$\forall t_1: T_1; t_2, t_3: T_2 \cdot (t_1 R t_2 \wedge t_1 R t_3 \Rightarrow t_2 = t_3) \wedge \operatorname{dom} R = T_1$$

Exercise 7.1

If sysprog = {archiver, editor, filer, compiler, linker}, then classify the
following five functions.

(i) {(archiver, 2), (editor, 3)}.
(ii) {(archiver, 3), (editor, 3), (compiler, 3), (linker, 3), (filer, 3)}.
(iii) {(archiver, 4), (editor, 4)}.
(iv) {(archiver, 1)}.
(v) {(archiver, 6), (compiler, 9), (editor, 12), (linker, 3), (filer, 84)}.

An **injective function** is a function whose inverse is also a
function. For example,

$$\{(1, 17), (2, 12), (3, 18), (4, 19)\}$$

is an injective function since its inverse

$$\{(17, 1), (12, 2), (18, 3), (19, 4)\}$$

is also a function, while

$$\{(8, 41), (9, 53), (10, 77), (11, 53)\}$$

is not injective since its inverse

$$\{(41, 8), (53, 9), (77, 10), (53, 11)\}$$

is not a function because of the multiple occurrences of 53 as the first element in its pairs.

Injective functions can again be classified as partial or total. A function R over $T_1 \times T_2$ is a partial injective function if

$$(\forall t_1 \colon T_1; t_2, t_3 \colon T_2 \cdot (t_1 R t_2 \wedge t_1 R t_3) \Rightarrow t_2 = t_3) \wedge$$
$$(\forall t_1, t_3 \colon T_1; t_2 \colon T_2 \cdot (t_2 R^{-1} t_1 \wedge t_2 R^{-1} t_3) \Rightarrow t_1 = t_3).$$

A function R over $T_1 \times T_2$ is a total injective function if

$$(\forall t_1 \colon T_1; t_2, t_3 \colon T_2 \cdot (t_1 R t_2 \wedge t_1 R t_3) \Rightarrow t_2 = t_3) \wedge \text{dom } R = T_1 \wedge$$
$$(\forall t_1, t_3 \colon T_1; t_2 \colon T_2 \cdot (t_2 R^{-1} t_1 \wedge t_2 R^{-1} t_3) \Rightarrow t_1 = t_3).$$

Exercise 7.1

If *processnames* = {process1, process2, process3, process4} and *range* is 1..4, then classify the following functions.

   (i) {(1, process1)}.
  (ii) {(1, process1), (2, process1)}.
 (iii) {(1, process1), (2, process2), (3, process1), (4, process4)}.
 (iv) {(1, process1), (2, process2), (3, process3), (4, process4)}.
  (v) {(1, process1), (3, process1)}.

A function is said to be **surjective** if its range is the whole of the set from which the second elements of its pairs are taken. For example, if *computers* is the set

$$\{\text{VAXA}, \text{VAXB}, \text{VAXC}, \text{PDP11}\},$$

then the function

$$\{(1, \text{VAXA}), (3, \text{VAXB}), (7, \text{VAXC}), (9, \text{VAXC}), (11, \text{PDP11})\}$$

is a surjective function over $\mathbf{N} \times$ *computers* since its range is

$$\{\text{VAXA}, \text{VAXB}, \text{VAXC}, \text{PDP11}\}.$$

Again surjective functions can be total or partial. A function R over $T_1 \times T_2$ is a **partial surjection** if

$$(\forall t_1\colon T_1;\, t_2,\, t_3\colon T_2 \cdot (t_1 R t_2 \wedge t_1 R t_3) \Rightarrow t_2 = t_3) \wedge \text{rng } R = T_2,$$

and a function R over $T_1 \times T_2$ is a **total surjection** if

$$(\forall t_1\colon T_1;\, t_2,\, t_3\colon T_2 \cdot (t_1 R t_2 \wedge t_1 R t_3) \Rightarrow$$
$$t_1 = t_3) \wedge \text{rng } R = T_2 \wedge \text{dom } R = T_1.$$

thus, if *monitors* is the set

{monitor1, monitor2, monitor3, monitor4, monitor5}

and *reactors* is the set

{reactor1, reactor2, reactor3},

then

{(monitor1, reactor1), (monitor2, reactor2),

(monitor3, reactor3), (monitor4, reactor3)}

is a partial surjection and

{(monitor1, reactor1), (monitor2, reactor2), (monitor3, reactor2),

(monitor4, reactor3), (monitor5, reactor1)}

is a total surjection.

A final important category of function is one which is both injective and surjective. These are known as **bijective functions**. A function R over $T_1 \times T_2$ is a partial bijective function if

$$(\forall t_1\colon T_1;\, t_2,\, t_3\colon T_2 \cdot (t_1 R t_2 \wedge t_1 R t_3) \Rightarrow t_2 = t_3) \wedge$$
$$(\forall t_1,\, t_3\colon T_1;\, t_2\colon T_2 \cdot (t_2 R^{-1} t_1 \wedge t_2 R^{-1} t_3) \Rightarrow t_1 = t_3) \wedge \text{rng } R = T_2.$$

A function R over $T_1 \times T_2$ is a total bijective function if

$$(\forall t_1\colon T_1;\, t_2,\, t_3\colon T_2 \cdot (t_1 R t_2 \wedge t_1 R t_3) \Rightarrow t_2 = t_3) \wedge$$
$$(\forall t_1,\, t_3\colon T_1;\, t_2\colon T_2 \cdot (t_2 R^{-1} t_1 \wedge t_2 R^{-1} t_3) \Rightarrow t_1 = t_3) \wedge \text{rng } R = T_2 \wedge$$
$$\text{dom } R = T_1.$$

An example of a total bijective function over {monitor1, monitor2, monitor3} $\times$ {reactor1, reactor2, reactor3} is

{(monitor1, reactor2), (monitor2, reactor1),
                                                  (monitor3, reactor3)}.

Its inverse is a function, its domain is the set from which the first elements of its pairs is taken, and its range is the set from which the second element of its pairs is taken.

Exercise 7.3

Classify the following finite functions. Assume that

> supplier = {Jones, Wilson, Brown, Thomas},
>
> depot = {Cardiff, London, Sheffield, Manchester},
>
> product = {nut, bolt, hanger, screw}.

(i) {(nut, 1), (bolt, 4), (hanger, 7), (screw, 4)}.

(ii) {(Jones, Cardiff), (Wilson, London), (Brown, Sheffield), (Thomas, Manchester)}.

(iii) {(Jones, bolt), (Wilson, bolt), (Wilson, nut), (Brown, hanger), (Thomas, screw)}.

(iv) {(Jones, nut)}.

(v) {(Jones, bolt), (Wilson, hangar)}.

Example 7.2

The following is an excerpt from the system specification of a monitoring system for a chemical plant. What type of function can be used to model the operation of the plant?

> The monitoring system is intended to monitor the operation of five chemical reactors. Every reactor is connected to only one cluster of temperature and pressure sensors, a cluster that is in use is only connected to one reactor; not all the clusters are necessarily in use at the same time.

The fact that a reactor is connected to a cluster can be modelled by a total injective function over *reactors* × *clusters*, where *reactors* is the set of reactors in the monitoring system and *clusters* is the set of clusters in the system. If all the clusters in the system were always in use, then the function would be total and bijective.

Functions can be applied to an element in their domain to yield an element from their range. This is written as the function name followed by the element name. Thus, if *connected* is a function over *computers × lines* and has a value

{(VAXA, comm1), (VAXB, comm2),

(VAXC, comm3), (VAX4, comm1)},

then *connected VAXA* is equal to *comm1*.

Since functions are only a special type of relation the operators which were described in the previous chapter can be used. For example, if the partial injective function *has_account* over *customers × account_numbers* models the fact that a customer has an account and the partial function *is_located* over *account_numbers × banks* models the fact that an account is held in a bank, then the function

has_account; is_located

can be used to model the relationship between a customer and his bank and the expression

$^\#$((overdraft_customers ◁ (has_account; is_located))

▷ {ManchesterA})

represents the number of overdraft accounts at the *ManchesterA* branch, where *overdraft_customers* is the set of customers who have overdrafts. The movement of an account of a customer *cust* from a branch to another branch *new_branch* can be written as

is_located' = is_located ⊕ (has_account cust, new_branch).

Two functions which will be used frequently in the rest of this book are *pred* and *succ*. They are both over $N_1 \times N$. *Pred* returns the predecessor of its argument while *succ* returns its successor. Thus, the functions are

$$\text{pred} = \{(1, 0), (2, 1), (3, 2), (4, 3), \ldots\}$$
$$\text{succ} = \{(1, 2), (2, 3), (3, 4), (4, 5), \ldots\}.$$

7.2 Higher-order functions

The functions already described in this chapter have been comparatively simple. Normally, they have involved ranges and domains which contain simple objects such as natural numbers or monitor names. While such functions are adequate for a large proportion of specifications, there is often a need for more complicated functions.

As an example consider the memory allocation subsystem of an operating system which keeps track of the addresses of processes in memory. A process will be characterized by its start address and its finish address. If processes are characterized by name, then they can be modelled by a function which maps process names to $\mathbf{N} \times \mathbf{N}$.

Example 7.3

The partial function *memory_map* maps process names p into pairs which represent the start address and finish address of processes. These addresses are expressed in bytes. Write an expression which gives the number of processes that occupy more than 2000 bytes of storage. Assume that *addresses* is the set of all possible addresses in memory.

The expression will be the cardinality of the set of processes whose pairs differ by more than 2000. This is expressed as

$^{\#}\{\text{proc: dom memory\_map} \mid \exists a,b\colon \text{addresses} \cdot (b - a) > 2000 \wedge (a, b) = \text{memory\_map proc}\}.$

Example 7.4

Write down a predicate which describes the result of removing all processes with a length greater than 10 000 bytes from *memory_map*.

The predicate will relate the value of *memory_map* before removal of the specified processes with its value after removal of the processes. It involves subtracting all those processes with a length greater than 10 000 from *memory_map*. The predicate will be:

memory_map' = {proc: dom memory_map | ∃*a*,*b*: addresses · (*b* − *a*) > 10 000 ∧ (*a*, *b*) = memory_map proc} ◁ memory_map

Another example of the use of more complicated functions occurs in the modelling of part of a stock-control system which deals with commodities stored at various warehouses. The fact that a series of commodities is stocked at a warehouse can be modelled by means of a partial function *stores* which maps warehouse names to a set of commodity codes. In order to extract the commodities stored at, say, Manchester, all that would need to be written would be

stores Manchester.

Example 7.5

Assume that as part of the stock control system described above a command is required which displays the number of different commodities stored at a location *city*. Write down an expression involving *stores* which gives the required number.

The expression will be the cardinality of the set to which the function *stores* maps *city*. This will be

$^{\#}$(stores city).

Example 7.6

The customer for the stock-control system described above requires that a facility be provided which enables new commodity codes for a new city to be added to a particular warehouse. Assume that the user types in the set of new commodity codes *comm_codes* and a new city *city_name*. Write a predicate which expresses the effect of this on *stores*.

The command will have the effect of forming the union of *stores* with the pair (*city_name, comm_codes*). Formally expressed, this will be

stores′ = stores ∪ (city_name, comm_codes).

Another frequent use of complicated functions involves functions where the type of the domain or the type of the range is itself a function. These are known as **higher-order functions**. An example of the use of a higher-order function might occur in a system for keeping track of reservations for a set of rooms in a hotel. The fact that a room is to be occupied by a guest might be modelled by a function which maps room numbers into guest names. However, if one wishes to keep track of the occupancy of rooms over a time period, then a further function *bookings* is required which maps dates into the previous function. A simple example will make this clear. Let us make the gross simplifying assumptions that the hotel has only three rooms; that booking details are kept for only two days in advance, and that dates are expressed as an integer relative to the beginning of the year. If the value of the function is

$$\{(24, \{(1, \text{Jones}), (2, \text{Ince})\}),$$
$$(25, \{(1, \text{Wilson}), (2, \text{Timms}), (3, \text{Yeo})\})\}$$

then the function maps day 24 into the function {(1, Jones), (2, Ince)} which maps room numbers into occupant's names and maps day 25 into the function {(1, Wilson), (2, Timms), (3, Yeo)} which again maps room numbers into occupants' names. Each element of the function is a pair. The first element is a date and the second element is a function which maps room numbers into the names of occupants. Thus, if the name of the occupant of room *room_no* for date *day* is required, then

bookings day room_no

would be written

Example 7.7

An operation required for the hotel booking system outlined above is that of adding a new day *newday* to the function *bookings*. When this day is added the rooms in the hotel for that day will be assumed to be not booked. Write down the predicate which describes this event.

The effect is straightforward. The new value of *bookings* will be the union of the old value together with a pair made up of *newday* and the empty set. The latter signifies no bookings for that day. This is formally expressed as

bookings' = bookings ∪ {(newday, { })}.

7.3 Modelling a version-control system using higher-order functions

A version-control system is a software tool which keeps track of different versions of a software system. Many large software systems exist in a considerable number of different versions. There are a number of reasons for this: one reason is that a software system may be required to operate in a number of different hardware configurations; each configuration may require a slightly different version of the original system. Another reason is that, as a software system evolves during maintenance, changes will be made to that system; after a time all the changes are normally aggregated and a new version of the system formed and distributed to its users.

The text of part of a specification for a very simple

version-control system is shown below, and the formal specification of the effect of each command is interspersed with this text. The effect of errors is not included in the specification.

    1. The purpose of the configuration management system is to keep track of the large number of different versions of software systems produced by International Software Packages Inc.

    2. Each version of a named software system is given a unique integer identification. The first version has the value 1.

    3. Each version of the software system will contain a number of named program units. Each program unit will exist as a series of different versions. These will be uniquely identified by an integer. The first version of a program unit has the value 1.

The statement of requirements has, so far, indicated that two sets of objects will be required. The first set *system_names* will be the set of all possible system names which are to exist in a number of different versions. The second set will be the set of all possible program unit names *program_unit_names*.

    A function is also required which maps program unit names into version numbers; this function is used to relate the units making up a system to the version numbers of units. Also a function *sys_versions* is required which maps *system_names* into functions which map system-version numbers into the former type of function; this function is used to relate system names to the version numbers of systems and the program units that makeup the system. It is assumed that **N** will be the set from which program-unit version numbers and system-version numbers are taken. Thus, the structure of *sys_versions* is

a function mapping elements of *system_names* into
  a set of functions each of which map elements of **N** into
    a set of functions which map elements of *program_unit_names* into
      the set **N**.

    4. A version is formed from a previous version in three ways: first, by replacing existing program units in a version

with new versions for those program units; second, by removing program units from the version; third, by adding program units to a version.

5. A number of different commands are to be provided as part of the version control system. These are detailed below.

5.1 The SETUP command

This command sets up the first version of a system. The user provides the system name and a list of program units and the version control system stores the program unit names as the first version of the system. The system will assume that the program unit names entered will be the initial versions.

Assuming that the name of the set of program unit names provided is *uns_provided* and the name of the new system is *sys_nm,* then the result of this command can be specified formally as

sys_versions' =
sys_versions $\cup$ {(sys_nm, {(1, {unit:uns_provided $\cdot$ (unit, 1)})})}.

5.2 The DISPLAY command

This command expects the version number and the name of a system. It will then display the names of the program units which make up that version of the system.

If *sys_nm* is the name of the system and *version_no* the version number, then the set of displayed program units is given as

$$dom(sys\_versions \ sys\_nm \ version\_no).$$

5.3 The DIFF command

This command expects a version number n of a system together with the system name. It will then display those program units which are not in the nth version of the system but which are in the $(n + 1)$th version.

If *sys_nm* is the name of the system, then the set produced by this command will be

$$dom(sys\_versions \ sys\_nm(n + 1))$$
$$- dom(sys\_versions \ sys\_nm \ n).$$

The first set dom *(sys_versions sys_nm(n + 1))* gives the program unit names that participate in version $n + 1$ of the system; *dom(sys_versions sys_nm n)* gives the program unit names that participate in version n of the system.

5.4 The COMMON command

This command expects a version number n of a system together with the system name. It will then display those program units which are in both the nth version of the system and in the $(n + 1)$th version.

This command is relatively simple to specify; the common modules are given by the intersection of the expressions formed in the last command specification. It will hence be

$$\text{dom(sys\_versions sys\_nm}(n + 1)) \cap \text{dom(sys\_versions sys\_nm } n).$$

5.5 NUMIN command

This command expects the version number of a system and a system name. It then displays the number of program units in the system.

Again the effect of this command is relatively simple to specify. The expression required is

$$^{\#}(\text{sys\_versions sys\_nm } n).$$

5.6 The NUMVERSIONS command

This command displays the number of current versions of a system. The command expects a system name.

Again the effect of this command is relatively simple to specify. It is given by

$$^{\#}(\text{sys\_versions sys\_nm}).$$

5.7 The FORMVERSION command

This command forms a new version of a software system. The user provides the name of the system together with a set of program unit names and corresponding program-unit version numbers. The effect of the command is to form a new version of the system comprising the program units.

If the name of the system is given by *sys_nm* and the set of pairs representing program unit names and version numbers is *unit_set,* then the effect of the command can be specified as

$$\text{sys\_versions' sys\_nm} = \text{sys\_versions sys\_nm} \cup$$
$$\{(^{\#}(\text{sys\_versions sys\_nm}) + 1, \text{unit\_set})\}.$$

5.8   The OCCUPIES command
This command expects a program-unit name and a system name. It will display the number of versions of the software system in which the program unit participates.

The number of versions of the software system which contain the program unit is given by

$$^{\#}\{\text{version\_num}: \mathbf{N} \mid \text{unit\_name} \in \text{dom}$$
$$(\text{sys\_versions sys\_nm version\_num})\}$$

where *unit_name* is the name of the program unit provided and *sys_nm* is the name of the system.

7.4   Functions as lambda expressions

An alternative way of writing functions which is often used in mathematics is known as a **lambda expression**. The general form of a lambda expression is

$$\lambda \text{ Signature} \mid \text{Predicate} \cdot \text{Term}.$$

It has a similar form to the notation for constructive set specification. The signature establishes the types of the variables used. The predicate gives a condition which each first element of every pair in the function must satisfy; the term gives the form of the second element of each pair in the function. An example of a lambda expression is

$$\lambda m: \mathbf{N} \mid m > 4 \cdot m + 5.$$

It denotes the infinite function

$$\{(5, 10), (6, 11), \dots ,\}.$$

Another example is

$$\lambda x: 0..10 \mid (x, x^2)$$

which is a finite function which maps natural numbers between 0 and 10 to a pair whose first element is the natural number and the second element its square, i.e.

$$\{(0, (0, 0)), (1, (1, 1)), (2, (2, 4)), \ldots, (10, (10, 100))\}.$$

In general, a lambda expression maps types made up from variables of the signature into the expression represented by the term for which the predicate is true. Thus,

$$\lambda a, b, c: \mathbf{N} \mid a + b = c \cdot a^2 + b^2 + c^2$$

specifies the function

$$\{((0, 0, 0), 0), ((0, 1, 1), 2), ((1, 0, 1), 2), ((1, 1, 2), 6), \ldots\}$$

since each (a, b, c) in every pair satisfies the predicate $a + b = c$ and the second element of each pair is $a^2 + b^2 + c^2$.

Exercise 7.4

If *files* is the set

$$\{upd, text, ed1, ed2, ed3, tax1, tax2\}$$

and *users* the set

$$\{Timms, Jones, Wilkins, Wilson\}$$

and *size* is a partial function over *files* × **N** with the value

$$\{(upd, 45), (text, 175), (ed1, 105), (ed2, 95)\},$$

then write down the values of the following expressions.

   (i) $\lambda x: \mathbf{N} \mid x < 3 \cdot x^2$.
   (ii) $\lambda x: 3..15 \mid x^2 \leq 9 \cdot x$.
   (iii) $2..4 \lhd (\lambda x: \mathbf{N} \mid x < 10 \cdot x)$.
   (iv) $(\lambda x: \mathbf{N} \mid x < 10 \cdot x^2) \oplus \{(3, 8), (4, 17)\}$.
   (v) $\lambda x: \text{rng } size \mid x > 53 \cdot x + 10$.
   (vi) $\lambda x: \text{rng } size \mid x = \text{rng } size$.
   (vii) $\{2, 3\} \lhd \lambda x: \mathbf{N} \cdot x^2$.
   (viii) $size; (\lambda x: \mathbf{N} \mid x > 100 \cdot x + 10)$.
   (ix) $(\lambda x: \mathbf{N} \mid x > 5 \wedge x < 10 \cdot x) \cup (\lambda x: \mathbf{N} \mid x^2 = 16 \cdot x^3)$.

7.4.1   *Curried functions*

One of the powerful facilities that lambda abstraction allows the specifier is known as **currying**. As an example of this consider the function

$$\lambda x : \mathbf{N} \cdot \lambda y : \mathbf{N} \cdot x + y.$$

This represents the infinite function which forms the sum of two natural numbers. This function can be regarded as a function which maps natural numbers into a function which itself maps natural numbers into natural numbers. Not only does this allow the specifier to write

$$(\lambda x : \mathbf{N} \cdot \lambda y : \mathbf{N} \cdot x + y) 8 \; 9$$

which delivers 17, but also allows the specifier to generate a family of functions. For example, the function that adds three to a number can be written as

$$(\lambda x : \mathbf{N} \cdot \lambda y : \mathbf{N} \cdot x + y) 3.$$

This generates the function

$$\{(0, 3), (1, 4), (2, 5), \ldots ,\}$$

and the function that adds 2098 to a number can be written as

$$(\lambda x : \mathbf{N} \cdot \lambda y : \mathbf{N} \cdot x + y) 2098.$$

This treatment of functions with two or more arguments is named after the logician H. B. Curry.

7.5   Sequences as functions

In many system specifications there is a need to model the fact that a series of objects is to be associated with natural numbers and an ordering implied. For example, the excerpts from the following specifications all indicate some ordering is inherent in the relations that are being described.

> . . . , Each message to be printed at the remote printer will be queued according to the priority of the message.

> . . . , There will be a 200 consecutive memory slots. Each program currently awaiting execution will occupy adjacent

memory slots. The programs will be stored in ascending order of size.

..., On receipt of the LISTSUM command the program will print out stock identities in descending order of stock-holding.

Because such situations are very common in specifications they can be modelled using a special function known as a **sequence**. A sequence of type T is a partial function from N_1 to T where the domain of the function is of the form $1..n$. For example, if *files* is the set

$$\{upd, tax1, tax2, edtax, newupd, oldupd, credit1, credit2\},$$

then

$\{(1, upd)\}$

$\{(1, tax1), (2, upd), (3, oldupd), (4, credit1)\}$

$\{(1, tax1), (2, credit2), (3, credit2)\}$

$\{(1, edtax), (2, oldupd), (3, credit1),$

$\qquad\qquad\qquad (4, credit2), (5, edtax), (6, credit1)\}$

are all examples of sequences of files. Formally, a sequence is a function which maps members of **N** to members of a set T and is defined as

$$\text{dom } S = 1..\,^{\#}S \wedge \text{rng } S \subseteq T,$$

i.e. a sequence of objects of type T is a function from natural numbers to T such that the domain of the function is the set of numbers from 1 to the cardinality of the function and the range is taken from T. This definition ensures that the sequence will contain the consecutive numbers from 1 to $^{\#}S$ in the domain of the function.

Given this definition it is relatively straightforward to extract an element from a sequence. For example, if *print_queue* is a sequence of files then *printqueue(1)* or *printqueue1* gives the first element of the sequence while *printque* $^{\#}$*printqueue* gives the final element of the sequence.

A number of operators can be defined which operate on sequences. The first is the *head* operator which is a function that returns the first object in a sequence. This can be defined using the lambda form as

$$\lambda s\colon S \mid s \neq \{\} \cdot s \; 1$$

where s is a sequence of objects of an arbitrary type. The operator *front* returns the first $n-1$ elements of a sequence of length n. It is defined as

$$\lambda s\colon S \mid s \neq \{\} \cdot (1..^{\#}s - 1) \lhd s$$

Example 7.8

The *tail* operator extracts from a sequence of length n the last $n-1$ elements. Use the *succ* function to define *tail*.

The *tail* operator is defined as

$$\lambda s\colon S \mid s \neq \{\} \cdot \{0\} \lhd (\mathrm{succ}; s).$$

The *succ* function is composed with s in order to subtract one from the first element of each pair. This gives a function which is identical to s except that the first element of each pair has been decreased by one. The first element of this sequence can then be removed using the domain subtraction operator.

Finally, the function *last* can be defined. *last* gives the last element of a sequence s and is defined as

$$\lambda s\colon S \mid s \neq \{\} \cdot s^{\#}s.$$

Example 7.9

A system specification for an operating system requires that the computer operator be able to remove the nth to mth entries in a queue of programs awaiting execution. Define a function using lambda notation which, when applied to a sequence of programs, gives the set of nth to mth programs.

The definition is

$$\lambda n, m: \mathbf{N}; s: S \mid n > 0 \wedge m \geq n \wedge m \leq {}^{\#}s \cdot \text{rng}(n..m \triangleleft s)$$

where s is a sequence of programs. The predicate $n > 0 \wedge m \geq n \wedge m \leq {}^{\#}s$ specifies the condition under which the function is applied since if n and m are out of range or $n > m$, then the function is undefined.

The functions defined above have all involved retrieving items from sequences. There is also a need for sequences to be constructed from other sequences. This is the function of the **concatenation** ⌢ operator. It takes two sequences and places the second sequence after the first. Thus, if *first* is the sequence

$$\{(1, \text{file1},), (2, \text{file7})\}$$

and *second* is the sequence

$$\{(1, \text{newfile}), (2, \text{oldupd}), (3, \text{oldtax}), (4, \text{newed})\},$$

then *first⌢second* is

$$\{(1, \text{file1},), (2, \text{file7}), (3, \text{newfile}),$$
$$(4, \text{oldupd}), (5, \text{oldtax}), (6, \text{newed})\}.$$

The definition of ⌢ follows.

$$\{(1, a_1), (2, a_2), \ldots, (n, a_n)\} \frown \{(1, b_1), (2, b_2), \ldots, (m, b_m)\} =$$
$$\{(1, a_1), (2, a_2), \ldots, (n, a_n), (n+1, b_1), (n+2, b_2), \ldots, (n+m, b_m)\}$$

$$\{\}^\frown A = A^\frown\{\} = A.$$

The first two lines define concatenation for two non-empty sequences and the third line defines concatenation when one of the sequences is empty.

7.6 Applying sequences in specifications—a print spooler

A computer operating system normally has more requests for printing facilities than printing facilities available. In order to cope with this the operating system of the computer will ensure that when a program produces any output it is first copied to a file. This file joins all other files awaiting printing in a queue or set of queues. The following specification describes the operator facilities available for manipulating such queues.

Spool queues—operator facilities

1. A number of commands will be available for the computer operator which enable him to manipulate queues or items in a queue.

2. Each output peripheral connected to the computer will be associated with a queue.

3. The SIZE command will return the number of entries in a queue.

4. The EMPTYSIZE command will return the number of queues which are empty together with the name of the peripheral associated with each queue.

5. The REMOVE command will remove a specified file from the queue associated with a particular peripheral.

6. The ADD command will remove all the items from a queue associated with a peripheral and add them to the end of another queue.

7. The MOVE command will remove an item from a queue associated with a peripheral and place it at the end of another queue.

8. The TOTALQUEUE command will return with the number of queues currently active, i.e. those queues which contain at least one entry.

Operators of the computer system will normally specify a peripheral name when using the above commands. For example, the operator will be more interested in the size of a queue associated with a particular peripheral than the number of items in a particular named queue. Thus, it seems natural to model the spooling system by means of a partial function from peripheral names to sequences of spool files. This can be done because each peripheral is associated with only one queue. If this were not the case, then a relation would have to be used. Therefore, let us assume the existence of a partial function *peripheral_assoc* which maps *peripheral_names* to a sequence of files. Each command can be specified in terms of operations on this function. In the specification that follows it is assumed that the operator has typed in a valid command and we are not concerned with error-processing.

The SIZE command assumes that the operator has typed in *periph_name* as a peripheral and the system returns the value of the queue size in *size*. The effect of the command can be specified in terms of the predicate

$$\text{periph\_name} \in \text{dom peripheral\_assoc} \land$$
$$\text{size} = {}^{\#}(\text{peripheral\_assoc periph\_name}) \land$$
$$\text{peripheral\_assoc}' = \text{peripheral\_assoc}.$$

The first conjunct states that the peripheral has a queue associated with it, the second conjunct establishes the value of *size,* and, lastly, the third conjunct specifies the fact that the command does not affect *peripheral_assoc.*

The EMPTYSIZE command will form a set of peripheral names *periph_set* such that the function *peripheral_assoc* maps each element of the set to an empty sequence. The number of queues currently empty *number_empty* will be equal to the cardinality of this set. The predicate expressing this is

$$\text{periph\_set} = \{\text{per: peripherals} \mid \text{peripheral\_assoc per} = \{\}\} \land$$
$$\text{number\_empty} = {}^{\#}\text{periph\_set} \land \text{peripheral\_assoc}' =$$
$$\text{peripheral\_assoc}.$$

Example 7.10

Specify the REMOVE command. Assume that the operator has typed a file name *file_name* and a peripheral name *periph_name.*

The REMOVE command can be specified by using the domain restriction operator

$$\text{periph\_name} \in \text{dom peripheral\_assoc} \land$$
$$\text{file\_name} \in \text{rng}(\text{peripheral\_assoc periph\_name}) \land$$

queue_posn =
(peripheral_assoc periph_name)$^{-1}$file_name $\wedge$

peripheral_assoc' periph_name = (1..(queue_posn −
1)$\lhd$peripheral_assoc periph_name) $\cup$

succ; ((queue_posn + 1..$^{\#}$(peripheral_assoc
periph_name))$\lhd$peripheral_assoc periph_name).

The first conjunct specifies that the peripheral name must
have a queue associated with it. The second conjunct
specifies that *file_name* should be in the queue associated
with *periph_name*. The third conjunct gives the position
in the queue of *file_name*. This is expressed using the
inverse of the sequence which represents the queue of
files. This, of course, assumes that the function is
bijective. If it were not, then the command would not be
meaningful as there would be more than one instance of
a file name in a particular queue. The final conjunct
defines the new sequence. It is the old sequence minus
the extracted item.

The ADD queue command will remove those elements from a
queue associated with a peripheral say *per1* and add them to the
queue associated with a second peripheral *per2*. The specification
is

per1 $\in$ dom peripheral_assoc $\wedge$ per2 $\in$ dom peripheral_assoc $\wedge$
peripheral_assoc' per2 =
(peripheral_assoc per2)$\frown$(peripheral_assoc per1) $\wedge$
peripheral_assoc' per1 = { }.

The first conjunct states that both peripherals must have queues
associated with them. The second conjunct states that the *per2*
queue becomes the old *per2* queue joined with the *per1* queue.
The final conjunct states that the *per1* queue becomes empty.

The MOVE command will remove an item *file_name* from the
queue associated with *per1* and place it at the end of the queue
associated with *per2*. The specification for this command is

per1 $\in$ dom peripheral_assoc $\wedge$ per2 $\in$ dom peripheral_assoc $\wedge$
file_name $\in$ rng (peripheral_assoc per1) $\wedge$
queue_posn = (peripheral_assoc per1)$^{-1}$ file_name $\wedge$
peripheral_assoc' per1 = (1..queue_posn $-$ 1) $\lhd$
(peripheral_assoc per1) $\cup$
succ; ((queue_posn + 1..$^{\#}$(peripheral_assoc per1)) $\lhd$
peripheral_assoc per1) $\wedge$
peripheral_assoc' per2 = peripheral_assoc per2 $\cup$
$\{(^{\#}$(peripheral_assoc per2) + 1, file_name)$\}$.

Example 7.11

Specify the TOTALQUEUE command.

This command can be specified by calculating the cardinality of the set of all peripherals which are mapped by *peripheral_assoc* to non-empty queues. If *tot_queues* is the total number of non-empty queues, then this command can be specified as the predicate

tot_queues =
$^{\#}\{$per: peripherals $|$ $^{\#}$(peripheral_assoc per) $> 0\}$ $\wedge$
peripheral_assoc' = peripheral_assoc.

The second conjunct specifies that the command does not affect *peripheral_assoc*.

8 Induction and recursive specification

8.1 Recursive specification

Assume that we need to specify a function which gives the sum of the first n natural numbers; how could that be specified? The first attempt might be to combine natural language with a small degree of mathematical formalism.

> The function *sum* maps elements of N_1 into elements of N_1. For a given n it produces the sum of the first n natural numbers.

A second attempt might be to list the function explicitly

$$\{(1, 1), (2, 3), (3, 6), (4, 10), \ldots\}.$$

A third attempt might be to give a rule which relates elements of the domain to elements of the range

$$\text{sum } n = 1 + 2 + 3 \ldots n.$$

All these techniques have drawbacks when it comes to reasoning about properties. The major criticism of the first attempt is the same as that made about natural language in Chapter 2. Although the example above seems an eminently readable description, it soon gets out of hand for more complex mathematical structures. The criticism of the second attempt is the same that was made in Chapter 5 about specification by enumeration. The third attempt is an improvement over the other two but it still suffers from the fact that it is unwieldy to reason about.

In order to avoid this situation mathematicians have devised a method of specification known as **recursive specification**. Such a specification involves defining objects in term of themselves. The example of the sum function will make this technique clear.

Some values of the function follow.

$$\text{sum } 1 = 1$$
$$\text{sum } 2 = 1 + 2$$
$$\text{sum } 3 = 1 + 2 + 3$$
$$\text{sum } 4 = 1 + 2 + 3 + 4$$

$\vdots$

$$\text{sum } n - 2 = 1 + 2 + 3 + \ldots (n-3) + (n-2)$$
$$\text{sum } n - 1 = 1 + 2 + 3 + \ldots (n-3) + (n-2) + (n-1)$$
$$\text{sum } n \quad = 1 + 2 + 3 + \ldots (n-3) + (n-2) + (n-1) + n.$$

From this pattern it can be seen that each sum differs from its predecessor by only one number. For example, sum 4 is equal to sum 3 plus 4. Similarly, sum 3 is equal to sum $2 + 3$. Looking at the final entries it can be seen that *sum* $(n-1)$ is equal to *sum* $(n-2)$ plus $n-1$ and that *sum* n is equal to *sum* $(n-1)$, plus n. This suggests that we can define *sum* n as

$$\text{sum } n = \text{sum}(n-1) + n.$$

This has effectively defined sum in terms of itself. Unfortunately, there is one problem. If we apply the rule to sum(1) we get

$$\text{sum}(1) = \text{sum}(0) + 1.$$

What is the sum of the first zero natural numbers? Well, in order to find out, the rule could be applied again to give

$$\text{sum}(0) = \text{sum}(-1) + 0.$$

However, this is nonsense. What is needed is a definition which terminates the repeated application of the specification of sum. One convenient rule would be

$$\text{sum } 1 = 1$$

or

$$\text{sum } 0 = 0.$$

If one assumes the former, then the specifiation of sum would be

$$\forall n : \mathbf{N}_1 \cdot \text{sum } n = \text{sum}(n-1) + n \wedge \text{sum } 1 = 1.$$

This is known as a **recursive specification**. A recursive specification is a specification where a mathematical object is described in terms of itself.

Example 8.1

The factorial function *fact* maps numbers from $\mathbf{N}_1$ into $\mathbf{N}_1$. Informally, *fact n* can be defined as

$$\text{fact } n = n * (n - 1) * (n - 2) \ldots * 2 * 1.$$

Write down a recursive specification of *fact*.

By writing down the values of *fact* a general pattern can be discovered

fact $1 = 1$
fact $2 = 2 * 1$
fact $3 = 3 * 2 * 1$
$\vdots$
fact $n - 2 = (n - 2) * (n - 3) \ldots * 3 * 2 * 1$
fact $n - 1 = (n - 1) * (n - 2) * (n - 3) \ldots 3 * 2 * 1$
fact $n \quad = n * (n - 1) * (n - 2) * (n - 3) \ldots 3 * 2 * 1.$

It can be seen that the factorial of a number is equal to the factorial of the previous number times the number itself. This gives the recursive specification

$$\forall n : \mathbf{N}_1 \cdot \text{fact } n = n * \text{fact}(n - 1) \wedge$$
$$\text{fact } 1 = 1.$$

Although the specifications described have involved writing down values of functions and then spotting patterns, this was only used as a teaching device and tends to be quite tedious. Normally, a recursive specification can be derived by asking two very simple questions.

How can I express the specification of this (function, relation, or any mathematical structure) applied to an object in terms of applying the (function, relation, or any mathematical structure) to a slightly smaller object? If the object is a natural number *n,* then it often involves considering the specification in terms of $n - 1$. If the object is a set, then it often involves considering the specification in terms of a set with one of its members removed. If the object is a sequence, then it involves considering the sequence with one of its elements removed.

How can I express the specification in terms of an object which terminates the chain of recursive definitions? In the factorial case described in Example 8.1 this involves defining the factorial of one.

In order to illustrate this the development of a recursive specification for the set cardinality function $^{\#}$ is outlined below. The questions that the specifier must ask himself are written in italics.

How can I express the specification of this (function, relation, or any mathematical structure) applied to an object in terms of applying the (function, relation, or any mathematical structure) to a slightly smaller object?

This entails expressing the relationship between the cardinality function applied to a set and the same function applied to a smaller set from which an element has been removed. How is it possible to relate the cardinality of a set to the cardinality of the set formed by removing an element from the set? The answer is straightforward. By removing an element from a set all that happens is that its cardinality is decreased by one. This gives the recursive specification

$$\forall A: \mathbb{P}T \cdot {}^{\#}A = {}^{\#}(A - \{a\}) + 1 \qquad \text{where } a \in A$$

and where T is an arbitrary type.

How can I express the specification in terms of an object which terminates the chain of recursive definitions?

In this case the object that terminates the chain of reasoning will be the empty set. The cardinality of the empty set is zero; hence

$$^{\#}\{\ \} = 0$$

which gives the full specification as

$$\forall A: \ \mathbb{P}T \cdot {}^{\#}A = {}^{\#}(A - \{a\}) + 1 \wedge$$
$$^{\#}\{\ \} = 0 \qquad \text{where } a \in A.$$

Example 8.2

Write down a recursive specification of the intersection operator *intersect*. Assume that *intersect* is written with two operands as

$$\text{intersect } (S_1, S_2).$$

In deriving the specification, assume that operand S_1 is the element which is to be involved in the specification by removing one of its elements.

The questions to be asked are again written in italics.

How can I express the specification of this (function, relation or any mathematical structure) applied to an object in terms of applying the (function, relation, or any mathematical structure) to a slightly smaller object? This means establishing a relationship between *intersect* (S_1, S_2) and *intersect* $(S_1 - \{s\}, S_2)$. There are two cases to consider. The first is that s is contained in S_2. In this case

$$\forall S_1, S_2 \colon \; \mathbb{P}T \cdot \text{intersect } (S_1, S_2) =$$
$$\{s\} \cup \text{intersect } (S_1 - \{s\}, S_2).$$

The second case is that s is not contained in S_2. Now if s is not contained in S_2, then removing it from S_1 should make no difference to the intersection of S_1 and S_2. Hence,

$$\forall S_1, S_2 \colon \; \mathbb{P}T \cdot \text{intersect } (S_1, S_2) = \text{intersect } (S_1 - \{s\}, S_2).$$

How can I express the specification in terms of an object which terminates the chain of recursive definitions? The object to be used is the empty set so that it is necessary to define what *intersect*$(\{\ \}, S_2)$ will be. This is straightforward since the intersection of any set with the empty set is the empty set. Thus,

$$\text{intersect}(\{\ \}, S_2) = \{\ \}.$$

Recursive specifications can be applied to sequences as well. As an illustration consider the specification of the function *rev* which reverses the elements of a sequence.

How can I express the specification of this (function, relation, or any mathematical structure) applied to an object in terms of applying the (function, relation, or any mathematical structure) to a slightly smaller object? In this case let us assume that we have to relate *rev S* to *rev tail S*; this is because *tail S* is *S* with its first element removed. The reverse of a sequence *S* will be the reverse of its tail together with the head of the sequence concatenated at the end. Formally, this would be written as

$$\forall S\colon \text{Seq } T \cdot \text{rev } S = (\text{rev tail } S)^\frown\text{head } S$$

where *Seq T* is the set of all sequences of an arbitrary type *T*. *How can I express the specification in terms of an object which terminates the chain of recursive definitions?* The object in this case will be the empty sequence. The reverse of the empty sequence is the empty sequence. This gives the full specification of *rev* as

$$\forall S\colon \text{Seq } T \cdot \text{rev } S = (\text{rev tail } S)^\frown\text{head } S \wedge$$

$$\text{rev}\,[\,] = [\,].$$

Exercise 8.1

(i) Write down a recursive specification of the set–subset relation.
(ii) Write down a recursive specification of the function *addup* which maps a set of natural numbers into the natural number which is the sum of the numbers in the set.
(iii) Write down a recursive specification of the set union operator.
(iv) Write down a recursive specification of the $^\frown$ operator which appends two sequences together.
(v) Write down a recursive specification of the + operator which forms the sum of two natural numbers.

8.2 Numbers and induction

Consider the following statement.

> A plant monitoring system consists of a set of closely coupled monitors. Each monitor is connected to another

monitor. If a monitor is in a ready state, then the monitor connected to it is in a ready state.

What can be deduced from the known fact that the first processor is in a ready state? Since the first processor is connected to another processor then this processor is also in a ready state. Consequently, if this latter processor is in a ready state, then the processor connected to it is in a ready state and so on. We can deduce that all the processors are in a ready state. This rule of reasoning is known as **induction**. This section describes how induction can be used to prove properties of natural numbers. Later sections extend the idea to more complicated structures such as sets and sequences. Induction is particularly useful when proving properties of recursive specifications.

How can one formally express the induction rule of reasoning? A clue can be gained from the paragraph above which describes part of a monitoring system. What this paragraph states is that

$$\text{ready}(k\text{th monitor}) \Rightarrow \text{ready}((k + 1)\text{th monitor})$$

where ready is the predicate *monitor is in a ready state*. Given that the first monitor is in a ready state, it can be deduced that all monitors are in a ready state, i.e.

$$\forall \text{mon: monitors} \cdot \text{ready}(\text{mon}).$$

The full sequence of reasoning can be described more formally as

$$\text{ready}(1\text{st monitor}), \text{ready}(k\text{th monitor}) \Rightarrow$$

$$\text{ready}((k + 1)\text{th monitor}) \vdash \forall \text{mon: monitors} \cdot \text{ready}(\text{mon}).$$

In terms of natural numbers the induction rule of reasoning is just a very simple rewrite of the above with *ready* being replaced by any predicate p

$$p(1), p(k) \Rightarrow p(k + 1) \vdash \forall n: \mathbf{N}_1 \cdot p(n).$$

This states that, if a predicate is true for the number one and it can be inferred that if the predicate holds for the $(k + 1)$th natural number from the fact that it holds for the kth natural number, then it is possible to deduce that the predicate holds for all natural numbers apart from zero.

An alternative formulation of the induction principle starts with the natural number zero

$$p(0), p(k) \Rightarrow p(k+1) \vdash \forall n: \mathbf{N} \cdot p(n).$$

An example from mathematics should make the principle clearer. Assume that it is wished to demonstrate that the sum of the first k integers is $k * (k+1)/2$. This can be expressed as the predicate $p(k)$

$$p(k) \Leftrightarrow \text{sum}_k = k * (k+1)/2$$

where sum_k stands for the sum of the first k numbers. First, it is necessary to demonstrate that $p(1)$ is true. This is achieved by setting k to 1 in the predicate. This gives

$$p(1) \Leftrightarrow \text{sum}_1 = 1 * 2/2 = 1,$$

which states that $p(1)$ is true if the sum of the first natural number is one; this is obviously true; therefore $p(1)$ is true. The next step is to demonstrate that

$$p(k) \Rightarrow p(k+1),$$

i.e. if $p(k)$ is true, then $p(k+1)$ can be deduced. First, assume $p(k)$ is true, i.e.

$$p(k) \Leftrightarrow \text{sum}_k = k * (k+1)/2$$

is true. Now the sum of the first $k+1$ natural numbers sum_{k+1} is the sum of the first k natural numbers plus $k+1$. This can be expressed as

$$\text{sum}_{k+1} = \text{sum}_k + k + 1.$$

Since it has been assumed that sum_k is $k * (k+1)/2$, this can be expressed as

$$\text{sum}_{k+1} = k * (k+1)/2 + k + 1.$$

When the right-hand side of the equality has been simplified, it reduces to

$$\text{sum}_{k+1} = (k+1) * (k+2)/2$$

is true. Now this predicate is simply a restatement of p_k

$$\text{sum}_k = k * (k+1)/2$$

with k replaced by $k+1$, i.e. $p(k+1)$. Thus it has been

demonstrated that $p(k + 1)$ is true. Thus, it has been shown that $p(k + 1)$ is true, if it is assumed that $p(k)$ is true. Since $p(1)$ has also been demonstrated true then, by induction

$$\forall n: \mathbf{N}_1 \cdot p_n,$$

i.e., no matter what the value of n, the sum of the first n natural numbers is $n * (n + 1)/2$.

The proof can be laid out more formally as

1	$p(k) \Leftrightarrow \text{sum}_k = k * (k + 1)/2$	
2	$p(1) \Leftrightarrow \text{sum}_1 = 1$	$\{1\}$
3	$p(1)$	$\{2\}$
4	$\text{sum}_{k+1} = \text{sum}_k + k + 1$	
5	$p(k)$	assumption
6	$\text{sum}_k = k * (k + 1)/2$	$\{1, 5\}$
7	$\text{sum}_{k+1} = k * (k + 1)/2 + k + 1$	$\{4, 6\}$
8	$\text{sum}_{k+1} = (k + 1) * (k + 2)/2$	$\{7\}$
9	$p(k + 1) \Leftrightarrow \text{sum}_{k+1} = (k + 1) * (k + 2)/2$	$\{1\}$
10	$p(k + 1)$	$\{7, 9\}$
11	$\forall n: \mathbf{N}_1 \cdot p(n)$	$\{3, 5, 10\}.$

Line 1 establishes the equivalence of $p(k)$ and the predicate to be proved. Lines 2 and 3 establish the truth of $p(1)$. Line 4 states that the sum of the first $k + 1$ natural numbers is equal to the sum of the first k natural numbers plus $k + 1$. Line 5 states the assumption necessary for the use of induction. Since $p(k)$ is assumed to be true on line 5, $\text{sum}_k = k * (k + 1)$ is true by virtue of line 1. This is shown on line 6. Line 7 follows from substituting for sum_k in line 6 from line 4. Algebraic manipulation gives line 8. Line 9 is a restatement of line 1 with $k + 1$ substituted for k. Line 10 shows that, since $\text{sum}_{k+1} = (k + 1) * (k + 2)/2$ has been demonstrated on line 8, then $p(k + 1)$ is true. Finally, line 11 shows, since $p(1)$ has been demonstrated true and also $p(k) \Rightarrow p(k + 1)$ has been demonstrated true, then, by the induction rule,

$$p(1), p(k) \Rightarrow p(k + 1) \vdash \forall n: \mathbf{N}_1 \cdot p(n),$$

that

$$\forall n: \mathbf{N}_1 \cdot p(n)$$

has been demonstrated true, i.e.

$$\forall n: \mathbf{N}_1 \cdot \text{sum}_n = n * (n + 1)/2.$$

In a proof by induction the first assumption, in this case p_1, is known as the **base case**. The assumption that $p(k)$ is true is known as the **induction hypothesis**. The proof that $p(k) \Rightarrow p(k + 1)$ is known as the **induction step**.

The proof just discussed has been written down in almost painstaking detail. When you become fully confident in the use of induction, many of the steps can be telescoped to one step. The proof has been laid out in detail in order to demonstrate its structure. You should be confident that you follow each step since induction is quite a difficult concept.

Example 8.3

Show that the sum of the squares of the first n natural numbers is given by

$$n * (n + 1) * (2n + 1)/6.$$

Lay out your proof in the same way as the proof on page 212.

---

1 $p(k) \Leftrightarrow \text{sumsq}_k = k * (k + 1) * (2k + 1)/6$
2 $p(1) \Leftrightarrow \text{sumsq}_1 = 1$ {1}
3 $p(1)$ {2}
4 $\text{sumsq}_{k+1} = \text{sumsq}_k + (k + 1)^2$
5 $p(k)$ Assumption
6 $\text{sumsq}_k = k * (k + 1) * (2k + 1)/6$ {1, 5}
7 $\text{sumsq}_{k+1} = k * (k + 1) * (2k + 1)/6 + (k + 1)^2$ {4}
8 $\text{sumsq}_{k+1} = (k + 1) * (k * (2k + 1) + (k + 1) * 6)/6$ {7}
9 $\text{sumsq}_{k+1} = (k + 1) * (2k^2 + k + 6k + 6)/6$ {8}
10 $\text{sumsq}_{k+1} = (k + 1) * (k + 2) * (2k + 3)/6$ {9}
11 $p(k + 1) \Leftrightarrow \text{sumsq}_{k+1} =$ {1}
     $(k + 1) * ((k + 1) + 1) * (2(k + 1) + 1)/6$
12 $p(k + 1) \Leftrightarrow \text{sumsq}_{k+1} =$ {11}
     $(k + 1) * (k + 2) * (2k + 3)/6$
13 $p(k + 1)$ {10, 12}
14 $\forall n: \mathbf{N}_1 \cdot p(n)$ {3, 5, 13}.

Exercise 8.2

   (i) Prove by induction that, for all natural numbers,

$$2n > n.$$

   (ii) Prove using induction that the sum of the first n cubes of the natural numbers is

$$n^2 * (n + 1)^2/4.$$

   (iii) The factorial of a natural number fact(n) is defined as the product of the number and all the natural numbers which lie between the number and one, i.e.

$$\text{fact}(n) = n * (n - 1) * (n - 2), \ldots, 3 * 2 * 1.$$

   Show by induction that

$$1 * \text{fact}(1) + 2 * \text{fact}(2) \ldots + n * \text{fact}(n) = \text{fact}(n + 1) - 1.$$

   Answer each question by using the format of proof shown in Example 8.3.

8.3   Set induction

The previous section described the use of induction as a proof method for reasoning about natural numbers. It was formally stated as

$$p(1), p(k) \Rightarrow p(k + 1) \vdash \forall n: \mathbf{N}_1 \cdot p(n)$$

or in English as

> If we wish to prove that a predicate is true for all the natural numbers, first demonstrate that it holds for the number one. Next, show that, if the predicate holds for a natural number k, then it implies that it holds for the natural number $k + 1$.

This type of proof is a special case of a more general technique known as **structural induction**. There is a corresponding application of structural induction to sets; it is known as **set induction**.

Informally stated it is

> If it is required to prove a predicate true about any finite set
> A containing elements of type T, then first show that the
> predicate holds for the empty set. Next, show that, if the
> predicate holds for the set $A - \{a\}$ where $a \in A$, then it
> implies that the predicate holds for the set A.

Formally stated, this is

$$p(\{\ \}), a \in A, p(A - \{a\}) \Rightarrow p(A) \vdash \forall x \mathbb{P} T \cdot p(x).$$

An example of a proof by set induction follows. It demonstrates that the recursive definition of $\cap$, **intersect**, is correct. The definition is.

$\forall S_1, S_2 : \mathbb{P} T \cdot$

intersect$(\{\ \}, S_2) = \{\ \} \wedge$

intersect$(S_1, S_2) = \{e\} \cup$ intersect $\wedge (S_1 - \{e\}, S_2)$
    where $e \in S_2$ and $e \in S_1 \wedge$

intersect$(S_1, S_2) =$ intersect$(S_1 - \{e\}, S_2)$
    where $e \notin S_2$ and $e \in S_1$.

The predicate $p(A)$ to be demonstrated is

$$A \cap S = \text{intersect}(A, S).$$

1   $p(\{\ \}) \Leftrightarrow \{\ \} \cap S = \text{intersect}(\{\ \}, S)$
2   $p(\{\ \}) \Leftrightarrow \{\ \} = \{\ \}$ $\{1\}$
3   $p(\{\ \})$ $\{2\}$
4   $p(A - \{a\}) \Leftrightarrow (A - \{a\}) \cap S = \text{intersect}(A - \{a\}, S)$
5   $p(A - \{a\})$ Assumption
6   $(A - \{a\}) \cap S = \text{intersect}(A - \{a\}, S)$ $\{4, 5\}$
7   $a \in A$
8   $a \notin S$
9   $p(A) \Leftrightarrow A \cap S = \text{intersect}(A, S)$
10   $p(A) \Leftrightarrow A \cap S = \text{intersect}(A - \{a\}, S)$ $\{9\}$
11   $p(A) \Leftrightarrow A \cap S = (A - \{a\}) \cap S$ $\{6, 10\}$
12   $p(A) \Leftrightarrow A \cap S = A \cap S$ $\{11\}$
13   $p(A)$ $\{12\}$
14   $a \in S$
15   $p(A) \Leftrightarrow A \cap S = \{a\} \cup \text{intersect}(A - \{a\}, S)$
16   $p(A) \Leftrightarrow A \cap S = \{a\} \cup ((A - \{a\}) \cap S)$ $\{6, 15\}$

17 $p(A) \Leftrightarrow A \cap S = A \cap S$ {16}
18 $p(A)$ {17}
19 $\forall x \colon \mathbb{P}T \cdot p(x)$ {3, 5, 13, 18}

The first three lines establish the base case by substituting { } for A in the predicate p. Line 5 is the induction hypothesis. Since line 5 is assumed true, then the right-hand side of the equivalence in line 4 is true; this is shown on line 6. The inductive proof proceeds in two steps. First, a is assumed not to be in S. This leads to line 11 which can be simplified since a is not contained in S. This is shown in line 12 which establishes $p(A)$. The second part of the inductive proof assumes that a is in S. This leads to line 17 which uses the fact that

$$p(A) \Leftrightarrow A \cap S = (\{a\} \cup (A - \{a\})) \cap (S \cup \{a\}).$$

The equivalence between $(\{a\} \cup (A - \{a\})) \cap (S \cup \{a\})$ and $A \cap S$ holds because, since a is contained in A, then $\{a\} \cup (A - \{a\})$ reduces to A and, since a is in S, then $S \cup \{a\}$ reduces to S.

Example 8.4

Prove by induction that the specification of *subset* below is a correct specification of the subset operator

$\forall E, S \colon \mathbb{P}T \cdot$

$\text{subset}(\{\ \}, S) \Leftrightarrow T \wedge$

$\text{subset}(E, S) \Leftrightarrow \text{subset}(E - \{e\}, S\} \wedge (e \in E \text{ and } e \in S)$

$\text{subset}(E, S) \Leftrightarrow F \wedge (e \in E \text{ and } e \notin S).$

The predicate p to be proved is

$$p(A) \Leftrightarrow (\text{subset}(A, S) \Leftrightarrow A \subseteq S).$$

1    $p(\{\ \}) \Leftrightarrow ((\text{subset}(\{\ \}), S) \Leftrightarrow$
     $\{\ \} \subseteq S)$
2    $p(\{\ \}) \Leftrightarrow (T \Leftrightarrow T)$
3    $p(\{\ \})$ {2}
4    $a \in A$
5    $p(A - \{a\}) \Leftrightarrow (\text{subset}(A -$
     $\{a\}, S) \Leftrightarrow A - \{a\} \subseteq S)$

6	$p(A - \{a\})$	Assumption
7	$\text{subset}(A - \{a\}, S) \Leftrightarrow A - \{a\} \subseteq S$	$\{5, 6\}$
8	$a \in S$	
9	$p(A) \Leftrightarrow (\text{subset}(A, S) \Leftrightarrow$ $A \subseteq S)$	
10	$p(A) \Leftrightarrow (\text{subset}(A, S) \Leftrightarrow$ $A - \{a\} \subseteq S)$	$\{9\}$
11	$p(A) \Leftrightarrow (\text{subset}(A - \{a\}, S) \Leftrightarrow$ $A - \{a\} \subseteq S)$	$\{10\}$
12	$p(A)$	$\{7, 11\}$
13	$a \notin S$	
14	$p(A) \Leftrightarrow (\text{subset}(A, S) \Leftrightarrow A \subseteq S)$	
15	$p(A) \Leftrightarrow (F \Leftrightarrow F)$	$\{14\}$
16	$p(A)$	$\{15\}$
17	$\forall x: \mathbb{P}T \cdot p(x)$	$\{12, 15\}.$

Lines 1 to 3 establish the base case. Lines 4 to 7 establish the inductive assumption. There are two cases to consider: the first is when $a \in S$; the second case is when $a \notin S$. The first case is examined in lines 8 to 12. Line 9 is the definition of $p(A)$. Line 10 follows from line 9 because

$$A - \{a\} \subseteq S \Leftrightarrow A \subseteq S.$$

Line 11 follows from line 10 by applying the definition of subset. Line 12 establishes the truth of $p(A)$ since line 7 had already established the truth of: $\text{subset}(A - \{a\}, S) \Leftrightarrow A - \{a\} \subseteq S$ from the inductive assumption. Lines 13 to 16 complete the proof for $a \notin S$. Line 15 follows from line 14 since, if there is an element a which is in A but not in S, then $A \subseteq S$ is false; $\text{subset}(A, S)$ is then also false from the third line of its definition.

8.4 Sequence induction

There is an equivalent rule for induction which involves sequences. It is

$$p(\{\ \}), p(\text{tail } S) \Rightarrow p(S) \vdash \forall x: \text{seq } T \cdot p(x)$$

where T is the type of the elements of the sequence S. This is similar to the rules for induction over natural numbers or sets. The empty sequence plays the part of 0 or $\{\}$ in the corresponding rules for natural numbers and sets. As an example consider the definition of the *rev* function which reverses a sequence

$$\mathrm{rev}(\{\,\}) = \{\,\} \wedge$$

$$\mathrm{rev}\,S = \mathrm{rev}(\mathrm{tail}\,S)^\frown \mathrm{head}\,S.$$

Assume that, given this definition, it is wished to prove that

$$^\#S = {}^\#\mathrm{rev}\,S.$$

This is equivalent to an inductive proof of the predicate p where

$$p(S) \Leftrightarrow {}^\#S = {}^\#\mathrm{rev}\,S.$$

The inductive proof on S follows.

1   $p(\{\,\}) \Leftrightarrow {}^\#\{\,\} = {}^\#\mathrm{rev}\{\,\}$
2   $p(\{\,\}) \Leftrightarrow 0 = 0$ $\{1\}$
3   $p(\{\,\})$ $\{2\}$
4   $p(\mathrm{tail}\,S) \Leftrightarrow {}^\#\mathrm{tail}\,S = {}^\#\mathrm{rev}\,\mathrm{tail}\,S$
5   $p(\mathrm{tail}\,S)$ Assumption
6   ${}^\#\mathrm{tail}\,S = {}^\#\mathrm{rev}\,\mathrm{tail}\,S$ $\{4, 5\}$
7   $p(S) \Leftrightarrow {}^\#S = {}^\#\mathrm{rev}\,S$
8   $p(S) \Leftrightarrow {}^\#S = {}^\#(\mathrm{rev}(\mathrm{tail}\,S)^\frown\mathrm{head}\,S)$ $\{7\}$
9   $p(S) \Leftrightarrow {}^\#S = {}^\#(\mathrm{rev}\,\mathrm{tail}\,S) + 1$ $\{8\}$
10 $p(S) \Leftrightarrow {}^\#(\mathrm{head}\,S^\frown\mathrm{tail}\,S) = {}^\#(\mathrm{rev}\,\mathrm{tail}\,S) + 1$ $\{9\}$
11 $p(S) \Leftrightarrow 1 + {}^\#\mathrm{tail}\,S = {}^\#(\mathrm{rev}\,\mathrm{tail}\,S) + 1$ $\{10\}$
12 $p(S) \Leftrightarrow {}^\#\mathrm{tail}\,S = {}^\#(\mathrm{rev}\,\mathrm{tail}\,S)$ $\{11\}$
13 $p(S)$ $\{6, 12\}$
14 $\forall x\colon \mathrm{seq}\,T \cdot p(x)$ $\{13\}$

Lines 1 to 3 establish the base case. Lines 4 to 6 establish the inductive assumption. Lines 7 to 8 simplify $p(S)$. Line 8 applies the definition of *rev*. The simplification in line 9 is based on the fact that the cardinality of a sequence concatenated with a single element is 1 plus the cardinality of the sequence. Line 10 splits the sequence S into the sequence formed by concatenating the head of the sequence together with its tail. Line 11 follows from the fact that the cardinality of a sequence is equal to 1 plus the cardinality of the tail of the sequence. Finally $p(S)$ is established on line 13 from the predicate in line 6 and the simplification in line 12.

Part III

9 The specification language Z

Although in the previous chapters computer systems have been described in precise terms, there has been little stress on the syntax of the mathematical notations used. This part of the book remedies this state of affairs. It describes a language called Z which is based on typed set theory and which allows a concise expression of the functional properties of computer systems. One of the principal features of Z is an object known as a **schema**.

9.1 Schemas

The pattern *signature | predicate* has occurred a large number of times in the previous chapters. For example,

$$\{n: \mathbf{N} \mid n > 3 \cdot n^2\}$$

is the infinite set of squares of the natural numbers greater than 3, and

$$\exists \text{mon: monitors} \mid \text{mon} \in \text{dom is\_connected}$$

is an example of a predicate which asserts that there exists a monitor which is in the domain of the relation *is_connected*. Also,

$$\lambda \text{mon: monitors} \mid \text{mon} \in \text{dom is\_monitoring} \cdot \text{mon}$$

is an example of a lambda expression which is the identity relation on the domain of *is_monitoring*. The pattern

$$\text{signature} \mid \text{predicate}$$

occurs so many times in specifications that Z has a special name for it. It is known as a *schema* and is written in two forms. The first form encloses the signature and predicate in a box-like structure. An example of this is

$$
\begin{array}{|l}
\hline
a: \mathbf{N} \qquad \text{Signature} \\
b: \mathbb{P}\mathbf{N} \\
\hline
a \in b \qquad \textit{Predicate} \\
\hline
\end{array}
$$

The signature of variables is written above the middle line while predicates are written below the middle line. The signature introduces variables and assigns them a set theoretic type. This is similar to declarations in a programming language such as Pascal. For example, in Pascal the declaration

> new_height: INTEGER;
>
> coefficient: REAL;

introduces the variable *new_height* and states that it will contain integers and introduces the variable *coefficient* and states that it will contain real numbers. In the same way the schema above introduces two variables a and b and states that a will be a natural number and b will be a set of natural numbers. The only difference between the programming language declarations and those found in a schema is that since a computer has a finite store the range of values of the former is limited.

The predicate of a schema refers to the variables in the schema or global variables in other schemas and relates the values of these variables to each other. For example, the predicate in the schema above asserts that a is contained in b.

An alternative, linear form for schemas is constructed by listing the signature followed by the predicate with | marking their separation and with the whole enclosed in square brackets. Thus, an alternative to the box structure shown above would be

$$[a: \mathbf{N}; b: \mathbb{P}\mathbf{N} \mid a \in b].$$

Whenever a series of predicates are written in a schema with each one on a separate line, then the total predicate represented by that schema is the conjunction of the predicates on each line.

For example, the schema

$$
\begin{array}{|l}
\hline
a, b: \mathbf{N} \\
c: \mathbb{P}\mathbf{N} \\
\hline
a \in c \\
b \in c \\
\hline
\end{array}
$$

is equivalent to

$$
\begin{array}{|l}
\hline
a, b: \mathbf{N} \\
c: \mathbb{P}\mathbf{N} \\
\hline
a \in c \land b \in c \\
\hline
\end{array}
$$

or

$$[a, b: \mathbf{N}; c: \mathbb{P}\mathbf{N} \mid a \in c \land b \in c].$$

Schemas will need to be named because they will be referred to in other schemas. Naming is achieving by labelling a schema box with a name, for example,

$$
\begin{array}{|l}
\hline
\text{mon\_condition} \\
\hline
\text{mon\_no: } \mathbf{N} \\
\text{available\_monitors: } \mathbb{P}\mathbf{N} \\
\hline
\text{mon\_no} \in \text{available\_monitors} \\
\hline
\end{array}
$$

The equality symbol $\triangleq$ is also used to label the linear form of a schema; for example,

mon_condition $\triangleq$

[mon_no: **N**; available_monitors: $\mathbb{P}$**N**

$\mid$ mon_no $\in$ available_monitors]

is equivalent to the above schema. The signature in a schema can introduce variables of any set-theoretic type. They range from natural numbers up to complicated higher-order functions. Whenever functions and relations are defined in a signature, their type is designated by the types of their domain and range together with a symbol which gives the type of the function or relation. A full list of symbols used to distinguish types of functions follows

$$\leftrightarrow \qquad \text{a relation}$$
$$\nrightarrow \qquad \text{a partial function}$$
$$\rightarrow \qquad \text{a total function}$$
$$\rightarrowtail\!\!\!\!\!\rightarrow \qquad \text{a partial injection}$$
$$\rightarrowtail \qquad \text{a total injection}$$

Some examples of schemas using such signatures are

```
┌─accounts──────────────────────────────────────┐
│  holds_account: account-no ↦ customer         │
│───────────────────────────────────────────────│
│  holds_account ≠ { }                          │
└───────────────────────────────────────────────┘
```

(where { } is the null set)

```
┌─upd───────────────────────────────────────────┐
│  customer_no: N                               │
│  up_group: (N → N) → (N → N)                   │
│───────────────────────────────────────────────│
│  #dom dom up_group > 50                        │
└───────────────────────────────────────────────┘
```

```
┌───────────────────────────────────────────────┐
│  squareadd: N → N                             │
│───────────────────────────────────────────────│
│  ∀n: N · squareadd n = n² + 12                 │
└───────────────────────────────────────────────┘
```

The first schema *accounts* is named and contains a partial function *holds_account* in its signature. Its predicate asserts that there will be at least one element in the function. The second named schema *upd* introduces two variables *customer_no* and *up_group*. The former is a natural number while the latter is a higher-order function which takes its domain from functions which map natural numbers into natural numbers and its range from functions which map natural numbers to natural numbers. The predicate asserts that the cardinality of the domain of the functions which are in the domain of *up_group* is greater than 50. Lastly, the unnamed schema introduces a total function *squareadd* which is

$$\{(0, 12), (1, 13), (2, 16), (3, 21), \ldots, \}.$$

Example 9.1

Write down a schema *block_inv* which introduces two variables. The first variable is a partial function *block_own* which maps natural numbers into sets of natural numbers. The second variable is a natural number, *max_blocks*. The schema should include a predicate which states that *block_own* will never map a natural number into a set whose cardinality is greater than *max_blocks*.

```
block_inv
block_own: N ⇸ PN
max_blocks: N

∀n: dom block_own · #(block_own n) ≤ max_blocks
```

Example 9.2

A fragment of the natural-language specification for a filing system follows.

> There will never be more than 30 users of the file system who currently own files, no user is allowed to own more than 25 files, and no file is allowed to be bigger than 500 blocks.

In a Z specification the file store of the system is modelled by a relation *stores* which relates user names with file names and a relation *occupies* which relates file names to natural numbers which represent the blocks that the files occupy. Write down a schema which is equivalent to this description.

---

file-sys
stores: user_names ↔ file_names
occupies: filenames ↔ **N**

$^{\#}$dom stores ≤ 30
∀name: dom stores · $^{\#}$(stores⟦{name}⟧) ≤ 25
∀file: dom occupies · $^{\#}$(occupies ⟦{file}⟧) ≤ 500

9.2 The structure of Z specifications

One of the major features of Z is that it provides a framework within which a specification can be developed and presented incrementally. A full Z specification can be constructed from other schemas which themselves can be expressed in terms of other schemas etc. Each subsidiary schema can be referred to by schemas which use it.

This is similar to the presentation of a software design or a program. A well written program will consist of a series of program units which can be read and understood in isolation. A Z specification will consist of schemas which can be developed and presented incrementally with individual schemas being able to be understood in isolation.

9.2.1 Schema inclusion

The means by which schemas can be referred to by other schemas is known as **schema inclusion**. As an example consider the schema *set_inv*.

---

set_inv
upper, lower: **ℙN**
max_size: **N**

$^{\#}$upper + $^{\#}$lower ≤ max_size

which introduces two sets of natural numbers, *upper* and *lower,* and states that the sum of their cardinalities will never exceed *max_size.* If this schema is required by another schema, then it is written in the signature part of the schema which requires it. For example, the schema *midd_inv* refers to *upper* and *lower* and hence uses *set_inv*.

```
┌─midd_inv──────────────────────────────────────┐
│ middle: ℙN                                     │
│ set_inv                                        │
│ ─────────────────                              │
│ middle ⊂ upper ∪ lower                         │
└────────────────────────────────────────────────┘
```

Since it uses *upper* and *lower* from *set_inv,* the schema is included in *midd_inv.* The effect of including one schema in the signature of another schema is to form the union of their signatures and to conjoin their predicates. Thus, *midd_inv* is equivalent to

```
┌─midd_inv──────────────────────────────────────┐
│ middle: ℙN                                     │
│ upper, lower: ℙN                               │
│ max_size: N                                    │
│ ─────────────────                              │
│ middle ⊂ upper ∪ lower                         │
│ #upper + #lower ≤ max_size                     │
└────────────────────────────────────────────────┘
```

9.2.2 *Events and observations in Z*

Z specifications describe three types of entities: states, observations, and events. A **state** is the mathematical structure which models a system. An **event** is an occurrence which is of interest to the specifier. For example, in the specification of a queue subsystem typical events would be: the addition of an entry to a queue; the deletion of a queue; or the calculation of queue length. In the specification of a filing system, typical events would be: the creation of a file; the deletion of a file; or the reading of a file. An **observation** is a set theoretic variable whose value can be examined before and after an event has occurred. Typical examples of observations are: a function modelling a file store; a relation modelling the fact that a system user owns a file; and a set of books in an automated library system. States are made up of observations.

There are two types of properties of a state that a Z specification is intended to reflect. The first is static properties. These are predicates which always hold over the course of time no matter what event occurs. These are often known as **invariants**. The second type of property are those which characterize the effect of an event. These properties are embodied in **observations**.

An example will make this clearer. Suppose that it was necessary to specify a system which kept track of students who have handed in a homework assignment. This can be characterized by a state consisting of three sets: the set of all students; the set of students who have handed in assignments; and the set of students who have not handed in assignments.

There are two static properties. The first is that the union of the set of students who have handed in an assignment and the set of students who have not handed in an assigment is equal to the set of students in the class. The second static property is that, since a student cannot simultaneously have handed in an assignment and not have handed in an assignment, then the intersection of the set of students who have handed in an assignment and the set of those who haven't is the empty set.

These properties can be characterized by the schema $\Delta class\_homework$

$\Delta class\_homework$

$class, handed\_in, not\_handed\_in: \mathbb{P}\ students$
$class', handed\_in', not\_handed\_in': \mathbb{P}\ students$

$handed\_in \cup not\_handed\_in = class$
$handed\_in \cap not\_handed\_in = \{\ \}$
$handed\_in' \cup not\_handed\_in' = class'$
$handed\_in' \cap not\_handed\_in' = \{\ \}$

This contains the state *class, handed_in, not_handed_in*: $\mathbb{P}$ *students*. The observations which make up the state are assigned a set theoretic type $\mathbb{P}$ *students* and the predicates characterize the properties of the observations which must always be true. Primes are used, as in the second part of the book, to indicate the value of the observations after an operation occurs. For example, the schema states that before any event occurs the union of *handed_in* and *not_handed_in* will be equal to *class*

$$handed\_in \cup not\_handed\_in = class,$$

while after any event has occurred the union of *handed_in'* and *not_handed_in'* will be equal to *class'*

$$handed\_in' \cup not\_handed\_in' = class'$$

The schema is preceded by the symbol Δ in order to indicate that it represents invariant properties of a system. This is one of the conventions in writing Z schemas which will be further described in Chapter 10.

The dynamic properties of the system are again characterized by: the names of observations made before an event occurs; the names of those observations which can be made after the event; and a predicate which relates them.

For example, in the student-assignment specification assume that there are two events. The first is that of a student *stud?* handing in an assignment. The second event is that of a student *stud?* leaving the class. The first event *hand_in* can be expressed as the schema

```
 hand_in
 stud?: students
 Δclass_homework

 stud? ∈ not_handed_in
 not_handed_in' = not_handed_in − {stud?}
 handed_in' = handed_in ∪ {stud?}
 class' = class
```

The signature contains the observations that can be made before and after the *hand_in* event. Primed observations are those made after an event. The inclusion of the schema Δ*class_homework* adds the invariant properties of the student assignment system. The first predicate states that the student must not already have handed in an assignment. The second and third predicates describe the fact that the student who has handed in an assignment is removed from the *not_handed_in* set and placed in the *handed_in* set. The final predicate asserts that the membership of the class is unaffected by the *hand_in* event.

The schema *hand_in* shown above contains another example of a Z convention. Inputs to a schema are described by terminating them with a question mark. Thus, *stud?* is an input which alters the state of the system is terminated by a question mark.

The second event: that of removing a student from the class is characterized by the schema *remove*

```
┌─remove─────────────────────────────────────────┐
│ stud?: students                                 │
│ Δclass_homework                                 │
│ ───────────────────────────                     │
│ stud? ∈ class                                   │
│ class' = class − {stud?}                        │
│ handed_in' = handed_in − {stud?}                │
│ not_handed_in' = not_handed_in − {stud?}        │
└─────────────────────────────────────────────────┘
```

If *stud?* is contained in either *handed_in* or *not_handed_in*, then the student is removed from one of the sets.. Notice that if *stud?* is not contained in *handed_in*, then

$$handed\_in' = handed\_in$$

and, similarly, if *stud?* is not in *not_handed_in*, then

$$not\_handed\_in' = not\_handed\_in.$$

The full Z specification of any system will consist of a set of schemas together with sentences which introduce the sets which are referred to in the schemas but not specifically defined. For example, in the homework system this would only include the set *students*. Thus, the homework system outlined above would consist of the schemas: Δ *class_homework*, *hand_in*, and *remove* together with the sentence

Let *students* be the set of all students.

Example 9.3

A filing subsystem consists of a series of files which are owned by users of an operating system. Each file occupies a series of blocks of storage. The filing system can be modelled by means of a partial function *owns*(users $\rightarrowtail$ $\mathbb{P}$file_names), the partial function *occupies*(file_names $\rightarrowtail$ $\mathbb{P}$block_nos), the set *users* which contains all possible user names, the set *system_users* which is a subset of *users,* the set *block_nos* which is the set of all possible block numbers, the set *file_names* which contains all possible file names, and the set *free_blocks* which is a subset of *block_nos*. *Owns* models the fact that a user currently owns a series of files; *occupies* models the fact that a file occupies a series of blocks on a file storage device. *System_users* are those users who are currently allowed to use the system. No more than *no_users* are allowed to use the system. Write down the natural-language sentence which introduces the types and a Z specification for the file system which characterizes its static properties. Make the artificial assumption that each file name created by a user is unique.

The sentences which introduce the types are

> Let *users* be the set of all possible user names.
> Let *file_names* be the set of all possible file names.
> Let *block_nos* be the set of all possible block numbers.

The static properties of the system are

> The number of users must not exceed *no_users*, if a file is known to the system as occupying a series of blocks, then it is owned by a user; all blocks that make up a file are not free blocks; only system users are allowed to own files; and, finally, no two files are allowed to share blocks.

```
┌─file_system────────────────────────────────────────────┐
│ owns: users ↦ ℙfile_names                              │
│ occupies: file_names ↦ ℙblock_nos                      │
│ system_users: ℙ users                                   │
│ free_blocks: ℙblock_nos                                 │
│ no_users: N                                             │
├─────────────────────────────────────────────────────────┤
│ #system_users ≤ no_users                                │
│ ∀file: dom occupies · ∃us: dom owns · file ∈ owns us   │
│ ∀file: dom occupies; block: block_nos · block ∈        │
│ occupies file ⇒ block ∉ free_blocks                     │
│ dom owns = system_users                                 │
│ ∀fs1, fs2: rng owns · fs1 ≠ fs2 ⇒ fs1 ∩ fs2 = { }      │
└─────────────────────────────────────────────────────────┘
```

Given the schema shown in Example 9.3, a number of events can be defined in terms of their effect on the filing subsystem. These events correspond to commands employed by users. For example, an event which, for a given user *usname?*, removes one of his files *fname?* can be defined as

```
┌─remove──────────────────────────────────────────────────┐
│ file_system                                             │
│ file_system'                                            │
│ usname?: users                                          │
│ fname?: file_names                                      │
├─────────────────────────────────────────────────────────┤
│ usname? ∈ system_users                                  │
│ fname? ∈ owns usname?                                    │
│ system_users' = system_users                            │
│ free_blocks' = free_blocks ∪ occupies fname?            │
│ occupies' = {fname?} ◁ occupies                          │
│ owns' = owns ⊕ {usname? ↦ owns usname? − {fname?}}     │
│ no_users' = no_users                                    │
└─────────────────────────────────────────────────────────┘
```

where file_system' is

```
┌─file_system'────────────────────────────────────────────┐
│ owns': users ↦ ℙfile_names                             │
│ occupies': file_names ↦ ℙblock_nos                     │
```

$$systems\_users': \mathbb{P}users$$
$$free\_blocks': \mathbb{P}block\_nos$$
$$no\_users': \mathbf{N}$$

$$^{\#}system\_users' \leq no\_users'$$
$$\forall file: dom\ occupies' \cdot \exists us: dom\ owns' \cdot file \in owns'\ us$$
$$\forall file: dom\ occupies'; block: block\_nos \cdot block \in$$
$$occupies'\ file \Rightarrow block \notin free\_blocks'$$
$$dom\ owns' = system\_users'$$
$$\forall fs1, fs2: rng\ owns' \cdot fs1 \neq fs2 \Rightarrow fs1 \cap fs2 = \{\ \}$$

The first predicate states that the user who employs the command must be a system user. The second predicate states that the name of the file to be deleted must be owned by the user whose name is *usname?*. The third predicate states that the set of system users is unchanged by the event. The fourth predicate states that *free_blocks* is updated by adding to it those blocks which were contained in the file to be removed. The fifth predicate states that the file name is removed from the *occupies* function since it no longer occupies any blocks. The sixth predicate removes the file from the *owns* function since the user no longer owns the file. The final predicate states that the maximum number of users is unchanged by by the event.

The addition of a file *fname?* by a user *usname?* can be defined by the schema *add*

---
add

file_system
file_system'
usname?: users
fname?: file_names

$$fname? \notin owns\ usname?$$
$$usname? \in system\_users$$
$$system\_users' = system\_users$$
$$free\_blocks' = free\_blocks$$
$$owns'\ usname? = owns\ usname? \cup fname?$$
$$occupies' = occupies \cup (fname?, \{\ \})$$
$$no\_users' = no\_users$$

Example 9.4

Write down a schema which describes the effect of removing a user *usname* and all his files from the file store.

┌─remove_user─────────────────────────────────────┐
file_system
file_system'
usname?: users

─────────────────────────

usname? ∈ system_users
system_users' = system_users − {usname?}
owns' = {usname?} ⊲ owns
occupies' = owns usname? ⊲ occupies
free_blocks' = free_blocks ∪ {block: block_nos |
∃fname: file_names · fname ∈ owns usname? ∧
block ∈ occupies fname}
└───┘

The first predicate asserts that the user is one of the current system users. The third predicate asserts that after the *remove_user* event all the instances of *usname?* are removed from *owns*. The fourth predicate asserts that after the *remove_user* event all the files owned by *usname?* have been removed. Lastly, the fifth predicate asserts that after the *remove_user* event the free blocks occupied by those files owned by *usname* are returned to the store of free blocks.

9.3   Some examples of schema use

The previous section described the use of schemas in characterizing events of interest to a system specifier. This is the major use of schemas. However, there are a number of subsidiary uses for schemas. This section describes these uses.

First, a Z schema can define and constrain a constant or a series of constants. For example, the schema *file_sys_consts*

```
┌─file_sys_consts─────────────────────────────┐
│ max_file_size, max_no_files: N              │
│─────────────────────────────────────────────│
│ max_file_size = 1000                        │
│ max_no_files > 20 ∧ max_no_files ≤ 25       │
└─────────────────────────────────────────────┘
```

introduces the constants *max_file_size* and *max_no_files*. The first line of the predicate gives *max_file_size* the value 1000, while the second line constrains the value of *max_no_files* to lie between 20 and 25.

Other examples of constant declarations follow without explanation.

```
┌─restricted_nodes────────────────────────────┐
│ important_nodes: Pnodes                      │
│─────────────────────────────────────────────│
│ #important_nodes ≤ 10                        │
└─────────────────────────────────────────────┘
```

```
┌─original_block──────────────────────────────┐
│ block_slots, cylinder_slots: Pblocks        │
│─────────────────────────────────────────────│
│ block_slots = 1..15000                      │
│ cylinder_slots = 1..250                     │
└─────────────────────────────────────────────┘
```

A schema can also be used to define explicitly a function. For example, the schema *square_def* defines the square function

```
┌─square_def──────────────────────────────────┐
│ square: N → N                               │
│─────────────────────────────────────────────│
│ ∀n: N · square n = n²                       │
└─────────────────────────────────────────────┘
```

where the predicate is $\forall n: \mathbf{N} \cdot \text{square } n = n^2$.

The major point to notice about this definition is the use of the universal quantifier. It states that the predicate *square* $n = n^2$ holds for all values of **N**.

```
┌─file_funcs──────────────────────────────────┐
│ file_size: Pblocks → N                      │
│ user_number: Pusers → N                     │
```

$$\forall b: \mathbb{P}\text{blocks} \cdot \text{file\_size } b = {}^{\#}b$$
$$\forall u: \mathbb{P}\text{users} \cdot \text{user\_number } u = {}^{\#}u$$

Relations can also be defined in the same way as functions. The schema *new_rel* defines the relation *plus_up*

____new_rel_____
plus_up: $\mathbf{N} \leftrightarrow \mathbf{N}$

$\forall n, i: \mathbf{N} \cdot n \text{ plus\_up } i \Leftrightarrow n + i = 10$
_____

It states that n is related to i only when their sum is 10. Notice that = is not used in the predicate to define the relation but $\Leftrightarrow$ is used since the left and right-hand sides of the quantified expression are predicates.

Finally, sets can be defined in Z schemas. The schema *archiver_s* defines a set *arch_files*

____archiver_s_____
arch_files: $\mathbb{P}\text{file\_names}$
expiry_date: $\text{file\_names} \nrightarrow \mathbf{N}$

arch_files $= \{\text{name: file\_names} \mid \text{expiry\_date name} > 365\}$
_____

Further examples of set definition follow without explanation.

_____
odd_nos: $\mathbb{P}\mathbf{N}$

odd_nos $= \{n: \mathbf{N} \cdot 2 * n + 1\}$
_____

____priv_file_sys_____
privileged_files: $\mathbb{P}\text{file\_names}$
secure_user: user_names

privileged_files $= \{\text{fname: file\_names} \cdot$
                       $\text{fname} \in \text{owns}[\![\{\text{secure\_user}\}]\!]\}$
_____

This chapter has briefly introduced the ideas behind the Z specification language. It is clear that the language itself is nothing but a convenient way of displaying what can be a large amount of very shallow mathematical text. The format of function definitions, set specifications, and predicates exactly mirrors that described in Part II of this book. What is different is the use of schemas and schema inclusion to present a concise formulation of a system specification. Subsequent chapters will briefly describe the operations available in Z; outline how schemas are themselves objects which can be manipulated in a similar way to sets, relations, and functions; and, lastly, describe a large example of the use of Z in system specification.

10 Operations and objects in Z

You will already have noticed that there is very little difference between the notation used in Part II of this book and that employed in Z schemas. The purpose of this chapter is to review the mathematical objects informally described in part II, define these objects formally using Z, and introduce a few new operators which have not been previously described.

10.1 Numbers and sets of numbers

There are no built-in sets in Z. Nevertheless, it is safe to assume that the symbol $\mathbf{N}$ denotes the set of natural numbers. Some specifications require the set of natural numbers minus zero; this is denoted by $\mathbf{N}_1$ which is defined as

$$
\begin{array}{|l}
\hline
\mathbf{N}_1 \colon \mathbb{P}\mathbf{N} \\
\hline
\mathbf{N}_1 = \mathbf{N} - \{0\} \\
\hline
\end{array}
$$

All the built-in operators and sets of Z are defined in a similar way; notice that no name is given to the schema.

The standard operators on natural numbers are defined in Z using a schema framework. There are a number of important points to notice about these schemas. First, the operators are defined as functions using lambda expressions. Second, the schema shown illustrates how any binary operator can be defined in Z. A binary operator is written with underscores on either side of the operator, both in the signature and predicate part of the schema. For example, the addition operator $+$ is defined as a total function

$$ \_ + \_ : \mathbf{N} \times \mathbf{N} \to \mathbf{N} $$

in the signature of the schema which follows and is defined as a lambda expression.

$$\_ + \_ = \lambda m, n: \mathbf{N} \cdot \text{succ}^n m$$

in the predicate of its schema where *succ* is the successor function described in Chapter 7.

$$\_ + \_, \_ * \_ : \mathbf{N} \times \mathbf{N} \to \mathbf{N}$$
$$\_ - \_ : \mathbf{N} \times \mathbf{N} \nrightarrow \mathbf{N}$$
$$\_ \leq \_ : \mathbf{N} \leftrightarrow \mathbf{N}$$

$$\_ + \_ = \lambda m, n: \mathbf{N} \cdot \text{succ}^n m$$
$$\_ * \_ = \lambda m, n: \mathbf{N} \cdot (\_ + m)^{n-1} m$$
$$\_ - \_ = \lambda m, n: \mathbf{N} \cdot \text{pred}^n m$$
$$\_ \leq \_ = \text{succ}^*$$

$+$ thus defines the function

$$\{((0, 0), 0), ((0, 1), 1), ((1, 1), 2), \ldots \}$$

which takes an ordered pair and delivers the sum of the numbers in the pair. This enables the specifier to curry such functions to construct total functions which contain one argument. For example, the function

$$(\_ + 3)$$

adds three to its argument.

This is used in the definition of $*$ where multiplication is defined as repeated addition since

$$(\_ + m)$$

is a function which adds m to its argument and the $(n-1)$ fold composition of this function

$$(\_ + m)^{n-1}$$

when applied to m forms $m * n$ by adding m to itself $(n-1)$ times. Less than or equal $\leq$ is defined by the reflexive transitive closure of the homogeneous function *succ*.

The relational operators $>$, $<$, and $\geq$ are not formally defined in Z. They can be built up from $\leq$. For example, $>$ is the inverse of $\leq$.

A set of consecutive natural numbers can be defined in Z using the .. operator. The full definition follows,

$$\_\,..\,\_ : \mathbf{N} \times \mathbf{N} \to \mathbb{P}\mathbf{N}$$

$$m\,..\,n = \{i : \mathbf{N} \mid m \le i \wedge i \le n\}$$

10.2 Sets

All the standard operators on sets are defined in Z. Difference, union, intersection, subset, and proper subset are defined as follows.

$[T]$

$$\_-\_\,,\,\_\cup\_\,,\,\_\cap\_ : (\mathbb{P}T) \times (\mathbb{P}T) \to (\mathbb{P}T)$$

$$\forall S_1, S_2 : \mathbb{P}(T) \cdot$$
$$S_1 - S_2 = \{x : T \mid x \in S_1 \wedge x \notin S_2\}$$
$$S_1 \cup S_2 = \{x : T \mid x \in S_1 \vee x \in S_2\}$$
$$S_1 \cap S_2 = \{x : T \mid x \in S_1 \wedge x \in S_2\}$$

$[T]$

$$\_\subset\_\,,\,\_\subseteq\_ : \mathbb{P}(T) \leftrightarrow \mathbb{P}(T)$$

$$\forall S_1, S_2 : \mathbb{P}(T) \cdot$$
$$S_1 \subseteq S_2 \Leftrightarrow (\forall x : T \cdot x \in S_1 \Rightarrow x \in S_2)$$
$$S_1 \subset S_2 \Leftrightarrow (S_1 \neq S_2 \wedge S_1 \subseteq S_2)$$

There are a number of points to note about these definitions. First, $-$, $\cap$, and $\cup$ are defined as operators which have two arguments that are subsets of a particular type T. It is irrelevant what the type of T is. It could be a set of files, a set of chemical reactors, or a set of accounts. The T surrounded by square brackets above a schema indicates that the definition holds for all types.

Two operators not described previously are generalized union $\bigcup$ and generalized intersection $\bigcap$. The generalized union of a power set of a particular type is the union of all the elements of the sets contained in the set which is its argument. For example,

$$\bigcup\{\{1,2\}, \{1,2,3,4\}, \{1,2,5,16,78\}\}$$

is

$$\{1,2,3,4,5,16,78\}.$$

The generalized intersection of a power set of a particular type is the intersection of all the elements of the sets contained in the set which is its argument. For example,

$$\bigcap\{\{1,2\}, \{1,2,3,4\}, \{1,2,5,16,78\}\}$$

is

$$\{1,2\}$$

and

$$\bigcap\{\{1,4,45\}, \{2,34,89\}, \{203,888\}\}$$

is

$$\{\}.$$

Their definitions are shown below. They are functions which have a power set of a power set as their domain type and a power set as their range type.

$[T]$

$$\bigcup\_, \bigcap\_ : \mathbb{P}(\mathbb{P}T) \rightarrow \mathbb{P}T$$

$$\bigcup SS = \{x: T \mid \exists S: SS \cdot x \in S\}$$
$$\bigcap SS = \{x: T \mid \forall S: SS \cdot x \in S\}$$

These are unary operators so that only one underscore is used in their definition.

Example 10.1

Write down a schema which defines a binary operator □ which takes two sets and returns the cardinality of their intersection. Do not name the schema.

[T]

$$\_\,\square\,\_ : \mathbb{P}(T) \times \mathbb{P}(T) \to \mathbf{N}$$

$$\forall S_1, S_2 : \mathbb{P}(T) \cdot$$
$$S_1 \,\square\, S_2 = {}^{\#}(S_1 \cap S_2)$$

Notice that there is no need to formally define $\cap$ within the schemas as it can be assumed that it has already been defined.

Example 10.2

Define an binary operator @ which takes as its first operand a set of natural numbers and as its second operand a natural number. Its result is the number of natural numbers in the first operand which are less than the second operand.

$$\_\,@\,\_ : \mathbb{P}(\mathbf{N}) \times \mathbf{N} \to \mathbf{N}$$

$$\forall S_1 : \mathbb{P}(\mathbf{N}); s : \mathbf{N} \cdot$$
$$S_1 \,@\, s = {}^{\#}\{n : \mathbf{N} \mid n \in S_1 \wedge n < s\}$$

A final operator which is occasionally used in Z specifications is the arbitrary set element operator μ. This takes a set as an argument and has a result which is any element in the set. Thus,

$$\mu\{1, 2, 3, 4\}$$

could be either $1, 2, 3,$ or 4.

10.3 Relations

Relations can also be used in Z specifications. A relation between two types T_1 and T_2 is written in the signature part of a

Z schema as

$$T_1 \leftrightarrow T_2.$$

Thus, a relation *has_blocks* over *programs* and subsets of *block_nos* would have a signature

$$\text{has\_blocks: programs} \leftrightarrow \mathbb{P} \text{ block\_nos}.$$

The identity relation of a set S whose elements are of type T is defined in Z as

$$\text{id}: \mathbb{P}(T) \rightarrow (T \leftrightarrow T)$$

$$\text{id } S = \{x: T \mid x \in S \cdot (x \mapsto x)\}$$

This schema states that *id* is a function which takes a subset of a type T and produces a relation over $T \times T$. The relation is the set of ordered pairs (x, x) made up of elements of the operand of *id*. The symbol $\mapsto$ is normally used in Z documents to stand for an ordered pair. Thus,

$$\{1 \mapsto 2, 2 \mapsto 3, 3 \mapsto 5\}$$

is equivalent to

$$\{(1, 2), (2, 3), (3, 5)\}.$$

All the operators described in Part II can be defined in Z. The two forms of relational composition are defined as

$$[T_1, T_2, T_3]$$

$$\_; \_, \_ \circ \_ : (T_1 \leftrightarrow T_2) \times (T_2 \leftrightarrow T_3) \rightarrow (T_1 \leftrightarrow T_3)$$

$$R_1; R_2 = \{t_1: T_1; t_3 T_3 \mid (\exists t_2: T_2 \cdot (t_1, t_2) \in R_1 \wedge (t_2, t_3) \in R_2)\}$$
$$R_2 \circ R_1 = R_1; R_2$$

Since the definition of composition is true whatever the types of T_1, T_2, and T_3 they are enclosed in square brackets. Domain and range restriction operators can be similarly defined in Z

$$[T_1, T_2]$$

$$\_ \triangleright \_, \_ \triangleright\!\!\!- \_ : (T_1 \leftrightarrow T_2) \times \mathbb{P}(T_2) \rightarrow (T_1 \leftrightarrow T_2)$$
$$\_ \triangleleft \_, \_ \triangleleft\!\!\!- \_ : \mathbb{P}(T_1) \times (T_1 \leftrightarrow T_2) \rightarrow (T_1 \leftrightarrow T_2)$$

$$R \triangleright S_2 = \{t_1\colon T_1; t_2\colon T_2 \mid t_1 R t_2 \wedge t_2 \in S_2\}$$
$$S_1 \triangleleft R = \{t_1\colon T_1; t_2\colon T_2 \mid t_1 R t_2 \wedge t_1 \in S_1\}$$
$$R \triangleright\!\!\!\!\!\!- S_2 = R \triangleright (T_2 - S_2)$$
$$S_1 -\!\!\!\!\!\!\triangleleft R = (T_1 - S_1) \triangleleft R$$

The relational overriding and the relational image operators are similarly defined

$[T_1, T_2]$

$$\_ \oplus \_ : (T_1 \leftrightarrow T_2) \times (T_1 \leftrightarrow T_2) \rightarrow (T_1 \leftrightarrow T_2)$$

$$R_1 \oplus R_2 = (\mathrm{dom}\, R_2 -\!\!\!\!\triangleleft R_1) \cup R_2$$

$[T_1, T_2]$

$$\_\llbracket\_\rrbracket : (T_1 \leftrightarrow T_2) \times (\mathbb{P} T_1) \rightarrow (\mathbb{P} T_2)$$

$$R\llbracket S \rrbracket = \{y\colon T_2 \mid \exists x\colon S \cdot x R y\}$$

Finally, iteration and transitive closure can be defined in Z. Iteration is the repeated application of relational composition to a single relation. It is defined recursively

$[T]$

$$\mathrm{iter}\colon \mathbf{N} \times (T \leftrightarrow T) \rightarrow (T \leftrightarrow T)$$

$$0 \,\mathrm{iter}\, R = \mathrm{id}\, T$$
$$(\mathrm{succ}\, n) \,\mathrm{iter}\, R = R; (n \,\mathrm{iter}\, R)$$

The first line of the predicate states that the zeroth iterate of a relation is the identity relation on its domain. The second line states recursively that the $(n + 1)$th iterate of a relation is equal to the composition of the relation and its nth iterate. Given this definition of iteration, transitive closure operators can be defined

$[T]$

$$\_^*, \_^+ : (T \leftrightarrow T) \rightarrow (T \leftrightarrow T)$$

$$R^* = \bigcup\{n\colon \mathbf{N} \cdot n \,\mathrm{iter}\, R\}$$
$$R^+ = \bigcup\{n\colon \mathbf{N}_1 \cdot n \,\mathrm{iter}\, R\}$$

Example 10.3

A file store of a computer is modelled by means of a relation over users and files. The static properties of the file store are embodied in the schema *file_sys* shown below

```
┌─file_sys──────────────────────────────────┐
│ file_store: users ↔ files                  │
│ system_users: ℙusers                       │
├────────────────────────────────────────────┤
│ #rng file_store ≤ 1000                     │
│ ∀us: users · #(file_store[{us}]) ≤ 50      │
│ #system users ≤ 150                        │
└────────────────────────────────────────────┘
```

Using natural language describe the properties embodied in the schema.

The first predicate states that there may be no more than 1000 entries in the file store. This limits the number of files in the store. The second predicate states that for all users the number of pairs with the user's name as the first element must be less than or equal to 50. This limits the number of files which can be owned by an individual user to no more than 50. The third predicate states that there will be no more than 150 users of the system.

Example 10.4

Define a Z schema which describes the event which occurs when adding a set of user files *files_to_be_added?* to the file store defined in Example 10.3. The name of the user whose files are to be added is *us?*. Assume the schema is called *add_files* and has *file_sys'* included in it.

```
┌─add_files─────────────────────────────────┐
│ file_sys                                   │
│ file_sys'                                  │
│ us?: users                                 │
│ files_to_be_added?: ℙ files                │
└                                            ┘
```

us? ∈ system_users
∀file: files_to_be_added? · (us? ↦ file) ∉ file_store
file_store' = file_store ∪ {file: files_to_be_
added? · (us? ↦ file)}

The operation is achieved by adding to the file store the set of all pairs which have the user name as the first element and each file to be added as the second element.

Example 10.5

Define a Z schema which describes the event of removing the set of user files owned by the user *us?* from the file store defined in Example 10.3. Assume that the schema is called *remove_files* and has *file_sys* and *file_sys'* included in it.

┌─remove_files──────────────────────────────────┐
│ file_sys   │
│ file_sys'   │
│ us?: users   │
│   │
│ us? ∈ system_users   │
│ file_store' = {us?} ⊲ file_store   │
└───┘

The removal of the files is achieved by using the domain subtraction operator.

10.4 Functions and sequences

10.4.1 *Functions*

Since functions are only a special type of relation the set and relation operators described in the previous subsection can all be used with Z objects that are declared as functions. The symbols used to denote types of functions and their definitions follow.

The four major symbols used to identify functions are $\rightarrow$, $\nrightarrow$, $\rightarrowtail$, and $\nrightarrowtail$, $\rightarrow$ is used to declare total functions; $\nrightarrow$ is used to declare partial functions; $\rightarrowtail$ is used to declare total injective functions; finally, $\nrightarrowtail$ is used to declare partial injective functions.

Whenever a function is written in a signature, its type should be written using one of the above operators. For example, the schema *mon_sys* which follows describes the static or invariant properties of a chemical reactor monitoring system. Each monitoring computer is attached to a named cluster of monitoring instruments such as thermocouples or pressure sensors. Furthermore, each monitoring instrument is attached to a particular reactor, although one reactor may have a number of instruments attached.

---
mon_sys

attached: computers $\nrightarrowtail$ clusters
connected: clusters $\nrightarrowtail \mathbb{P}$ instruments
monitors: instruments $\nrightarrow$ reactors
max_clust, max_comps: **N**

$^{\#}$dom attached $\leq$ max_comps
$\forall x$: dom connected $\cdot$ $^{\#}$connected $x \leq$ max_clust
$\forall x, y$: rng connected $\cdot$ $x \neq y \Rightarrow x \cap y = \{\ \}$
$\cup$ rng connected = dom monitors
rng attached = dom connected

Computers is the set of all possible computer names, *clusters* is the set of all possible names of clusters of instruments, and *instruments* is the set of all possible instruments names.

Attached, connected, and *monitors* are all functions since computers are only connected to one cluster, clusters are attached to a unique set of instruments, and each instrument is attached to only one reactor. Moreover, *attached* is an injective function since one cluster is connected to only one computer; *connected* is also an injective function since each distinct set of instruments is connected to only one cluster. Note that *monitors* is not injective because one reactor may have any number of instruments attached to it.

There are five predicates in *mon_sys* which express the static properties of the monitoring system. The first asserts that the number of computers attached to clusters will never be more than *max_comps*; the second asserts that the maximum number of instruments in any one cluster will be *max_clust*; the third asserts that no instrument will be connected in two or more clusters; the fourth asserts that all instruments in a cluster are attached to a reactor; finally, the fifth asserts that all the clusters that are attached to instruments are connected to a computer.

Example 10.6

The computer system for monitoring the progress of salesmen in a computer company is to be developed. Each salesman reports to a sales manager in the company who, in turn, reports to one of two sales directors. For efficiency reasons no more than 10 salesmen report to a sales manager. Each salesman in the company is responsible for up to 50 customers. No salesman reports to more than one sales manager, no sales manager reports to more than one sales director, and no customer is visited by more than one salesman. Construct a schema *sales* which describes the static properties of the salesman system. Assume the signature of the schema includes.

$$\text{dir\_responsible: directors} \rightarrowtail \mathbb{P} \text{ managers,}$$

$$\text{man\_responsible: managers} \rightarrowtail \mathbb{P} \text{ salesmen,}$$

$$\text{sales\_responsible: salesmen} \rightarrowtail \mathbb{P} \text{ customers.}$$

---

sales

dir_responsible: directors $\rightarrowtail \mathbb{P}$ managers
man_responsible: managers $\rightarrowtail \mathbb{P}$ salesmen
sales_responsible: salesmen $\rightarrowtail \mathbb{P}$ customers
director_staff: $\mathbb{P}$ directors
managerial_staff: $\mathbb{P}$ managers
sales_staff: $\mathbb{P}$ salesmen
current_customers: $\mathbb{P}$ customers

$\forall$dir: dom dir_responsible ·
  dir_responsible dir $\subseteq$ managerial_staff

∀man: dom man_responsible ·
$^{\#}$man_responsible man ≤ 10 ∧
man_responsible man ⊆ sales_staff
∀sales_m: dom sales_responsible ·
$^{\#}$sales_responsible sales_m ≤ 50 ∧
sales_responsible sales_m ⊆ current_customers
$^{\#}$director_staff = 2
∀x, y: rng man_responsible · $x \neq y \Rightarrow x \cap y = \{\}$
∀x, y: rng sales_responsible · $x \neq y \Rightarrow x \cap y = \{\}$
∀x, y: rng dir_responsible · $x \neq y \Rightarrow x \cap y = \{\}$

where *directors* is the set of all possible director names, *managers* is the set of all possible manager names, *salesmen* is the set of all possible salesman names, and *customers* is the set of all possible customers who are visited by salesmen. All the functons are partial since not every value from *directors, managers, salesmen,* and *companies* will occur in their domains. All the functions are injective since each element in the range of the functions is associated with only one element of the domain.

10.4.2 Sequences

Since sequences play an important part in any computer system, Z has notational facilities for representing sequences and a series of operators which take sequences as operands. A sequence in Z is defined as

$[T]$

seq: $\mathbb{P}T \rightarrow (\mathbf{N} \nrightarrow T)$

seq $t = \{f: \mathbf{N} \nrightarrow t \mid \text{dom} f = 1 .. {}^{\#}f\}$

A sequence then is a partial function which maps natural numbers from 1 up to the cardinality of the function, into objects which have a type T. Thus,

$$\{1 \mapsto 3, 2 \mapsto 6, 3 \mapsto 9, 4 \mapsto 11\}$$

is a sequence of natural numbers and

$$\{1 \mapsto \text{updatefile}, 2 \mapsto \text{edits}, 3 \mapsto \text{newtaxfile}\}$$

is a sequence of file names. The length of a sequence S in Z is given by $^{\#}S$. In Z the normal way to express sequences is to use square brackets to enclose the elements of the sequence; for example, the sequence

$$[\text{updatefile}, \text{edits}, \text{newtaxfile}]$$

is equivalent to the preceding sequence which was expressed using the $\mapsto$ notation.

When sequences are declared in a signature of a schema, the type of the elements which make up the sequence are preceded by the letters *seq*. For example, the schema *file-queue*.

---
file_queue

in_queue, out_queue: seq files

$^{\#}$in_queue $< {}^{\#}$out_queue

---

declares two objects which are sequences of files and states that the length of the first sequence *in_queue* is less than that of *out_queue*.

There is often a need to use sequences which can never be empty. These are defined by

$[T]$

$\text{seq}_1 : \mathbb{P}T \rightarrow (\mathbf{N} \nrightarrow T)$

$\text{seq}_1 t = \text{seq } t - \{\{\}\}$

The concatenation of sequences is achieved by means of the ⌢ operator. It takes two operands which are sequences and joins the second operand to the end of the first operand. Thus, if a and b are sequences of any type, then

$$a^\frown b$$

adds b to the end of a. The ⌢ operator can also be used to add single elements to the beginning or end of a queue. Thus, if a is a queue whose elements are of type T and t is of type T, then

$$[t]^\frown a$$

adds t to the front of a and

$$a \widehat{\ } [t]$$

adds t to the end of a.

As an example of the use of queues, consider the device handler for a moving-head disc unit. This is activated by a series of read/write instructions. These instructions give the address of the data to be read or written together with the address of a fixed area of store from which data is to be written to or read from. Since disc access will always take a longer time than store access, there will almost invariably be a number of requests waiting to be satisfied.

The device handler can be modelled by means of two sequences. The first would hold read requests; the second would hold write requests. The elements of the queue will be pairs consisting of a disc address and a memory address. Thus, the queues can be represented in a signature as

> read_queue, write_queue:
>   seq(disc_addresses × memory_addresses)

where *disc_addresses* is the set of all possible disc addresses and *memory_addresses* is the set of all possible memory addresses.

Sequence selection operators can be defined in Z as follows

$[T]$

> head, last: seq $T \rightarrow T$
> tail, front: seq $T \rightarrow$ seq T
>
> ---
>
> head = λs: seq $T \mid s \neq [\,] \cdot (s1)$
> front = λs: seq $T \mid s \neq [\,] \cdot \{^{\#}s\} \lhd s$
> tail = λs: seq $T \mid s \neq [\,] \cdot \{0\} \lhd (\text{succ}; s)$
> last = λs: seq $T \mid s \neq [\,] \cdot s(^{\#}s)$

All the operators are defined as lambda expressions. *head* returns the first element from a sequence. *tail* returns all but the first element of a list. *front* returns all but the last element of a sequence and *last* removes the last element of a sequence. The predicate $s \neq [\,]$ in each lambda expression ensures that all the functions are defined for non-empty lists.

Example 10.7

During the operation of a computer operating system, users will be continually creating and deleting files. In a distributed operating system the files that will be deleted or created may be held on a computer remote from the one on which the user is working. The file store of each computer will contain blocks of storage which are currently used in files and blocks of storage which are free for newly created files.

During the operation of the distributed system a packet of blocks released from the deletion of files by users of other computers will be received by a computer together with blocks released by users of that computer. These blocks will be queued in the order in which they were received. There will be no more than 30 computers in the distributed system. How would you model the distributed file store together with the queues of released blocks? Ignore any requirement to model the creation of files. Write down a schema which describes the static properties of the system.

The file store of each computer can be modelled by means of a disjoint set of blocks. The first set contains those blocks in use; the second set contains those blocks available for new files.

Each computer will be associated with a queue of blocks. Each entry of a queue will consist of a set of blocks. These queues can be modelled by means of a sequence of sets of blocks. The schema which describes the static properties of the system follows.

```
┌─ file_return ──────────────────────────────────────┐
│ connected_computers: ℙ computers                    │
│ free_file_stores: computers ⇸ ℙ blocks              │
│ used_file_stores: computers ⇸ ℙ blocks              │
│ waiting_delete: computers ⇸ seq(ℙ blocks)           │
├─────────────────────────────────────────────────────┤
│ connected_computers = dom free_file_stores          │
│ dom free_file_stores = dom used_file_stores         │
```

dom free_file_stores = dom waiting_delete
$^{\#}$connected_computers ≤ 30
$\forall$comp: connected_computers $\cdot$
free_file_stores comp $\cap$ used_file_stores comp = {}
$\forall$comp: connected_computers $\cdot$
$\forall x, y$ rng waiting_delete comp $\cdot$
$x \neq y \Rightarrow x \cap y = \{\}$
$\forall$comp: connected_computers $\cdot$
$\forall x$: rng waiting_delete comp $\cdot x$
$\subseteq$ used_file_stores comp

The free blocks in each computer together with the used blocks for each computer are modelled by the partial functions *free_file_stores* and *used_file_stores*. The queues of blocks waiting to be relinquished to the free block store of each computer are modelled by means of the partial function *waiting_delete*.

Example 10.8

Write down the sehema *return_block* which describes the event of returning the first set of blocks of file storage to free storage from the queue of returned blocks associated with the computer *comp_name?*.

---return_block---
file_return
file_return'
comp_name?: computers
----
comp_name? $\in$ connected_computers
waiting_delete comp_name? $\neq [\ ]$
connected_computers' = connected_computers
free_file_stores' = free_file_stores $\oplus$
{comp_name? $\mapsto$ free_file_stores (comp_name?) $\cup$
head(waiting_delete comp_name?)}

used_file_stores' = used_file_stores ⊕
  {comp_name? ↦ used_file_stores (comp_name?)
  − head(waiting_delete comp_name?)}
waiting_delete' = waiting_delete ⊕
  {comp_name? ↦ tail(waiting_delete
  comp_name?)}

The first predicate states that the computer *comp_name?*
must be one of the connected computers. The second
predicate states that the queue must not be empty. The
third predicate states that the operation does not alter
the number or names of the computers in the distributed
system. The fourth predicate describes the addition of
the queued block numbers to the free store associated
with the computer *comp_name?* The fifth predicate
describes the removal of the queued block numbers from
the used store associated with the computer *comp_
name?* Finally, the sixth predicate describes the removal
of the first element from the queue associated with the
computer *comp_name?*

A useful set of basic operations would include those which
retrieve the first n elements of a sequence or the last n elements
of a sequence. These are defined in Z as *for* and *after*. They
follow.

$[T]$

after, for: (seq T) × **N** → (seq T)

∀s: seq T; n: **N** ·
  s after n = succ$^{\#s-n}$; s
  s for n = (1..n) ⊲ s

10.5 Modelling a back-order system

This subsection concludes the description of basic Z facilities. It
illustrates the use of many of these facilities in the specification of

part of a typical commercial data-processing system. The specification is to be produced from the statement of requirements.

10.5.1 *The statement of requirements*

1. The back-order subsystem is to provide facilities for the processing of orders for commodities associated with gardening which are received by a wholesaler and which cannot be immediately satisfied by the wholesaler from stock.

2. On each day of operation a number of orders are received by the wholesaler. The majority of these orders are normally satisfied by withdrawing items from stock. However, some items will be temporarily out of stock.

3. When an order for an article is received which cannot be satisfied, the order is placed on a queue of orders for that article. The place where the order is inserted in the queue will depend on the importance of the customer who places the order. Some customers, for example large chain stores, are regarded as more important than other customers, so a priority list of customers must be maintained.

4. The following series of commands should be provided as part of the back-order subsystem.

4.1   NUMBER_QUEUE
This command displays the reference number of each customer who has ordered a quantity of a commodity that is out of stock. The customers, together with their associated order number, are displayed in the same order in which they occur in the commodity queue. The enquiries clerk who types in the command will provide the reference number of the commodity.

4.2.   TOTAL_QUEUE
This command displays the total number of orders for a particular out-of-stock commodity. The enquiries clerk who types in the command will provide the reference number of the commodity.

4.3 TOTAL_ALL_QUEUE

This command displays the total number of commodities which are currently ordered but are out of stock.

4.4 INSERT_CUSTOMER

The subsystem shall keep account of each possible customer for commodities. Associated with each customer is a priority. Customers with a high priority will have their orders satisfied before customers with a low priority. The purpose of this command is to insert a new customer into the system together with an associated priority. The order clerk types in a customer number and a priority.

4.5 DELETE_CUSTOMER

This command removes a single customer from the list of customers. The order clerk types in the customer number.

4.6 MOVE_CUSTOMER

This command alters the priority of a customer. The order clerk types in the customer number and a new priority.

4.7 REMOVE_PRODUCT

Very occasionally the wholesaler is notified by a manufacturer that a particular commodity is no longer produced. This command removes such commodities from the subsystem. The order clerk types in the commodity number that is no longer produced.

4.8 NEW_PRODUCT

Whenever a manufacturer decides to produce a new commodity, the number of that commodity is added to the subsystem. The order clerk types in the number of the new commodity.

4.9 NUMBER_STOCKED

This command displays the number of commodities that are currently stocked.

Should the priorities of the customers be unique? If so the position of individual orders belonging to a customer is unambiguously fixed in relation to orders from other customers. However, the ordering of orders from the same customer within the back-orders queues is not specified. We shall assume that, when a series of orders from the same customer are in a back-order queue, they are placed in ascending order of quantity. This has the dubious advantage that, when a consignment of a product is received by the wholesaler, then a number of smaller orders may be satisfied rather than one or two large orders.

What should happen if a customer is removed from those customers currently known to the subsystem by the DELETE_ CUSTOMER command and a number of back-orders for that customer are stored on a back-orders queue? Obviously, the statement of requirements is incomplete. Something will have to be done as a back-order will normally correspond to an order to a manufacturer which may have to be cancelled. In this case a print-out of orders from the deleted customer will be produced.

What should happen when the REMOVE_PRODUCT command is typed? There may be some orders for this product which can never be satisfied. It is clear that the customers for this product who have orders on the back-order queue will need to be notified or a substitute product sent. The statement of requirements is thus incomplete. We shall assume that a print-out of customer and order numbers for that product will be produced when that product is deleted from the subsystem.

What should happen when the MOVE_CUSTOMER command is typed? The effect of the command is to change the priority of a customer. Does this mean that the queue of back-orders from this customer should take account of the change? For example, if the customer is given a new higher priority should his back-orders be moved up a back-order queue? The statement of requirements is incomplete in this respect. We shall assume that the back-order queue will be adjusted.

10.5.2 Specifying the static properties of the system

The major part of the statement of requirements is concerned with queues of back-orders. These queues can be modelled by sequences. The whole collection of queues, each queue associated with a product, can be modelled by means of a partial function that maps product numbers to sequences which model the back-order queues for that product.

The statement of requirements also refers to items in stock.

This means that the association between a product and a number in stock should be modelled. This is achieved by means of a partial function that maps product numbers to the number in stock of that particular product.

Finally, the subsystem will need to keep track of customer priorities. Since each customer has a unique priority, the association between a customer and a priority can be modelled by means of a partial injection which maps customer numbers to priorities. Assuming that

>   *product_nos* is the set of all possible product numbers,
>   *cust_nos* is the set of all possible customer numbers,
>   *priority_nos* is the set of all possible priorities,
>   *order_nos* is the set of all possible order numbers,

the system can be characterized by the schema signature

```
┌─back_orders───────────────────────────────────────────────┐
│  queues: product_nos ⤚↠ seq order_nos
│  has_priority: cust_nos ⤚↠ priority_nos
│  stocks: product_nos: ↦ N
│  back_orders_no: order_nos ↦ N
│  back_orders_cust: order_nos ↦ cust_nos.
```

queues maps *product_nos* into the sequence of customer order numbers each of which correspond to an order for a commodity. *Has_priority* associates a customer number with the priority of the customer. *Stocks* maps a product number into the quantity in stock of that product. *Back_orders_no* maps an order number into the quantity ordered of a product and *back_orders_cust* maps an order number into the number of the customer who is associated with the order.

Example 10.9

Write down in natural language the properties of the back-order subsystem which must be true throughout its operation.

The list of properties is

(i) Each commodity that is stocked must be associated with a possibly empty back-orders queue.
(ii) Each order number in a queue element corresponds to an existing back-order.
(iii) The number in stock of a commodity must always be less than the number ordered in the first element of the queue for that commodity
(iv) Each order number in a queue element is unique.
(v) The orders should be in order of customer priority.

The invariants can be specified as

dom queues = dom stocks

dom back_orders_no = dom back_orders_cust =

$\bigcup${pr: dom queues $\cdot$ rng queues pr}

$\forall$pr: dom stocks | queues pr $\neq$ [] $\cdot$ stocks pr < head queues pr

$\forall$pr1, pr2: dom queues $\cdot$

pr1 $\neq$ pr2 $\Rightarrow$ rng(queues pr1) $\cap$ rng(queues pr2) = { }

$\forall$pr: dom queues $\cdot$ $\forall i, j$: dom queues pr $\cdot$

$i < j \Rightarrow$ has_priority back_orders_cust queues pr i

> has_priority back_orders_cust queues pr j.

This gives the schema

```
┌─back_orders─────────────────────────────────────┐
│ queues: product_nos ⇸ seq order_nos             │
│ has_priority: cust_nos ⇸ priority_nos            │
│ stocks: product_nos ⇸ N                          │
│ back_orders_no: order_nos ⇸ N                    │
│ back_orders_cust: order_nos ⇸ cust_nos           │
└──────────────────────────────────────────────────┘
```

dom queues = dom stocks

dom back_orders_no = dom back_orders_cust =

$\bigcup$ {pr: dom queues · rng queues pr}

$\forall$pr: dom stocks | queues pr $\neq$ [ ] · stocks pr < head
  queues pr

$\forall$pr1, pr2: dom queues ·

  pr1 $\neq$ pr2 $\Rightarrow$ rng(queues pr1) $\cap$ rng(queues pr2) = { }

$\forall$pr: dom queues · $\forall i, j$: dom queues pr ·

  $i < j \Rightarrow$ has_priority back_orders_cust queues pr i

  > has_priority back_orders_cust queues pr j

Given this schema, a number of events can be specified. Each
event corresponds to a command typed in by a clerk.

The NUMBER_QUEUE command can be specified as the
event *number_queue* which occurs when the command is typed.

---

number_queue

back_orders

back_orders'

cust_display!: seq cust_nos

ord_numbs_display!: seq order_nos

product?: product_nos

---

product? $\in$ dom queues

queues' = queues

has_priority' = has_priority

stocks' = stocks

back_orders_no' = back_orders_no

back_orders_cust' = back_orders_cust

cust_display! = (queues product?); back_orders_cust

ord_numbs_display! = queues product?

---

product? is the product number typed by the clerk. Two
sequences are formed: *cust_display!* contains the customer

numbers of those customers who have back orders for *product?*, *ord_numbs_display!* contains the order numbers of the back-orders for *product?*. The first predicate asserts that the product is known to the subsystem. The second to sixth predicates state that the subsystem will remain unchanged by the event. The seventh and eighth predicates define the sequences *cust_display!* and *ord_numbs_display!*.

The TOTAL_QUEUE command can be specified by the schema *total_queue:* it describes the event that occurs when the command is typed. *product?* represents the product number typed and *number!* represents the total number of queue entries for *product?*

```
┌─total_queue──────────────────────────────────────┐
│ back_orders                                        │
│ back_orders'                                       │
│ product?: product_nos                              │
│ number!: N                                         │
├────────────────────────────┤
│ product? ∈ dom queues                              │
│ queues' = queues                                   │
│ has_priority' = has_priority                       │
│ stocks' = stocks                                   │
│ back_orders_no' = back_orders_no                   │
│ back_orders_cust' = back_orders_cust               │
│ number! = #(queues product?)                       │
└────────────────────────────────────────────────────┘
```

The TOTAL_ALL_QUEUE command can be specified by the schema *total_all_queue.*

```
┌─total_all_queue──────────────────────────────────┐
│ back_orders                                        │
│ back_orders'                                       │
│ total_number!: N                                   │
├────────────────────────────┤
│ queues' = queues                                   │
│ has_priority' = has_priority                       │
│ stocks' = stocks                                   │
│ back_orders_no' = back_orders_no                   │
│ back_orders_cust' = back_orders_cust               │
│ total_number! = #{prod: dom queues | queues prod ≠ []} │
└────────────────────────────────────────────────────┘
```

The first five predicates are straightforward; they describe the fact that the subsystem is unaffected by the event. The final predicate is more complicated. It states that the total number of individual commodities which are on order is the cardinality of the set of products associated with back-order queues which are not empty.

Example 10.10

Define a schema *insert_customer* which describes the event that occurs when the INSERT_CUSTOMER command is typed.

```
┌─insert_customer──────────────────────────────────────┐
│ back_orders                                           ┐
│ back_orders'
│ customer?: cust_nos
│ priority?: priority_nos
├───────────────────────────────────────────────
│ customer? ∉ dom has_priority
│ priority? ∉ rng has_priority
│ queues' = queues
│ stocks' = stocks
│ back_orders_no' = back_orders_no
│ back_orders_cust' = back_orders_cust
│ has_priority' = has_priority ∪
│    {(customer?, priority?)}                           ┘
```

customer? is the name of the customer and *priority?* is the associated priority of the customer. The first predicate asserts that the customer must be a new customer. The second predicate asserts that priority must be unique. The third to sixth predicates state that *queues, stocks, back_orders_no,* and *back_orders_cust* are unchanged by the event. Finally, the last predicate uses the set union operator to show the addition of the pair corresponding to the new customer with a new priority to *has_priority*.

The DELETE_CUSTOMER command can be specified as the schema *delete_customer* which describes the event that occurs when this command is typed. The number of the customer to be deleted is *customer?*.

```
┌─delete_customer─────────────────────────────────────┐
│ back_orders                                          │
│ back_orders'                                         │
│ customer?: cust_nos                                  │
├──────────────────────────────────────────────────────┤
│ customer? ∈ dom has_priority                         │
│ has_priority' = {customer?} ⊲ has_priority           │
│ stocks' = stocks                                     │
│ back_orders_cust' = back_orders_cust ⊳ {customer?}   │
│ back_orders_no' = (dom back_orders_cust') ⊲ back_    │
│    orders_no                                         │
│ dom queues' = dom queues                             │
│ ∀p: dom queues' ·                                    │
│ queues'p = squash(queues p ⊳ {o: order_nos |        │
│    back_orders_cust o = customer?})                  │
└──────────────────────────────────────────────────────┘
```

The first six predicates are relatively simple. The seventh predicate states that each of the queues after the *delete_customer* event will contain the elements in the queues before the event minus those associated with customer.

The MOVE_CUSTOMER command can be specified by means of the schema *move_customer:* This describes the event of altering a customer priority. *customer?* is the name of the customer whose priority is to be changed and *new_priority?* is the new value of the priority.

```
┌─move_customer───────────────────────────────────────┐
│ back_orders                                          │
│ back_orders'                                         │
│ customer?: cust_nos                                  │
│ new_priority?: priority_nos                          │
├──────────────────────────────────────────────────────┤
│ customer? ∈ dom has_priority                         │
│ new_priority? ∉ rng has_priority                     │
│ stocks' = stocks                                     │
│ back_orders_no' = back_orders_no                     │
```

$$back\_orders\_cust' = back\_orders\_cust$$
$$has\_priority' = has\_priority \oplus \{(customer?, new\_$$
$$\quad priority?)\}$$
$$dom\ queues' = dom\ queues$$
$$\forall prod: dom\ queues \cdot$$
$$\quad rng\ queues'\ prod = rng\ queues\ prod$$

The first predicate states that the customer must already have been allocated a priority number. The second predicate asserts that the new priority must not already be assigned to a current customer. The sixth predicate asserts that the new priority has been assigned. The seventh predicate asserts that no new_ product queues are created and no queues are deleted. The eighth predicate states that the individual entries in each queue remain unchanged. It is a temptation to include a predicate which shows the subsequent movement of items in each queue due to the re-assignment of a new priority to a customer. However, the schema *back_orders'* includes a predicate which ensures that the correct ordering is maintained.

Example 10.11

Write down a schema *remove_product* which describes the event that occurs when the REMOVE_PRODUCT command is typed and when there is stock held for the product that is to be removed.

```
remove_product
back_orders
back_orders'
prod?: product_nos
lucky_customer!: cust_nos
notified_customers!: Pcust_nos

stocks prod? > 0
prod? ∈ dom queues
has_priority' = has_priority
lucky_customer! = back_orders_cust queues prod?1
```

$$
\begin{array}{l}
\text{notified\_customers!} = \text{back\_orders\_cust} \llbracket \text{rng queues} \\
\quad \text{prod?} \rrbracket - \text{lucky\_customer!} \\
\text{stocks}' = \{\text{prod?}\} \lhd \text{stocks} \\
\text{queues}' = \{\text{prod?}\} \lhd \text{queues} \\
\text{back\_orders\_no}' = (\text{rng queues prod?}) \lhd \text{back\_} \\
\quad \text{orders\_no} \\
\text{back\_orders\_cust}' = (\text{rng queues prod?}) \lhd \text{back\_} \\
\quad \text{orders\_cust}
\end{array}
$$

The name of the commodity which has been discontinued is *prod?*. If there is stock of the commodity in the wholesaler's warehouse, then the first customer on the back-order queue for the commodity *lucky_customer!* will receive the stock of that commodity.

Example 10.12

Write down a schema *new_product* which describes the event that occurs when the NEW_PRODUCT command is typed.

$$
\begin{array}{l}
\underline{\text{new\_product}} \\
\text{back\_orders} \\
\text{back\_orders}' \\
\text{new\_product?}: \text{product\_nos} \\
\hline
\text{new\_product?} \notin \text{dom queues} \\
\text{has\_priority}' = \text{has\_priority} \\
\text{back\_orders\_no}' = \text{back\_orders\_no} \\
\text{back\_orders\_cust}' = \text{back\_orders\_cust} \\
\text{queues}' = \text{queues} \cup \{(\text{new\_product?}, [\,])\} \\
\text{stocks}' = \text{stocks} \cup \{(\text{new\_product?}, 0)\}
\end{array}
$$

new_product? is the name of the product which is typed in by the clerk who uses the command.

11 The Z schema calculus

11.1 Schemas as objects

Schemas are a convenient way of organizing the description of specifications. They have a form that replicates a pattern found throughout discrete mathematics described in the early parts of this book. For example, the comprehensive set specification

$$\{\text{file}: \text{sys\_files} \mid \text{file} \in \text{accessed super\_user}\}$$

is reflected in the schema

$$
\begin{array}{|l}
\hline
\text{file}: \text{sys\_files} \\
\hline
\text{file} \in \text{accessed super\_user} \\
\hline
\end{array}
$$

while the function

$$\lambda s: \text{seq}(\text{file\_updates}) \mid {}^{\#}s > 3.s(1)$$

is partly reflected in the schema

$$
\begin{array}{|l}
\hline
\text{file}: \text{seq}(\text{file\_updates}) \\
\hline
{}^{\#}s > 3 \\
\hline
\end{array}
$$

and the predicate

$$\forall \text{file}: \text{sys\_files}; \text{us}: \text{normal\_users} \mid \neg(\text{file is\_owned us})$$

is reflected in the schema

$$
\begin{array}{|l}
\hline
\text{file}: \text{sys\_files} \\
\text{us}: \text{normal\_users} \\
\hline
\neg(\text{file is\_owned us}) \\
\hline
\end{array}
$$

This equivalence between schemas and comprehensive set specification, predicates, and lambda abstractions means that these three entities are interchangeable with schemas. For example, the schema

```
┌─special_invoice─────────────────────────────────────┐
│ name: invoice_names                                  │
│ special_category, not_supplied: ℙ invoice_names      │
│ ────────────────────                                 │
│ name ∈ not_supplied ∨ name ∈ special_category        │
└──────────────────────────────────────────────────────┘
```

when enclosed in curly brackets

$$\{\text{special\_invoice}\},$$

is equivalent to the comprehensive set specification

{name: invoice_names; special_category, not_supplied:

ℙ invoice_names | name ∈ not_supplied ∨ name ∈

special_category}

which is the set of all invoice names which are either in the *not_supplied* set or in the *special_category* set.

Predicates and schemas are also interchangeable. For example, a schema such as

```
┌─normal_invoice──────────────────────────────────────┐
│ name: invoice_names                                  │
│ ────────────────────                                 │
│ name ∈ current_invoices                              │
└──────────────────────────────────────────────────────┘
```

can be preceded by a quantifier and followed by a period and a predicate. For example,

$$\exists \text{normal\_invoice} \cdot \text{name} \subseteq \text{special\_category}$$

$$\forall \text{normal\_invoice} \cdot \text{name} \subseteq \text{reserved\_invoices}.$$

The period is read as an implication so that the above predicates are equivalent to

∃name: invoice_names | name ∈ current_invoices

⇒ name ⊆ special_category

∀name: invoice_names | name ∈ current_invoices

⇒ name ⊆ reserved_invoices.

A schema can also be quantified by just writing the quantifier in front of the schema name; thus

$$\exists \text{normal\_invoice}$$

is equivalent to

$$\exists \text{name: invoice\_names} \cdot \text{name} \in \text{current\_invoices}$$

and

$$\forall \text{normal\_invoice}$$

is equivalent to

$$\forall \text{name: invoice\_names} \cdot \text{name} \in \text{current\_invoices}.$$

Finally, a schema can form part of a lambda expression. For example, a schema such as

```
__distributed_directory_____
  all_users, normal_users, system_users: ℙ user_names
 _____
  normal_users ∩ system_users = { }
  (normal_users ∪ system_users) ⊆ all_users
```

can be preceded by λ and followed by a period and an expression involving the variables of the signature. Thus,

$$\lambda \text{ distributed\_directory} \cdot {}^{\#}\text{normal\_users}$$

is a function which returns the number of normal users defined in the schema *distributed_directory*. It is equivalent to:

$$\lambda \text{ all\_users, normal\_users, system\_users: } \mathbb{P} \text{ user\_names} \mid$$
$$\text{normal\_users} \cap \text{system\_users} = \{ \} \wedge (\text{normal\_users} \cup$$
$$\text{system\_users}) \subseteq \text{all\_users} \cdot {}^{\#}\text{normal\_users}.$$

The function

$$\lambda \text{ distributed\_directory} \cdot \text{system\_users}$$

returns the set of system users in a distributed directory. Such a function which delivers one of the variables that make up a signature is known as a **projection function**.

Exercise 11.1

The schema *file_queue* describes the properties of the subsystem of an operating system concerned with the off-line printing of results and reports that have been generated by terminated user programs.

```
┌─file_queue─────────────────────────────────────────────┐
│ waiting_jobs: output_peripherals ↦ seq(print_files)     │
│ current_priority: output_peripherals ⇻ print_priorities │
│ maxqsize: N                                             │
├─────────────────────────────────────────────────────────┤
│ dom waiting_jobs = dom current_priority                 │
│ ∀s: dom waiting_jobs ·                                   │
│ #waiting_jobs s ≤ maxqsize                              │
└─────────────────────────────────────────────────────────┘
```

Write down

- (i) The function which returns the waiting jobs in the file queue.
- (ii) The assertion that in the *file_queue* subsystem there isn't a queue longer than *maxqsize*.
- (iii) The function which returns the number of output peripherals in the *file_queue* subsystem.
- (iv) The set of all file_queues . . . .

Schemas can be written using the box notation above or can be enclosed in brackets. For example, the schema

```
┌─S──────────────────────────────────────────────┐
│ Sys_users, Normal_users: N                      │
├─────────────────────────────────────────────────┤
│ Sys_users + Normal_users ≤ 120                  │
└─────────────────────────────────────────────────┘
```

can be written as

S ≙ [Sys_users, Normal_users:

$$N \mid Sys\_users + Normal\_users \leq 120].$$

11.2 Extending and manipulating schemas

Chapter 9 described how schemas can be incorporated into other schemas by means of schema inclusion. This allows a much more concise form of presentation and enables a specification to be presented at a number of levels of abstraction. However, the precise semantics of schema inclusion have not yet been described.

The result of including one schema within another is to form another schema which contains the union of the signatures of both schemas with the predicates of both schemas conjoined together. For example, if the schema *files* is

```
┌─files───────────────────────────────────────────┐
│ sys_files, user_files, stored_files: ℙ file_names │
│ ─────────────────────────                         │
│ sys_files ∪ user_files = stored_files             │
│ sys_files ∩ user_files = { }                      │
└─────────────────────────────────────────────────┘
```

and the schema *tapes* is

```
┌─tapes───────────────────────────────────────────┐
│ sys_tapes, user_tapes, stored_tapes: ℙ tape_names │
│ ─────────────────────────                         │
│ sys_tapes ∪ user_tapes = stored_tapes             │
│ sys_tapes ∩ user_tapes = { }                      │
└─────────────────────────────────────────────────┘
```

then

```
┌─whole_file──────────────────────────────────────┐
│ files                                            │
│ tapes                                            │
│ max_files, max_tapes: N                          │
│ ─────────────────────────                        │
│ #stored files ≤ max_files                        │
│ #stored_tapes ≤ max_tapes                        │
└─────────────────────────────────────────────────┘
```

is equivalent to the schema

```
┌─whole_file──────────────────────────────────────┐
│ sys_files, user_files, stored_files: ℙ file_names │
│ sys_tapes, user_tapes, stored_tapes: ℙ tape_names │
│ max_files, max_tapes: N                           │
│ ─────────────────────────                         │
│ sys_files ∪ user_files = stored_files             │
│ sys_files ∩ user_files = { }                      │
│ sys_tapes ∪ user_tapes = stored_tapes             │
```

> sys_tapes ∩ user_tapes = { }
> #stored_files ≤ max_files
> #stored_tapes ≤ max_tapes

Any duplicated names in the schemas which are joined in this way are replaced by a single instance of the name provided they are of the same type. These names must be of the same type.

A schema can also be primed. This has the effect of placing a prime above each variable in both the signature and predicate parts of a scheme. Thus, if the schema *cust* is

```
__cust_____
  ordinary_cust, priority_cust, registered_cust: ℙ customers

  ordinary_cust ∩ priority_cust = { }
  ordinary_cust ∪ priority_cust = registered_cust
```

which represents the relationships between categories of customer in a commercial data-processing application, then *cust'* is

```
__cust'_____
  ordinary_cust', priority_cust', registered_cust': ℙ customers

  ordinary_cust' ∩ priority_cust' = { }
  ordinary_cust' ∪ priority_cust' = registered_cust'
```

These schemas can then be combined to form a schema which describes the invariant properties of the system in terms of the observations *ordinary_cust, priority_cust,* and *registered_cust*

```
  _____
  cust
  cust'
```

This is equivalent to the schema

```
  _____
  ordinary_cust, priority_cust, registered_cust,
  ordinary_cust', priority_cust', registered_cust': ℙ customers

  ordinary_cust ∩ priority_cust = { }
  ordinary_cust ∪ priority_cust = registered_cust
  ordinary_cust' ∩ priority_cust' = { }
  ordinary_cust' ∪ priority_cust' = registered_cust'
```

Schemas can also be extended by adding to their signatures or predicates. Adding a new declaration to a signature is achieved by following the schema name by a semicolon and the new declaration. For example, if the schema *permanent_files* is

```
┌─permanent_files───────────────────────────────────┐
│ pfile_directory: ℙ files
│ master_file: files
│ ─────────────────────────
│ master_file ∈ pfile_directory
└───────────────────────────────────────────────────┘
```

then the schema

$$\text{new} \triangleq [\text{permanent\_files}; \text{user\_directory}: \mathbb{P} \text{ files}]$$

would be

```
┌─new───────────────────────────────────────────────┐
│ user_directory, pfile_directory: ℙ files
│ master_file: files
│ ─────────────────────────
│ master_file ∈ pfile_directory
└───────────────────────────────────────────────────┘
```

A predicate can be added to a schema by concatenating the schema's name with the symbol |, followed by the predicate to be added. Thus,

$$\text{new\_perm} \triangleq [\text{permanent\_files} \mid {}^{\#}\text{pfile\_directory} \le 200]$$

is equivalent to the schema

```
┌─newperm───────────────────────────────────────────┐
│ pfile_directory: ℙ files
│ master_file: files
│ ─────────────────────────
│ master_file ∈ pfile_directory
│ #pfile_directory ≤ 200
└───────────────────────────────────────────────────┘
```

and

$$\text{bigger\_perm} \triangleq [(\text{permanent\_files}; \text{user\_directory}: \text{files}) \mid$$

$${}^{\#}\text{pfile\_directory} \le 200 \ \wedge \ \text{user\_directory} \in$$

$$\text{pfile\_directory}]$$

is equivalent to

```
┌─bigger_perm─────────────────────────────┐
│ pfile_directory: ℙ files                │
│ master_file, user_directory: files      │
├─────────────────────────────────────────┤
│ master_file ∈ pfile_directory           │
│ #pfile_directory ≤ 200                   │
│ user_directory ∈ pfile_directory        │
└─────────────────────────────────────────┘
```

Two operators which are often useful in Z specifications are *tuple* and *pred*. Both of these operators operate on schemas. *Tuple* returns the ordered tuple of the variables of the schema upon which it operates. For example, if the schema *stud* is

```
┌─stud─────────────────────────────────────┐
│ class, absent, present: ℙ students       │
├──────────────────────────────────────────┤
│ class ∪ absent = students                │
│ class ∩ absent = { }                     │
└──────────────────────────────────────────┘
```

then *tuple stud* is the ordered tuple

$$(\text{class, absent, present}).$$

pred returns the predicate part of the schema upon which it operates. For example, *pred stud* is

$$\text{class} \cup \text{absent} = \text{students} \wedge \text{class} \cap \text{absent} = \{ \}.$$

11.3 Z schema conventions

When constructing Z specifications, a number of conventions are observed. These conventions dictate the form of schema and variable names and provide a visual cue to the reader about the function and nature of schemas and the variables used in schemas.

The first convention is concerned with schemas that describe events which change part of a system. The symbol Δ is used to precede a schema name to indicate the general properties of the schema that are unaffected by a series of events. As an example, consider the schema *spool_queue_sys* which describes the fact that all elements of a spool queue of files awaiting printing are temporary files

```
┌─spool_queue_sys──────────────────────────────┐
│ temp_files: ℙ files                                       │
│ spool_queue: seq(files)                                   │
│ ─────────────────────────────────                        │
│ rng spool_queue ⊆ temp_files                             │
└──────────────────────────────────────────────┘
```

The schema which describes the fact that this property will always hold is Δ*spool_queue_sys*

```
┌─Δspool_queue_sys─────────────────────────────┐
│ spool_queue_sys                                           │
│ spool_queue_sys′                                          │
└──────────────────────────────────────────────┘
```

which is, of course, equivalent to

```
┌─Δspool_queue_sys─────────────────────────────┐
│ temp_files, temp_files′: ℙ files                          │
│ spool_queue, spool_queue′: seq(files)                     │
│ ─────────────────────────────────                        │
│ rng spool_queue ⊆ temp_files                             │
│ rng spool_queue′ ⊆ temp_files′                           │
└──────────────────────────────────────────────┘
```

It can be used in any schema which does not affect the fact that all the files in a spool queue are temporary files. For example, the schema *remove_spool_file* describes the event of removing the first element of the spool queue

```
┌─remove_spool_file────────────────────────────┐
│ Δspool_queue_sys                                          │
│ removed_file!: files                                      │
│ ─────────────────────────────────                        │
│ removed_file! = head spool_queue                          │
│ spool_queue′ = tail spool_queue                           │
└──────────────────────────────────────────────┘
```

Example 11.1

A computerized library system at a university administers the loan of books to staff and students alike. Each user has a unique borrower number and each book in the library has a unique reference number. Staff can borrow no more than 20 books, while students can borrow no more than 10 books. There are no other users apart from staff and students. Write down a schema Δ*users* which describes the invariant properties of the library system. Assume that the fact that a user borrows a series of books is modelled by means of a relation over user names and book registration numbers.

The invariant properties of the system are

(i) The only users are staff and students.

(ii) A user cannot simultaneously be a member of staff and a student.

(iii) No member of staff can borrow more than 20 books.

(iv) No student can borrow more than 10 books.

These properties are embodied in the schema *users*

```
users
staff, students, all_users: ℙ borrower_numbers
borrows: borrower_numbers ↔ book_reference_numbers

staff ∪ students = all_users
staff ∩ students = { }
∀st: staff · #(borrows⟦{st}⟧) ≤ 20
∀stud: students · #(borrows⟦{stud}⟧) ≤ 10
```

The invariant properties can then be expressed as

```
Δusers
users
users'
```

Example 11.2

A system for monitoring the operation of a chemical plant is to be developed by a software house. The system will consist of a series of monitors (thermocouples, pressure tranducers) each of which will be attached to a chemical reactor. Each monitor is also connected to a single computer. A monitor is identified by a unique monitor name; each computer is identified by a unique computer name. There are two types of computers which will be used in the system. Type A computers are very powerful and are able to process signals from up to 200 monitors. Type B computers are less powerful, older computers which can process signals from up to 120 monitors. The fact that a computer is connected to monitors is modelled by a function from computer names to $\mathbb{P}$ monitor names. The fact that a monitor is attached to a reactor is modelled by means of a partial injective function which maps a monitor name to a monitoring point on a reactor. Write down a schema which describes the invariant properties of the proposed system.

The invariant properties are

> No computer can be both type A and type B.
> No type A computer can be connected to more than 200 monitoring points.
> No type B computer can be connected to more than 120 monitoring points.
> If *ta* is the number of type A computers in the system and *tb* is the number of type B computers in the system than $ta * 200 + tb * 120$ must be greater or equal to the number of connections to the reactors.
> No monitor is connected to more than one computer.

This can be expressed in the schema Δmon_sys

```
┌─ Δmon_sys ──────────────────────────────────────┐
│ mon_sys                                          │
│ mon_sys'                                         │
└──────────────────────────────────────────────────┘
```

where *mon_sys* is

```
_mon_sys_____
all_computers, typeAs, typeBs: ℙ computer_names
has_monitor: computer_names ⇸ ℙ monitor_names
is_connected: monitor_names ⤔ monitor_points
_____
all_computers = typeAs ∪ typeBs
dom is_connected =
   ∪ {c: dom has_monitor · has_monitor c}
typeAs ∩ typeBs = { }
∀comp: typeAs ·
   #(has_monitor comp) ≤ 200
∀comp: typeBs ·
   #(has_monitor comp) ≤ 120
#typeAs * 200 + #typeBs * 120 ≥
   #dom is_connected
∀co1, co2: rng has_monitor ·
   co1 ≠ co2 ⇒ co1 ∩ co2 = { }
```

A further convention involves schemas which describe objects or sets of objects which are not changed by events. Such schemas are named by preceding a schema name with the symbol ≡. Δ schemas are those which indicate invariant properties while ≡ schemas are used to describe parts of a system that do not change.

For example, consider the commercial data-processing system described by the signature

```
_dp_order_____
product_price: product_nos ⇸ prices
product_supplier: suppliers ↔ product_nos
product_stock: product_nos ⇸ N
order_level: product_nos ⇸ N
product_position: product_nos ⇸ warehouse_positions
order_product: order_nos ⇸ product_nos
back_orders: product_nos ⇸ ℙ order_nos
order_placed: order_nos ⇸ customer_nos
```

product_price models the association between a product and its price; *product_supplier* models the association between a supplier and a series of products that are supplied; *product_stock* models the association between a product and the amount of that product in stock; *order_level* models the association between a product and the minimum stock level below which it must never be allowed to drop. *product_position* models the association between a product and its position in the warehouse. It is used to generate picking lists. Such lists give the names of each product to be removed by warehouse staff in response to an order. They are arranged in ascending order of warehouse position. This enables warehouse staff to travel the warehouse in one smooth journey rather than travelling large distances from one end of the warehouse to the other. *Order_product* models the association between an order number and a product being ordered, *back_orders* is used to model the queues of orders for products which are not in stock, and *order_placed* models the association between an order and the customer that placed the order.

Some events in such a system will unaffect all the variables of the signature shown. For example, part of the system may be concerned with processing queries from order clerks. For such events the schema ≡dp_order can be defined as

$$
\begin{array}{|l}
\hline \_\equiv\text{dp\_order}\_\underline{\hspace{4cm}} \\
\text{dp\_order} \\
\text{dp\_order}' \\
\hline
\text{tuple dp\_order}' = \text{tuple dp\_order} \\
\hline
\end{array}
$$

For example, the schema which represents the event that occurs when an order clerk queries the system to obtain the number of *back_orders* for a particular product can be written as

$$
\begin{array}{|l}
\hline \_\text{back\_order\_query}\_\underline{\hspace{4cm}} \\
\equiv\text{dp\_order} \\
\text{product\_number?: product\_nos} \\
\text{number!: } \mathbf{N} \\
\hline
\text{product\_number?} \in \text{dom back\_orders} \\
\text{number!} = {}^{\#}\text{back\_orders product\_number?} \\
\hline
\end{array}
$$

A final convention concerns the variables in a signature. Some variables in the signature of a schema will represent input variables whose values are to be used by the event described by the schema. Other variables will represent output variables which will gain a value after the event described by the schema has occurred. For example, the schema

```
┌─ ≡updates ──────────────────────────────────────┐
│  customer_no?: N                                 │
│  account_balance!: N                             │
├──────────────────────────────────────────────────┤
│  customer_no? ∈ dom balance                      │
│  account_balance! = balance customer_no          │
└──────────────────────────────────────────────────┘
```

describes a query in a banking system where *balance* is a partial function which maps customer accounts into the balance of cash in that account. The query provides a customer account number *customer_no?* and the balance is returned in *account_balance!* In this schema *customer_no?* is an input variable while *account_balance!* is an output variable. In Z schemas the input variables are annotated with a question mark: output variables are annotated by an exclamation mark.

Exercise 11.2

A banking system is to be specified using Z. Each bank in the system contains a series of current accounts and deposit accounts. An account is identified by a unique number. An account is owned by a customer who is also uniquely identified by a customer name. A customer can own a number of accounts.

   (i) Write down a signature which describes the banking system.
  (ii) Write down the schema Δ*bank_sys* which describes the invariant relation between elements of the signature.
 (iii) Write down the schema ≡*bank_sys* which can be used in events which do not affect the variables of the system.
 (iv) Write down the schema *dep_customers_one* which describes the event that occurs when those customers who have at least one deposit account are listed.
  (v) Write down the schema *cur_customers_one* which describes the event that occurs when those customers who have at least one current account are listed.
 (vi) Write down the schema *both_accounts* which describes the

event that occurs when those customers who have at least one
current account and at least one deposit account are listed.

(vii) Write down a schema balance which describes the event that
occurs when the balance of a particular account is displayed.

11.4 Logical operators and schemas

Schemas can be combined together using the logical operators:
$\Leftrightarrow$, $\Rightarrow$, $\lor$, $\land$, and $\lnot$. The effect of applying a binary logical
operator on two schemas is to form a schema whose signature is
the union of the signature of the operands' signatures provided
that the types of shared variables agree. The predicate of the new
schema so formed is constructed by applying the logical operator
to the predicates of the schemas which are its operands.

For example, if the schema *accounts* is

```
┌─accounts────────────────────────────────────────────────┐
│ has_account: customer_names ↦ ℙ account_nos             │
│ large_holders: ℙ customer_names                         │
├─────────────────────────────────────────────────────────┤
│ ∀name: large_holders ·                                  │
│    #(has_account name) > 10                             │
└─────────────────────────────────────────────────────────┘
```

and if the schema *com_accounts* is

```
┌─com_accounts────────────────────────────────────────────┐
│ company_accounts: ℙ customer_names                      │
│ large_holders: ℙ customer_names                         │
├─────────────────────────────────────────────────────────┤
│ company_accounts ⊆ large_holders                        │
└─────────────────────────────────────────────────────────┘
```

then the schema all_accounts $\triangleq$ accounts $\land$ com_accounts is

```
┌─all_accounts────────────────────────────────────────────┐
│ company_accounts: ℙ customer_names                      │
│ large_holders: ℙ customer_names                         │
│ has_account: customer_names ↦ ℙ account_nos             │
├─────────────────────────────────────────────────────────┤
│ company_accounts ⊆ large_holders                        │
│ ∀name: large_holders ·                                  │
│    #(has_account name) > 10                             │
└─────────────────────────────────────────────────────────┘
```

When the negation operator is applied to a schema it only affects the predicate of the schema; for example, ¬*com_accounts* is

---
```
company_accounts: ℙ customer_names
large_holders: ℙ customer_names
```

```
¬company_accounts ⊆ large_holders
```

11.5 Using the schema calculus—a simple query system for a spare-parts data base

The Reliable Parts Company provide spare parts for garages in a major city. The parts are identified by a unique name. Many of the parts can only be fitted to one type of vehicle. However, some parts are able to be fitted to a range of vehicles. The garage also stocks a number of parts which are supplied by different manufacturers and which are equivalent in the sense that they can be fitted to the same type of car.

The spare-parts data base for this application can be modelled by the signature

---
```
vehicles_supplied: ℙ vehicles
supp_of_part: part_nos ↔ supplier_names
price_of_part: part_nos ↦ part_prices
in_stock: part_nos ↦ N
fitted_to: part_nos ↔ vehicles
substitute: part_nos ↔ part_nos
```
---

vehicles_supplied is the set of all vehicles that the company supplies spare parts for. The relation *supp_of_part* models the association between a part number and the suppliers who supply the part. *price_of_part* models the association between a part and its price. *in_stock* models the association between a part and the number in stock of the part. *fitted_to* models the association between a part and the vehicles it can be fitted to. Finally, *substitute* is a relation which models the association between a part and all the parts that can be substituted for it.

The part of the statement of requirements concerned with queries follows.

4.   Queries allowed

A number of queries can be typed in by a stores clerk

4.1   LIST_IN_STOCK

A stores clerk can type in the LIST_IN_STOCK command at a terminal and the system will respond by displaying all the part numbers and quantities in stock of all current parts.

4.2   IN_STOCK

A stores clerk can type in the IN_STOCK command at a terminal together with a part number. The system will respond by displaying the quantity in stock of the particular part whose number is typed, together with the number and quantities in stock of any substitute parts.

4.3   PRICE_PARTS

A stores clerk can type in the PRICE_PARTS command at a terminal together with a part number. The system will respond by displaying the price of the part whose number has been typed, together with the number and price of any substitutes.

4.4   SUPPLIER_PARTS

A stores clerk can type in the SUPPLIER_PARTS command at a terminal together with a part number. The system will respond by displaying the names of the suppliers of the part whose number has been typed.

4.5   PRINT_CAR_LIST

A stores clerk can type in the PRINT_CAR_LIST command at a terminal together with a vehicle name. The system will respond by printing the names of those parts which can be fitted to the vehicle.

The schema used to describe properties of the system will be called *db_prop*

```
┌─db_prop──────────────────────────────────────────┐
│ vehicles_supplied: ℙ vehicles                     │
│ supp_of_part: part_nos ↔ supplier_names           │
```

$$price\_of\_part: part\_nos \nrightarrow part\_prices$$
$$in\_stock: part\_nos \nrightarrow \mathbf{N}$$
$$fitted\_to: part\_nos \leftrightarrow vehicles$$
$$substitute: part\_nos \leftrightarrow part\_nos$$

$$dom\ supp\_of\_part = dom\ price\_of\_part$$
$$dom\ supp\_of\_part = dom\ in\_stock$$
$$dom\ supp\_of\_part = dom\ fitted\_to$$
$$dom\ substitute \subseteq dom\ supp\_of\_part$$
$$rng\ substitute \subseteq dom\ supp\_of\_part$$

The schema Δ*data_base* can be expressed in terms of *dp_prop*
s

$$\Delta data\_base \triangleq db\_prop' \wedge db\_prop.$$

'his schema which can be used in queries and which describes
ιe fact that the data base is unchanged is ≡*data_base*

___≡data_base_____
$$\Delta data\_base$$

$$tuple\ db\_prop' = tuple\ db\_prop$$

The schema *list_in_stock* describes the event that occurs when
the LIST_IN_STOCK command is typed

___list_in_stock_____
$$\equiv data\_base$$
$$names\_and\_quant!: part\_nos \nrightarrow \mathbf{N}$$

$$names\_and\_quant! = in\_stock$$

The schema *in_stock* describes the event that occurs when the
IN_STOCK command is typed

___in_stock_____
$$\equiv data\_base$$
$$typed\_no?: part\_nos$$
$$stocks!: part\_nos \nrightarrow \mathbf{N}$$

$$typed\_no? \in dom\ in\_stock$$
$$stocks! = (\{typed\_no?\} \cup$$
$$\quad substitute[\![\{typed\_no?\}]\!]) \lhd in\_stock$$

The schema *price_parts* describes the event that occurs when the PRICE_PARTS command is typed

```
┌─price_parts─────────────────────────────────────────┐
│ ≡data_base                                           │
│ typed_no?: part_nos                                  │
│ prices!: part_nos ↦ part_prices                      │
│ ─────────────────────────────────                    │
│ typed_no? ∈ dom in_stock                             │
│ prices! = ({typed_no?} ∪                             │
│    substitute⟦{typed_no?}⟧) ◁ price_of_part          │
└──────────────────────────────────────────────────────┘
```

The schema *supplier_parts* describes the event that occurs when the SUPPLIER_PARTS command is typed

```
┌─supplier_parts──────────────────────────────────────┐
│ ≡data_base                                           │
│ suppliers!: ℙ supplier_names                         │
│ typed_no?: part_nos                                  │
│ ─────────────────────────────────                    │
│ typed_no? ∈ dom in_stock                             │
│ suppliers! = supp_of_part⟦{typed_no?}⟧               │
└──────────────────────────────────────────────────────┘
```

Finally, the schema *print_car_list* describes the event that occurs when the PRINT_CAR_LIST command is typed

```
┌─print_car_list──────────────────────────────────────┐
│ ≡data_base                                           │
│ typed_vehicle?: vehicles                             │
│ parts_fitted!: ℙ part_nos                            │
│ ─────────────────────────────────                    │
│ typed_vehicle? ∈ vehicles_supplied                   │
│ parts_fitted! =                                      │
│ {parts: dom in_stock | typed_vehicle? ∈ fitted_to⟦{parts}⟧} │
└──────────────────────────────────────────────────────┘
```

Success or failure in a typed query can be associated with a schema *command_condition*

```
┌─command_condition───────────────────────────────────┐
│ report!: conditions                                  │
└──────────────────────────────────────────────────────┘
```

where *report!* gives an indication of the success and failure of an event. In the schemas described above there can be two types of error. First, the number of a part typed in by a clerk would not refer to a part whose details are stored in the data base. Second, a vehicle name is typed which is not supplied by the company. These errors can be defined by the schemas *part_error* and *vehicle_error*

```
┌─part_error─────────────────────────────────────┐
│ ≡data_base                                      │
│ command_conditions                              │
│ typed_no?: part_nos                             │
├─────────────────────────────────                │
│ typed_no? ∉ dom in_stock                        │
│ report! = invalid_part_no                       │
└─────────────────────────────────────────────────┘
```

```
┌─vehicle_error──────────────────────────────────┐
│ ≡data_base                                      │
│ command_conditions                              │
│ typed_vehicle?: vehicles                         │
├─────────────────────────────────                │
│ typed_vehicle ∉ vehicles_supplied               │
│ report! = invalid_vehicle_name                  │
└─────────────────────────────────────────────────┘
```

Finally, success can be defined as

```
┌─success────────────────────────────────────────┐
│ command_conditions                              │
├─────────────────────────────────                │
│ report! = success                               │
└─────────────────────────────────────────────────┘
```

The full effect of the commands can now be defined using the logical operators ∧ and ∨.

full_list_in_stock ≙ (list_in_stock ∧ success)

full_in_stock ≙ (in_stock ∧ success) ∨ part_error

full_price_parts ≙ (price_parts ∧ success) ∨ part_error

full_supplier_parts ≙ (supplier_parts ∧ success) ∨ part_error

full_print_car_list ≙ (print_car_list ∧ success) ∨ vehicle_error.

For example, *full_in_stock* is then equivalent to the complete schema

```
┌─full_in_stock──────────────────────────────────┐
│ vehicles_supplied, vehicles_supplied': ℙ vehicles
│ supp_of_part, supp_of_part': part_nos ↔ supplier_names
│ price_of_part, price_of_part': part_nos ⇸ part_prices
│ in_stock, in_stock': part_nos ⇸ N
│ fitted_to, fitted_to': part_nos ↔ vehicles
│ substitute, substitute': part_nos ↔ part_nos
│ typed_no?: part_nos
│ stocks!: part_nos ⇸ N
│ report!: conditions
├─────────────────────────────────────────────────
│ dom supp_of_part = dom price_of_part
│ dom supp_of_part = dom in_stock
│ dom supp_of_part = dom fitted_to
│ dom substitute ⊆ dom supp_of_part
│ rng substitute ⊆ dom supp_of_part
│ dom supp_of_part' = dom price_of_part'
│ dom supp_of_part' = dom in_stock'
│ dom supp_of_part' = dom fitted_to'
│ dom substitute' ⊆ dom supp_of_part'
│ rng substitute' ⊆ dom supp_of_part'
│ vehicles_supplied' = vehicles_supplied
│ supp_of_part' = supp_of_part
│ price_of_part' = price_of_part
│ in_stock' = in_stock
│ fitted_to' = fitted_to
│ substitute' = substitute
│ (typed_no? ∈ dom in_stock
│ stocks! = ({typed_no?} ∪
│    substitute⟦{typed_no?}⟧) ◁ in_stock
│    report! = success)
│ ∨ (typed_no? ∉ dom in_stock
│    report! = invalid_part_name)
└─────────────────────────────────────────────────┘
```

12 Z specifications in action—the University of Lincoln Library System

The purpose of this chapter is to demonstrate some of the power of the schema calculus in incrementally describing a system and to describe how error-processing can be accommodated in a Z specification. The final part of the chapter describes one way of organizing a Z specification and outlines how natural language can be used in conjunction with schemas. The specification described in the chapter is for an automated system for a university library. Only selected parts of the statement of requirements are shown; for example, parts 2.8 to 2.11 dealing with requirements for microfiche hard copy are omitted.

12.1 The statement of requirements

The University of Lincoln Library

1. Background

1.1 The library
The newly established University of Lincoln has a library serving a mixed community of students and staff. Currently, the system used to administer the loan of books is manual. This statement of requirements describes the functions of a proposed computer-based system.

1.2 The users
There are two types of users of the library: staff and students. Staff users are allowed to borrow up to 20 books; student users are allowed to borrow up to 10 books. Both are registered with the library when they join the University. The library currently keeps the name and address of each user on a card file. The borrowing period for both categories of user is 30 days.

1.3   The books

The library currently contains over 200 000 books. Details of each book are kept in a card file. Each card in the file gives the book's title, its author(s), and its classification number (ISBN number).

1.4   The replacement of the manual system

The manual system is to be replaced by a computer-based system. The system will consist of a centralized minicomputer together with a series of vdus together with plastic-tape readers and a printer. This equipment will be used by library assistants and will be positioned at the library issue desk.

Each book will contain a short, detachable length of tape which will contain a unique book registration number. This tape will be used to register the borrowing and returning of books. On registration with the library, users will also be issued with a user registration card which contains the user's name, address, and a unique registration number.

1.5   The borrowing of books

Users are allowed to borrow books and also reserve books which are currently out on loan. When a book is reserved the user who requires the book is added to a list of current users awaiting the book. When the book is returned, it is not immediately placed on the shelves if it is reserved but stored safely; the user at the top of the reservation list for the book is then notified and his name removed from the list.

1.6   Missing books

Occasionally, the library is notified that a book is missing. Usually this happens when a user cannot find a book on the shelves and no record of the book being borrowed can be discovered. When this happens the name of the book is placed on a missing list.

2.   The functions of the system

The following paragraphs describe the functions of the system. It should be borne in mind that errors will occur during the exercise of these functions; for example, the tape-reader occasionally malfunctions producing spurious data. Because of this each function should be associated with comprehensive error-checking.

2.1 The registration of new users

The system should allow a library assistant to register the name and address of a new user together with that user's registration number. The latter will be extracted from a list of unused numbers periodically produced by the system (see paragraph 2.6). When the name and address of the user have been entered the user has the borrowing rights of either a member of staff or a student. On successful completion of registration the library assistant will give the user a registration card containing his name, address, and user registration number. This will be filled out by hand.

2.2 The removal of existing users

The system should also be able to remove details of a user. For example, when a student user leaves the university, he no longer has any borrowing rights. The leaving user will provide a library assistant with his registration card. The assistant will then type in the user's registration number at a vdu. All details of the user corresponding to the registration number are expunged from the system.

2.3 Changing an address or name

The system should allow the library assistant to change the address or name of a user. The user provides his registration card and the library assistant uses the vdu to type his registration number and the new address or new name.

2.4 Registering a new book.

When a new book is purchased by the library it is first given to a librarian who assigns it an ISBN number and an unused registration number. This registration number is provided by a printout which is generated by the system (see paragraph 2.5). When this process is complete the book is given to a library assistant who registers the book with the system. The assistant types in at a vdu the registration number, the ISBN number, the title, and the author.

2.5 Generating unused book registration numbers

When a book is bought by the library, it is assigned a registration number which has not yet been assigned to any other catalogued book. A command should be provided which allows a library assistant to produce a print-out of currently unused numbers. The assistant should type in the number of registration numbers required and the system will provide the numbers in ascending order. At most 1000 numbers should be provided by the system at one time. The plan for the university library envisages that there will be no more than a million books in stock. Consequently, the registration numbers should have at most six digits.

2.6 Generating unused user registration numbers

When a user registers with the library, he or she will be allocated a user registration number which has not been allocated to any other user. These will be taken from a print-out produced by the system. A command should be provided which allows a library assistant to type in the number of unused user registration numbers that are required. The system will respond by printing the numbers in ascending order. No more than a thousand numbers should be provided. It is envisaged that no more than 10 000 users will ever be registered with the library at one time. Consequently, registration numbers should have no more than four digits.

2.7 Generating microfiche hard copy (*ISBN order*)

The library keeps details of its current books on a microfiche catalogue. Part of the microfiche contains a list of all currently catalogued books arranged in ascending order of ISBN number. Every month this catalogue is photographed for microfiche reproduction. In order to provide hard copy for this process a command should be provided which would enable a library assistant to print out all the catalogued books in the library in the above order.

⋮

2.12   Notification of overdue books

Each working day a list of borrowers who have borrowed books which are overdue is prepared. The library assistant responsible for this will load the remote printer with reminder forms. The system will then print the user name, address, book title, and registration number for every overdue book on each reminder form. These forms will then be sent out to the errant users. The system should only send out one reminder form for a particular overdue book.

> ⋮

2.21   The borrowing of books

When a book is borrowed the borrower gives his registration card to the library assistant on duty. The assistant then extracts the plastic tape from the book and places it in the tape reader. The user number is then typed in. A number of errors may occur during this operation.

> If the user has borrowed the maximum number of books allowed for that category of user, then an error message should be displayed.
>
> If the system does not recognize the user, then another error message should be displayed.
>
> Occasionally, a book is borrowed which the system recognizes as being missing. This usually is a result of the book being misfiled on the library shelves. When this happens the system should display an error message. The library assistant will then notify the system that a missing book has been found (see paragraph 2.30). Unless the book is reserved, it will normally be lent to the borrower.
>
> If a book is borrowed which is recognized as being already borrowed, then the system should display an error. When this occurs the library assistant should take appropriate action. For example, the book should be kept by the library and the borrower contacted.
>
> If an attempt is made to borrow a book which is reserved, then it should be put on one side and the system should regard the book as awaiting collection by the user who has reserved it.

2.22   The return of books

When a book is returned the tape contained in the book is placed in the tape reader and the system marks the book as being on the shelves. A number of errors may occur with this operation.

> The book may not have been borrowed and may be recognized by the system as being on the shelves. A suitable error message should be displayed.
>
> The system may not recognize the reader. For example, a reader who has been de-registered may return a book for a friend. A suitable error message should be displayed.
>
> The book may be on the list of missing books. A suitable error message should be displayed. The library assistant would then inform the system that a missing book has been discovered (paragraph 2.30).

After books are returned they are stored behind the issue desk and periodically returned to the shelves. However, if a returned book is reserved by another user, then the book is put to one side and the system will mark the book as awaiting collection by the user who reserved it.

⋮

2.30   Notification of found books

At certain times during the operation of the system a book which was believed missing could be discovered. In order to inform the system about this the library assistant should be able to type in the registration number of the book and the system would then mark that book as being on the shelves. If the book is currently reserved, the system should provide a message that it is reserved and add the book to the day's reserved books.

⋮

2.35   Notification of the return of reserved books

At the end of each day a library assistant will load the remote printer with notification forms. These forms will inform each user who has reserved a book that the book has been returned that day and is awaiting collection. Each notification form requires the name and address of the user and the title and registration number of the book.

12.2 The static properties of the system

The main objects manipulated by the library system will be books. The statement of requirements outlines the fact that each book will have a unique reference number: an ISBN number, a title, and an author. The statement of requirements also details the fact that books can either be borrowed, on the shelves of the library, or missing. Details for each book can be modelled by the schema *book_details*

```
┌─book_details────────────────────────────────┐
│ has_ISBN: book_nos ↦ ISBN_nos                │
│ has_title: book_nos ↦ titles                 │
│ has_author: book_nos ↦ author_names          │
└──────────────────────────────────────────────┘
```

where *book_nos* is the set of all possible book numbers, *ISBN_nos* is the set of all possible ISBN classification numbers, *titles* is the set of all possible titles, and *author_names* is the set of all possible author names.

Example 12.1

Write down a schema which describes the invariant properties of book details.

The invariant property of book details is that each book has a title, an author, and an ISBN number. This can be described by the schema *inv_book_details*

```
┌─inv_book_details────────────────────────────┐
│ book_details                                 │
├──────────────────────────────────────────────┤
│ dom has_ISBN = dom has_title = dom has_author │
└──────────────────────────────────────────────┘
```

Changes to book details can be described by the schema $\Delta book\_details$ where

$$\Delta book\_details \triangleq inv\_book\_details' \wedge inv\_book\_details.$$

The schema $\equiv book\_$describes events which leave the book details unaffected where

$\equiv$book_details $\triangleq$

Δbook_details | tuple book_details' = tuple book_details.

The schema *book_categories* describes the fact that books can be missing, on the shelves of the library, or borrowed.

```
┌─book_categories──────────────────────────────────┐
│   borrowed_books, shelf_books, missing_books,      │
│                                                     │
│                   catalogue_books: ℙbook_nos        │
└─────────────────────────────────────────────────────┘
```

where *catalogue_books* is the set of books owned by the library, *borrowed_books* are those that the system regards as being borrowed, *missing_books* are those books that the system regards as missing, and *shelf_books* are those books which the system regards as being borrowable.

The next step is to specify the static or invariant properties of book categories. These properties must hold no matter what events occur in the library system. Although not explicitly stated in the specification, a book can only be borrowed, on the shelves, or missing. It cannot be a combination of these categories; for example, it cannot be borrowed *and* on the shelves.

Given these static properties, the schema *inv_book_categories* can be written which describes these properties.

```
┌─inv_book_categories──────────────────────────────┐
│  book_categories                                    │
├─────────────────────────────────────────────────────┤
│  borrowed_books ∪ shelf_books ∪ missing_books =     │
│     catalogue_books                                 │
│  borrowed_books ∩ shelf_books = { }                 │
│  shelf_books ∩ missing_books = { }                  │
└─────────────────────────────────────────────────────┘
```

Finally, the schemas $\Delta book\_categories$ and $\equiv book\_categories$ can be defined

Δbook_categories $\triangleq$

inv_book_categories' $\wedge$ inv_book_categories

$\equiv$book_categories $\triangleq$

[Δbook_categories | tuple categories' = tuple categories].

Books can also be overdue. This can be described by the schema *overdue*.

```
┌─ overdues ──────────────────────────────────────┐
│ overdue_books: ℙbook_nos                        │
└─────────────────────────────────────────────────┘
```

Changes to overdue books and operations which do not affect overdue books can be defined by $\Delta overdues$ and $\equiv overdues$

$\Delta overdues \triangleq overdues' \wedge overdues$

$\equiv overdues \triangleq [overdues \mid tuple\ overdues' = tuple\ overdues]$.

Given the schemas which describe book details and book categories, the part of the library system dealing with books can be specified. The schemas *books* and *inv_books* can now be defined.

```
┌─ books ─────────────────────────────────────────┐
│ book_details                                    │
│ book_categories                                 │
│ overdues                                        │
│                                                 │
└─────────────────────────────────────────────────┘
```

```
┌─ inv_books ─────────────────────────────────────┐
│ inv_book_details                                │
│ inv_book_categories                             │
│ overdues                                        │
│ ───────────────────────                         │
│ dom has_title = catalogue_books                 │
│ overdue_books ⊆ borrowed_books                  │
└─────────────────────────────────────────────────┘
```

The first predicate in *inv_books* asserts that all catalogued books have a title. Since

$$dom\ has\_ISBN = dom\ has\_title = dom\ has\_author$$

is asserted in the included schema *inv_book_details*, this implies that every catalogued book has a title, an author name, and an ISBN number $\Delta books$ and $\equiv books$ can now be specified as

$\Delta books \triangleq inv\_books' \wedge inv\_books$

$\equiv books \triangleq [\Delta books \mid tuple\ books' = tuple\ books]$.

Users of the system can be described in a similar way. There are two types of users, staff users and student users. These can be modelled by means of the schema *users*

```
┌─users─────────────────────────────────────────────────┐
│ staff, students, library_users: ℙuser_nos              │
│ address_of: user_nos ⇸ addresses                       │
│ name_of: user_nos ⇸ user_names                         │
└────────────────────────────────────────────────────────┘
```

Where *library_users* is the whole community of users of the library, *user_names* is the set of all possible user names, *addresses* is a set of all possible addresses, and *user_nos* is the set of all possible user registration numbers. *Address_of* and *name_of* are functions which relate a user to his address and name.

One invariant property of users is that, since there cannot be any other type of user, the collection of staff users and student users forms the whole user population. Another invariant property is that each user has both a name and an address.

Another possible property is that no user can be both a staff user and a student user. However, this is not explicitly stated in the statement of requirements. There is a possibility that a member of staff is studying for a higher degree *and* is registered with the University as a student. The statement of requirements does not deal with this. The originator of the statement of requirements and library staff will have to be asked how the system should deal with this. Assuming that a member of staff cannot be simultaneously a student user and a staff user, the schema describing invariant properties of users *inv_users* can be defined

---

Example 12.2

Write down the schema *inv_users*.

First, since a user can either be a member of staff or a student, the whole user population of the library will be the union of *staff* and *students*. Second, since a user cannot be both a member of staff and a student, the intersection of *staff* and *students* will be the empty set. Third, since each user has a name and an addresss, the domain of *address_of* equals the domain of *name_of*.

```
┌─inv_users─────────────────────────────────────────┐
│ users                                              │
│ ─────────────                                      │
│ staff ∪ students = library_users                   │
│ staff ∩ students = { }                             │
│ dom address_of = dom name_of = library_users       │
└────────────────────────────────────────────────────┘
```

Finally, the two schemas: Δ*users* and ≡*users* can be defined

$$\Delta \text{users} \triangleq \text{inv\_users} \wedge \text{inv\_users}'$$

$$\equiv \text{users} \triangleq [\Delta \text{users} \mid \text{tuple users}' = \text{tuple users}].$$

To complete the description of the static properties it is necessary to describe the fact that users borrow books. The fact that a user is currently borrowing a book can be described by a relation *borrows* which is over *user_nos* × *book_nos*. The fact that a book is borrowed on a certain day can be modelled by a partial function *day_borrowed* which maps book numbers into days. These can be described by the schema *borrowings*. We shall assume that *days* are natural numbers measured from some base date, for example, 1st Jan 1900.

```
┌─borrowings──────────────────────────────────┐
│ borrows: user_nos ↔ book_nos                 │
│ day_borrowed: book_nos ⇸ days                │
└──────────────────────────────────────────────┘
```

The schema *inv_borrowings* describes the fact that an invariant property of borrowings is that every book borrowed by a user is associated with a day on which it was borrowed. Also that each book can only be borrowed by one user at a time.

```
┌─inv_borrowings──────────────────────────────────────┐
│ borrowings                                           │
│ ──────────────                                       │
│ dom day_borrowed = rng borrows                       │
│ ∀u1, u2: user_nos │ {u1, u2} ⊆ dom borrows ·         │
│   borrows [[{u1}]] ∩ borrows[[{u2}]] ≠               │
│   { } ⇒ u1 = u2                                       │
└──────────────────────────────────────────────────────┘
```

The schema Δ*borrowings* which describes changes to borrowing can be described by

$$\Delta\text{borrowings} \triangleq \text{inv\_borrowings}' \wedge \text{inv\_borrowings}.$$

Any event which does not change this schema can be described by the schema ≡*borrowings* defined as

≡borrowings ≜

[Δborrowings | tuple borrowings = tuple borrowings'].

The part of the system dealing with reservations can be described by the schema *reservations*

```
┌─reservations─────────────────────────────────────┐
│ reserve_lists: book_nos ⇸ seq user_nos            │
│ day_reserve: ℙbook_nos                            │
└───────────────────────────────────────────────────┘
```

day_reserve will contain the book numbers of those books which have been reserved and returned to the library; these books will be regarded by the system as being on the shelves of the library. At the end of each day *day_reserve* will be used to notify users that reserved books await collection at the library. The invariant properties of the part of the system dealing with reservations is described by *inv_reservations*

```
┌─inv_reservations─────────────────────────────────┐
│ reservations                                      │
│ ──────────────                                    │
│ day_reserve ⊆ {b: book_nos | #(reserve_lists b) > 0} │
└───────────────────────────────────────────────────┘
```

This states that the books that are regarded as being reserved and returned will be a subset of those books which have one or more users waiting for a book.

Δ*reservations* and ≡*reservations* can then be defined as

Δreservations ≜ inv_reservations' ∧ inv_reservations

≡reservations ≜

[Δreservations | tuple reservations' = tuple reservations].

The whole library system can then be partly described by the signature *sys*.

```
┌─sys─────────────────────────────────────────────┐
│ books                                            │
│ users                                            │
│ borrowings                                       │
│ reservations                                     │
│                                                  │
└──────────────────────────────────────────────────┘
```

The invariant properties which relate objects defined in *books, borrowings, overdues, reservations,* and *users* are

> All reserved books are borrowed by other users or are missing.
>
> A student user may borrow no more than 10 books.
>
> A staff user may borrow no more than 20 books.
>
> All books taken out by users are regarded as borrowed.
>
> Each catalogued book is associated with a possibly non-empty reservation list.
>
> All borrowed books are borrowed by library users.
>
> All reserved books are reserved by library users.

There is a further property which may hold but which the statement of requirements does not address. This is the number of books that a user may reserve. Again the originator of the statement of requirements or his staff will need to be interrogated. We shall assume that the number of books reserved for any user will not be limited.

Example 12.3

Write down a schema *inv_sys* which embodies both the properties specified above and the individual invariant properties of books, users, borrowings, and reservations.

```
┌─inv_sys─────────────────────────────────────────┐
│ inv_books                                        │
│ inv_users                                        │
│ inv_borrowings                                   │
│ inv_reservations                                 │
└──────────────────────────────────────────────────┘
```

$$\{b: \text{book\_nos} \mid {}^{\#}(\text{reserve\_lists } b) > 0\} \subseteq \text{borrowed\_books}$$
$$\cup \text{ missing\_books} \cup \text{day\_reserve}$$
$$\forall \text{stu: students} \cdot {}^{\#}\text{borrows}[\![\{\text{stu}\}]\!] \leq 10$$
$$\forall \text{sta: staff} \cdot {}^{\#}\text{borrows}[\![\{\text{sta}\}]\!] \leq 20$$
$$\text{rng borrows} = \text{borrowed\_books}$$
$$\text{catalogue\_books} = \text{dom reserve\_lists}$$
$$\text{dom borrows} \subseteq \text{library\_users}$$
$$\forall \text{book: catalogue\_books} \cdot$$
$$\quad \text{rng(reserve\_lists book)} \subseteq \text{library\_users}$$
$$\text{overdue\_books} \subseteq \text{borrowed\_books}$$
$$\text{day\_reserve} \subseteq \text{shelf\_books}$$

Given the schema described in Example 12.3, the schemas Δsys and $\equiv sys$ can be defined as

$$\Delta \text{sys} \triangleq \text{inv\_sys} \wedge \text{inv\_sys}'$$

$$\equiv \text{sys} \triangleq [\Delta \text{sys} \mid \text{tuple sys}' = \text{tuple sys}].$$

Finally, a schema *exceptions* can be defined. This describes the actions that are taken when an exception to normal processing occurs, for example, when an error occurs

$$\text{exceptions} \triangleq [\equiv \text{sys; message!: error\_types}].$$

message! will have differing values when exceptions occur. It will give an indication of the type of exception that has occurred. $\equiv sys$ is used in the definition of *exceptions* because the system does not change when an error is discovered.

If a successful operation occurs, then *message* will be given the value *ok*. This is defined by the schema *success*.

┌─success───┐
│ message!: error_types   │
│ ─────────────────────   │
│ message!: = ok   │
└──┘

12.3 The operations

A large bulk of the statement of requirements is concerned with the operation of the system. It deals with commands and occurrences such as a user returning a book. This section describes how to model these by means of events and observations.

Paragraph 2.1

Paragraph 2.1 of the statement of requirements describes the registration of a new user. There is a problem with this part of the statement of requirements: how do we know whether the user exists on the system given that we only know his or her name and address? There is a high probability that a user who has the same name and address as an existing user will be that user. However, in a University there are always a large number of shared houses and halls of residence where, say, two John Smiths may live. If this occurs then the library clerk has to discover whether the potential user already exists on the system. If so, then some form of admonishment is in order. If not, then a good strategy is to modify the user's address, for example by adding a room number, in the hope of making it unique and then re-register the details.

The schema which describes the fact that a typed name and address of a user may already exist in the library system is *add_and_name_in*.

```
┌─ add_and_name_in ──────────────────────────────┐
│ addr?: addresses                               │
│ name?: user_names                              │
│ users                                          │
├────────────────────────────                    │
│ ∃usno: user_nos · address_of usno = addr? ∧    │
│                                                │
│    name_of usno = name?                        │
└────────────────────────────────────────────────┘
```

The schema *add* will partially describe the successful registration of a user into the library system. Using $\equiv$*books*, $\equiv$*reservations*, and $\equiv$*borrowings* indicates that the event described by the schema does not affect the books, borrowings, and reservations of the system.

```
┌─ add ──────────────────────────────────────────┐
│ ≡books                                         │
│ ≡borrowings                                    │
│ ≡reservations                                  │
```

```
┌─Δusers──────────────────────────────────────────────────┐
│ success                                                  │
│ user?: user_names                                        │
│ us_no?: user_nos                                         │
│ us_addr?: addresses                                      │
├──────────────────────────────────────────────────────── │
│ us_no? ∉ library_users                                   │
│ address_of' = address_of ∪ {(us_no?, us_addr?)}         │
│ name_of' = name_of ∪ {(us_no?, user?)}                  │
│ library_users' = library_users ∪ {us_no?}              │
└──────────────────────────────────────────────────────────┘
```

This can then be used in the schema *insert_staff* which describes the insertion of staff details into the library system.

```
┌─insert_staff────────────────────────────────────────────┐
│ add                                                      │
├──────────────────────────────────────────────────────── │
│ staff' = staff ∪ {us_no?}                                │
│ students' = students                                     │
└──────────────────────────────────────────────────────────┘
```

Similarly, the insertion of a student into the system can be described by the schema *insert_student*.

```
┌─insert_student──────────────────────────────────────────┐
│ add                                                      │
├──────────────────────────────────────────────────────── │
│ students' = students ∪ {us_no?}                          │
│ staff' = staff                                           │
└──────────────────────────────────────────────────────────┘
```

The error that occurs when duplicate names and addresses are discovered can be defined by the schema *existing_user*

```
┌─existing_user───────────────────────────────────────────┐
│ add_and_name_in                                          │
│ exceptions                                               │
├──────────────────────────────────────────────────────── │
│ message! = existing_user_error                           │
└──────────────────────────────────────────────────────────┘
```

A further error can occur if the library clerk has allocated a new number to the user which has already been allocated to another user. This can be described by the schema *existing_number*

```
┌─existing_number──────────────────────────────────┐
│ us_no?: user_nos                                  │
│ exceptions                                        │
├───────────────────────                            │
│ us_no? ∈ library_users                            │
│ message! = existing_number_error                  │
└───────────────────────────────────────────────────┘
```

The events that are associated with paragraph 2.1 of the specification can now be fully defined as

$$\text{insert\_staff2.1} \triangleq (\text{insert\_staff} \wedge \neg\text{add\_and\_name\_in})$$
$$\vee \text{ existing\_user} \vee \text{existing\_number}$$

$$\text{insert\_student2.1} \triangleq (\text{insert\_student} \wedge \neg\text{add\_and\_name\_in})$$
$$\vee \text{ existing\_user} \vee \text{existing\_number}.$$

Paragraph 2.2

The removal of a student or staff user can be partly described by the schema *remove*

```
┌─remove────────────────────────────────────────────┐
│ ≡borrowings                                       │
│ ≡books                                            │
│ Δusers                                            │
│ Δreservations                                     │
│ success                                           │
│ us_no?: user_nos                                  │
├───────────────────────────────────────────────────│
│ us_no? ∈ library_users                            │
│ #borrows⟦{us_no?}⟧ = 0                            │
│ ∀book: dom reserve_list ·                         │
│   reserve_list′book =                             │
│   squash(reserve_list book ▷ {us_no?})            │
│ library_users′ = library_users − {us_no?}         │
└───────────────────────────────────────────────────┘
```

For a user to be removed successfully he must be already registered with the library system and he must no longer have any books out on loan. When the user is removed, all information about the books that he has reserved should be removed from the system.

This schema can then be used in the schemas *remove_student* and *remove_staff* which describe the act of removing a student and a member of staff from the system, respectively

┌─remove_student─────────────────────────────────────┐
│ remove   │
│ ─────────────────────────   │
│ students′ = students − {us_no?}   │
│ staff′ = staff   │
└───┘

┌─remove_staff───────────────────────────────────────┐
│ remove   │
│ ─────────────────────────   │
│ staff′ = staff − {us_no?}   │
│ students′ = students   │
└───┘

One error that can occur is when the user number is not recognized by the system.

┌─invalid_us_no──────────────────────────────────────┐
│ us_no?: user_nos   │
│ exceptions   │
│ ─────────────────────────   │
│ us_no? ∉ library_users   │
│ message! = non_existent_user_error   │
└───┘

Another error occurs when the user still has books out on loan

┌─books_on_loan──────────────────────────────────────┐
│ us_no?: user_nos   │
│ exceptions   │
│ ─────────────────────────   │
│ $^{\#}$borrows⟦{us_no?}⟧ > 0   │
│ message! = books_still_borrowed_error   │
└───┘

Paragraph 2.2 can now be fully defined as

remove_student2.2 ≙ remove_student ∨

$\qquad\qquad\qquad\qquad$ invalid_us_no ∨ books_on_loan

remove_staff2.2 ≙ remove_staff ∨

$\qquad\qquad\qquad\qquad$ invalid_us_no ∨ books_on_loan.

Paragraph 2.3

This paragraph is concerned with the change of address and name of a user.

Example 12.4

Specify the effect of paragraph 2.3.

Both the operation will leave the books in the library and the objects described in *borrowings* and *reservations* unchanged. A new address or new name is supplied together with the registration number of a user. This registration number must match one stored in the library system. The schema *change* partly describes the effect of a successful change of address or change of name.

```
┌─change────────────────────────────────────────┐
│ ≡books                                         │
│ ≡borrowings                                    │
│ ≡reservations                                  │
│ Δusers                                         │
│ success                                        │
│ us_no?: user_nos                               │
│ ─────────────────────────────────             │
│ us_no? ∈ library_users                         │
└────────────────────────────────────────────────┘
```

The schemas *change_address* and *change_name* specify the effect of a successful name change and address change.

```
┌─change_name───────────────────────────────────┐
│ change                                         │
│ new_name?: user_names                          │
│ ──────────────────────────────────            │
│ name_of' = name_of ⊕ {(us_no?, new_name?)}     │
└────────────────────────────────────────────────┘
```

```
┌─change_address────────────────────────────────┐
│ change                                         │
│ new_address?: user_addresses                   │
│                                                │
│ address_of' = address_of ⊕ {(us_no?, new_address?)} │
└────────────────────────────────────────────────┘
```

The only error that can occur with these events is when an invalid user registration number is typed by the library assistant. This has already been described in the schema *invalid_us_no* which was used to describe the event associated with paragraph 2.2. Paragraph 2.3 can hence be specified as

change_name2.3 $\triangleq$ change_name $\vee$ invalid_us_no

change_address2.3 $\triangleq$ change_address $\vee$ invalid_us_no.

Paragraph 2.4

This paragraph describes the insertion of book details into the library system. The library assistant provides: an ISBN number, a book title, and a registration number. The schema *insert_book* describes this process.

$$
\begin{array}{l}
\hline
\text{insert\_book} \\
\hline
\equiv\text{users} \\
\equiv\text{borrowings} \\
\equiv\text{reservations} \\
\equiv\text{overdues} \\
\Delta\text{book\_categories} \\
\Delta\text{book\_details} \\
\text{success} \\
\text{new\_ISBN?: ISBN\_nos} \\
\text{new\_title?: titles} \\
\text{new\_book\_no?: book\_nos} \\
\text{new\_author?: author\_names} \\
\hline
\text{new\_book\_no?} \notin \text{catalogue\_books} \\
\text{has\_ISBN}' = \text{has\_ISBN} \cup \\
\quad \{\text{new\_book\_no?} \mapsto \text{new\_ISBN?}\} \\
\text{has\_title}' = \text{has\_title} \cup \\
\quad \{\text{new\_book\_no?} \mapsto \text{new\_title?}\} \\
\text{has\_author}' = \text{has\_author} \cup \\
\quad \{\text{new\_book\_no?} \mapsto \text{new\_author?}\} \\
\text{missing\_books}' = \text{missing\_books} \\
\text{borrowed\_books}' = \text{borrowed\_books} \\
\text{shelf\_books}' = \text{shelf\_books} \cup \{\text{new\_book\_no?}\} \\
\hline
\end{array}
$$

$$\text{catalogue\_books}' = \text{catalogue\_books} \cup \{\text{new\_book\_no?}\}$$

The only error that can occur when the operation is carried out is a book registration number being provided that is already in use. This can be described by the schema *invalid_book_no*

┌─invalid_book_no─────────────────────────────┐
new_book_no?
exceptions
├───┤
new_book_no? ∈ catalogue_books
message! = invalid_book_registration_number_error
└───┘

Paragraph 2.4 can then be specified as

$$\text{insert\_book2.4} \triangleq \text{insert\_book} \lor \text{invalid\_book\_no}.$$

Paragraph 2.5

The operation of generating unused registration numbers does not change the library system. It forms a sequence of book numbers which are in ascending order. The range of the sequence is a subset of those natural numbers less than a million which are not already catalogue numbers. The schema which describes the successful event that corresponds to this operation is *provide_book_nos*

┌─provide_book_nos──────────────────────────────┐
≡sys
success
no_of_book_numbers?: **N**
unused_book_numbers!: seq **N**
├───┤
no_of_book_numbers? ≤ 1000
$^{\#}\{a: \mathbf{N} \mid a < 1\,000\,000 \land a \notin \text{catalogue\_books}\} \geq$
  no_of_book_numbers?
rng unused_book_numbers! ⊆
  $\{a: \mathbf{N} \mid a < 1\,000\,000 \land a \notin \text{catalogue\_books}\}$
∀i, j: dom unused_book_numbers! ·
  $i < j \Rightarrow$ unused_book_numbers!i <
  unused_book_numbers!j
$^{\#}$unused_book_numbers! = no_of_book_numbers?
└───┘

where *no_of_book_numbers?* is the number of book registration numbers required. The first predicate states that a maximum
of 1000 book numbers are to be provided by the library assistant.
The second predicate states that the number of unused numbers
must be greater than or equal to the number requested. The
third predicate establishes the fact that they will be unused. The
fourth predicate specifies that the sequence *unused_book_
numbers!* will be in ascending order. Finally, the fifth predicate
describes the fact that the number of book registration numbers
requested will be provided.

The first error that can occur is when the library assistant types
in a request to provide more than 1000 unused registration
numbers. This can be described by the schema *invalid_no_of_
books*

```
┌─ invalid_no_of_books ──────────────────────────────┐
│ no_of_book_numbers?: N                              │
│ exceptions                                          │
├─────────────────────────────                       │
│ no_of_book_numbers? > 1000                          │
│ message! = too_many_book_nos_error                  │
└─────────────────────────────────────────────────────┘
```

The second error that can occur is when not enough unused
book numbers remain to satisfy the command

```
┌─ not_enough_book_nos ──────────────────────────────┐
│ no_of_book_numbers?                                 │
│ exceptions                                          │
├─────────────────────────────                       │
│ #{a: N | a < 1 000 000 ∧ a ∉ catalogue_books} <     │
│   no_of_book_numbers?                               │
│ message! = too_few_book_numbers_available_error     │
└─────────────────────────────────────────────────────┘
```

The effect of paragraph 2.5 can now be specified as

provide_book_nos2.5 ≙ provide_book_nos

$\qquad\qquad\qquad$ ∨ invalid_no_of_books

$\qquad\qquad\qquad$ ∨ not_enough_book_nos.

Paragraph 2.6

This paragraph is similar to paragraph 2.5. Consequently, the
schemas will be similar.

Example 12.5

Specify the event described by paragraph 2.6 of the statement of requirements.

The event that occurs when unused user registration numbers are produced is described by the schema *provide_user_nos*

```
provide_user_nos_____
≡sys
success
no_of_user_numbers?: N
unused_user_numbers!: seq N
_____
no_of_user_numbers? ≤ 1000
#{a: N | a < 10 000 ∧ a ∉ library_users} ≥
   no_of_user_numbers?
rng unused_user_numbers! ⊆
   {a: N | a < 10 000 ∧ a ∉ library_users}
∀i, j: dom unused_user_numbers! ·
   i < j ⇒ unused_user_numbers!i <
   unused_user_numbers!j
#unused_user_numbers! = no_of_user_numbers?
```

The first error associated with this event occurs when the library assistant requests more than 1000 unused user numbers

```
invalid_no_of_users_____
no_of_user_numbers?: N
exceptions
_____
no_of_user_numbers? > 1000
message! = too_many_user_nos
```

The second error occurs when not enough user numbers are available to satisfy the request

```
not_enough_user_nos_____
no_of_user_numbers?: N
exceptions
_____
```

$\#\{a\colon \mathbf{N} \mid a < 10\,000 \land a \notin \text{library\_users}\} <$
no_of_user_numbers?
message! = too_few_user_numbers_available_error

Paragraph 2.6 can then be fully specified as

Provide_user_nos2.6 $\triangleq$ provide_user_nos

$\lor$ invalid_no_of_users

$\lor$ not_enough_user_nos.

Paragraph 2.7

This part of the statement of requirements implies that an ordering of entries for the microfiche hard copy is required. This means that a sequence has to be used to model the individual entries in the catalogue. These elements can be described by the schema *microfiche_elements*

```
┌─ microfiche_elements ──────────────────────┐
│ isbn: ISBN_nos                              │
│ titl: titles                                │
│ auth: author_names                          │
│ book: book_nos                              │
│ books                                       │
├─────────────────────────────────────────────┤
│ book ∈ catalogue_books                      │
│ isbn = has_ISBN book                        │
│ titl = has_title book                       │
│ auth = has_author book                      │
└─────────────────────────────────────────────┘
```

The set from which elements of the microfiche sequence are taken is then defined by

microfiche_entries =

$\{\text{microfiche\_elements} \cdot (\text{book}, \text{isbn}, \text{titl}, \text{auth})\}.$

The microfiche catalogue can be modelled by a sequence of elements which can be described by *microfiche_entries*. The effect of constructing the hard copy for the catalogue can be specified by the schema *form_microfiche*.

```
form_microfiche
≡sys
success
microfiche_copy!: seq microfiche_entries

rng microfiche_copy! = microfiche_entries
∀j, k: dom microfiche_copy! ·
    j < k ⇒ λ isbn microfiche_copy!
    j < λ isbn microfiche_copy! k
```

The predicate on the first line states that all the items in the microfiche hard copy will represent books which are in the library catalogue. The predicate written on the second and third lines describes the ordering outlined in paragraph 2.7. There will be no errors associated with this event. In this predicate the projection function *isbn* is used to extract elements from the tuples which make up the range of the sequence *microfiche_ copy!*.

Paragraph 2.12

The event described by paragraph 2.12 produces a list of reminders for all those library books which are overdue. Apart from the overdue books, it does not affect the library system. The statement of requirements does not specify any ordering of the reminder list; therefore, a set is chosen to represent it. The schema *form_overdue_list* describes the successful execution of this event. *day?* is the day on which the event occurs.

```
form_overdue_list
≡users
≡reservations
≡borrowings
≡book_details
≡book_categories
Δoverdues
success
books_found_overdue: ℙbook_nos
day?: days
overduereminders!:
    ℙ(usernames × addresses × titles × booknos)
```

$$books\_found\_overdue = \{no: book\_nos \mid no \in borrowed\_books$$
$$\wedge \; day? > day\_borrowed \; no + 30$$
$$\wedge \; no \notin overdue\_books\}$$

$$overdue\_reminders! = \{u: user\_names; \; a: addresses;$$
$$t: titles; \; b: book\_nos \mid$$
$$b \in books\_found\_overdue \; \wedge$$
$$u = name\_of \; borrows^{-1}[\![\{b\}]\!] \; \wedge$$
$$a = address\_of \; borrows^{-1}[\![\{b\}]\!] \; \wedge$$
$$t = has\_title \; b\}$$

$$overdue\_books' =$$
$$overdue\_books \cup books\_found\_overdue$$

No errors are associated with this event.

Paragraph 2.21

The successful borrowing of a book can be described as the schema *book_borrowed*.

```
┌─ book_borrowed ────────────────────────────────────────┐
│ ≡users                                                  │
│ ≡reservations                                           │
│ ≡book_details                                           │
│ ≡overdues                                               │
│ Δbook_categories                                        │
│ Δborrowings                                             │
│ success                                                 │
│ day?: days                                              │
│ us_no?: user_nos                                        │
│ book_no?: book_nos                                      │
├─────────────────────────────────────────────────────────┤
│ us_no? ∈ library_users                                  │
│ book_no? ∈ shelf_books                                  │
│ #(reserve_lists book_no?) = 0                           │
│ us_no? ∈ staff ⇒ #(borrows[[{us_no?}]]) < 20            │
│ us_no? ∈ students ⇒ #(borrows[[{us_no?}]]) < 10         │
│ shelf_books' = shelf_books − {book_no?}                 │
│ borrowed_books' = borrowed_books ∪ {books_no?}          │
└─────────────────────────────────────────────────────────┘
```

missing_books' = missing_books
catalogue_books' = catalogue_books
day_borrowed' = day_borrowed ∪
  {book_no? ↦ day?}
borrows' = borrows ∪ {us_no? ↦ book_no?}

For this event to occur successfully the user must be a registered library user, the book must be on the shelves, no user must have reserved the book to be borrowed, and the user must have borrowed less than his limit.

There are a number of errors associated with the borrowing of a book. First, the user may not be recognized by the system. This has already been described by the schema *invalid_us_no* which was used to describe paragraph 2.2 of the statement of requirements. Second, a borrower could have borrowed his limit of books

---

too_many_books_____
exceptions
us_no?: user_nos
_____
(us_no? ∈ staff ∧ $^{\#}$(borrows⟦{us_no?}⟧) = 20 ⇒
message! = staff_over_limit_error) ∨
(us_no? ∈ students ∧ $^{\#}$(borrows⟦{us_no?}⟧) = 10 ⇒
message! = student_over_limit_error)

Third, a book could already have been borrowed

---

already_borrowed_____
exceptions
book_no?: book_nos
_____
book_no? ∈ borrowed_books
message! = book_borrowed_error

Fourth, a book could be missing

---

missing_book_____
exceptions
book_no?: book_nos

> book_no? ∈ missing_books
> message! = book_missing_error

Fifth, a book could be reserved. In this case a message will be displayed, the book put to one side, and the book marked as awaiting collection. This can be described by the schema *book_reserved*

```
┌─book_reserved────────────────────────────────────┐
│ ≡books                                            │
│ ≡users                                            │
│ ≡borrowings                                       │
│ Δreservations                                     │
│ message!: error_types                             │
│ book_no?: book_nos                                │
├───────────────────────────────────────────────────┤
│ #(reserve_lists book_no?) > 0                     │
│ day_reserve' = day_reserve ∪ {book_no?}           │
│ shelf_books' = shelf_books ∪ {book_no?}           │
│ message! = book_already_reserved                  │
└───────────────────────────────────────────────────┘
```

Paragraph 2.21 can now be fully specified as

book_borrowed2.21 ≜ book_borrowed ∨ invalid_us_no

$\qquad\qquad\qquad\qquad\qquad$ ∨ too_many_books

$\qquad\qquad\qquad\qquad\qquad$ ∨ already_borrowed

$\qquad\qquad\qquad\qquad\qquad$ ∨ missing_book

Paragraph 2.22 $\qquad\qquad\qquad$ ∨ book_reserved.

The successful return of a book can be described by the schema *book_returned*

```
┌─book_returned────────────────────────────────────┐
│ ≡users                                            │
│ ≡book_details                                     │
│ ≡reservations                                     │
│ ≡overdues                                         │
│ Δbook_categories                                  │
│ Δborrowings                                       │
│ success                                           │
```

us_no?: user_nos
book_no?: book_nos

$^{\#}$(reserve_lists book_no?) = 0
us_no? ∈ library_users
book_no? ∈ borrowed_books
book_no? ∉ overdue_books
(us_no?, book_no?) ∈ borrows
borrowed_books' = borrowed_books − {book_no?}
shelf_books' = shelf_books ∪ {books_no?}
missing_books' = missing_books
catalogue_books' = catalogue_books
day_borrowed' = {book_no?} ⊲ day_borrowed
borrows' = borrows ▷ {book_no?}

The first five predicates establish the conditions that are to be true if a successful book return occurs. The first predicate states that the book must not be reserved; the second predicate states that the user must be a recognized library user; the third predicate states that the book must have been borrowed; the fourth predicate states that the book must not be overdue; finally, the fifth predicates states that the user returning the book must be the user who borrowed the book.

The sixth and seventh predicates establish the fact that the book is no longer borrowed and is on the shelves. The eighth and ninth predicates establish the fact that a successful borrowing does not affect the list of missing books and catalogued books. The tenth and eleventh predicates remove any trace of the fact that a book has been borrowed.

The first exception that is associated with the event occurs when the book returned is regarded by the system as being on the shelves of the library. This might occur when a library assistant forgot to notify the system when the book was borrowed

---
book_on_shelves
exceptions
book_no?

---

book_no? ∈ shelf_books
message! = not_borrowed_book_error

Second, the book may be regarded by the system as missing. This is described by the schema *missing_book* already defined in connection with paragraph 2.21. Third, the user registration number may not be recognized by the system. This is described by the schema *invalid_us_no* described in connection with paragraph 2.2, and *book_reserved* defined in connection with paragraph 2.21. Fourth, the user who returns a book may not be the user who borrowed the book. A message should be displayed for this and the library assistant should take an appropriate action. For example, finding out who actually borrowed the book and keying in the correct user registration number. This exception can be described by the schema *wrong_borrower*

```
wrong_borrower_____
us_no?: user_nos
book_no?: book_nos
exceptions
_____
(us_no?, book_no?) ∉ borrows
message! = wrong_borrower_error
```

Another important exception that can occur is a book being returned which is overdue. This can be specified by the schema overdue_book

```
overdue_book_____
≡users
≡book_details
≡borrowings
≡reservations
≡book_categories
Δoverdues
book_no?: book_nos
_____
book_no? ∈ overdue_books
overdue_books' = overdue_books − {book_no?}
message! = book_overdue_error
```

The library assistant will normally fine the borrower and then inform the system that the book has been returned. The event of returning a book can now be fully specified as

$$book\_returned2.22 \triangleq book\_returned \lor book\_on\_shelves$$
$$\lor book\_missing$$
$$\lor invalid\_us\_no$$
$$\lor book\_reserved$$
$$\lor wrong\_borrower$$
$$\lor overdue\_book.$$

Paragraph 2.30

Paragraph 2.30 is relatively easy to specify. The successful operation of notifying the system that a missing book has been found is described by the schema *notify_found_book*

```
┌─notify_found_book─────────────────────────────────┐
│ ≡users                                            │
│ ≡borrowings                                       │
│ ≡reservations                                     │
│ ≡book_details                                     │
│ ≡borrowings                                       │
│ Δbook_categories                                  │
│ book_no?: book_nos                                │
├───────────────────────                            │
│ book_no? ∈ missing_books                          │
│ #(reserve_lists book_no?) = 0                     │
│ shelf_books' = shelf_books ∪ {book_no?}           │
│ missing_books' = missing_books − {book_no?}       │
│ catalogue_books' = catalogue_books                │
│ borrowed_books' = borrowed_books                  │
└───────────────────────────────────────────────────┘
```

Example 12.6

What errors can occur when a library assistant notifies the system that a missing book has been found?

Two errors can occur: the book could already be marked as on the library shelves or it could be marked as borrowed.

The errors described in Example 12.6 can be described by the schemas, *shelf_book_found* and *borrowed_book_found*

```
┌─shelf_book_found─────────────────────────────────┐
│ exceptions                                        │
│ book_no?: book_nos                                │
│ ────────────────────────                          │
│ book_no? ∈ shelf_books                            │
│ message! = book_already_on_shelves                │
└───────────────────────────────────────────────────┘
```

```
┌─borrowed_book_found──────────────────────────────┐
│ exceptions                                        │
│ book_no?: book_nos                                │
│ ────────────────────────                          │
│ book_no? ∈ borrowed_books                         │
│ message! = book_already_borrowed                  │
└───────────────────────────────────────────────────┘
```

The missing book could be reserved for a user. In this case the library assistant should keep the book and the system notified. This can be achieved by the schema *book_reserved* described on page 314. The event of notifying a missing book can now be fully specified as

notify_found_book2.30 ≜

        notify_found_book ∨ shelf_book_found ∨

        borrowed_book_found ∨ book_reserved.

Paragraph 2.35

The successful completion of the event which describes the sending out of notification letters at the end of the working day is described by the schema *notification_return*

```
┌─notification_return──────────────────────────────┐
│ ≡book_details                                     │
│ ≡users                                            │
│ ≡borrowings                                       │
│ ≡book_categories                                  │
│ Δreservations                                     │
│ notifications!:                                   │
│     ℙ(user_names × addresses × titles × books_nos)│
└───────────────────────────────────────────────────┘
```

notifications! = {u: user_names; a: addresses; t: titles;

b: book_nos | $b \in$ day_reserve $\wedge$ t

= has_title $b \wedge a$

= address_of borrows$^{-1}[\![\{b\}]\!] \wedge u$

= name_of borrows$^{-1}[\![\{b\}]\!]$}

day_reserve$'$ = { }

$\forall$book: day_reserve. reserve_lists$'$ book =
tail reserve_lists book

The first predicate describes the set of all notifications to users. The second predicate describes the fact that at the end of the day the list of reserved books is cleared. The third predicate states that after the operation has been successfully completed all the queues for those books in the *day_reserve* set will have their first element removed.

12.4 Presenting a Z specification

The previous section detailed how Z schemas are devised for one application; the order of presentation was dictated by teaching considerations. This section provides some rules and tips for organizing a Z specification for presentation as a full project document.

A Z specification will consist of a number of objects which are to be manipulated, for example, books, users, radars, monitors, etc. The order in which a Z specification should be presented is

1. Given sets which are used in the specification.

2. For each type of object that is to be manipulated, inv, Δ, and $\equiv$ schemas should be defined.

3. Composite schemas which combine the schemas defined in the previous section should then be defined, together with the Δ and $\equiv$ schemas which define events on the composite schemas.

4. Schemas which describe the operations on the system should then be defined. They should be arranged in subsections which are related by the fact that they operate on one type of object. For example, in the library system

used in this chapter all schemas which represent operations on books should be grouped together. The schemas should be presented with any schemas which describe any errors or exceptions that occur.

It is important to point out that each schema should have associated with it a natural-language translation. This is important because the customer will refer to the Z specification during the validation process. It is clearly unreasonable to expect him to understand the mathematics involved. However, the natural-language commentary should only be regarded as supplementary to that presented in the schemas. It takes on the role of comments in a computer program.

If the Z specification described in the first three sections of this chapter were to be laid out using these informal rules, the first section of the Z document embodying this specification would include the list of all basic sets involved. It would start with

---

Given sets

titles is the set of all possible book titles.

ISBN_nos is the set of all possible ISBN category numbers.

author_names is the set of all possible author names.

book_nos = {1..999999}.

error_types = {existing_user_error,
    existing_number_error, invalid_us_no_error . . .

Since it is difficult to specify the exact nature of some sets it is allowable to describe them with statements such as: 'author_names is the set of all possible author names'. However, where it is possible to be exact about membership of a set you should be. For example, it is clear in the specification that the number of users of the library will not exceed 10 000. Hence the statement, user_nos = {1..9999}, can be written.

The next section of a Z document should deal with the objects that are to be described in the specification in the system. For example, the library system would start with the section 'Objects'.

Objects

```
┌─book_details──────────────────────────────┐
│ has_ISBN: book_nos ⤖ ISBN_nos             │
│ has_title: book_nos ⤖ titles              │
│ has_author: book_nos ⤖ author_names       │
└───────────────────────────────────────────┘
```

```
┌─inv_book_details──────────────────────────┐
│ book_details                              │
│───────────────────────────────────────────│
│ dom has_ISBN = dom has_title = dom has_author │
└───────────────────────────────────────────┘
```

A book has one ISBN number and one title and one author.

Δbook_details $\triangleq$ inv_book_details$'$ $\wedge$ inv_book_details

$\equiv$ book_details $\triangleq$ Δbook_details | tuple book_details$'$

= tuple book_details.

```
┌─book_categories───────────────────────────┐
│ borrowed_books, shelf_books, missing_books,│
│   catalogue_books: ℙbook_nos              │
└───────────────────────────────────────────┘
```

A book can be categorized as borrowed, missing, or on the shelves. The whole collection of books is in a catalogue.

```
┌─inv_book_categories───────────────────────┐
│ book_categories                           │
│───────────────────────────────────────────│
│ borrowed_books ∪ shelf_books ∪ missing_books = │
│ catalogue_books                           │
│ borrowed_books ∩ shelf_books ∩ missing_books = { } │
└───────────────────────────────────────────┘
```

The combined collection of books that are borrowed, books that are on the shelves, and missing books will appear in the main library catalogue. A book can only be regarded by the system as borrowed, on the shelves of the library, or missing. It cannot be regarded as a combination of any of these categories; for example, a book cannot be missing and on the shelves of the library. All catalogued books will have a title.

Δbooks $\triangleq$ inv_books $\wedge$ inv_books$'$

$\equiv$books $\triangleq$ [Δbooks | tuple books$'$ = tuple books].

The Z specification document will then contain schemas which describe users, borrowings, etc. This section of the library system specification will start as:

```
┌─sys─────────────────────────────────────────
│ books
│ users
│ borrowings
│ reservations
└─────────────────────────────────────────────
```

The library system will consist of books, users, information about reservations, and information about borrowings

```
┌─inv_sys─────────────────────────────────────
│ inv_books
│ inv_users
│ inv_borrowings
│ inv_reservations
├─────────────────────────────────────────────
│ {b: book_nos | #(reserve_lists b) > 0} ⊆
│     borrowed_books
│     ∪ missing_books ∪ day_reserve
│ ∀stu: students · #borrows⟦{stu}⟧ ≤ 10
│ ∀sta: staff · #borrows⟦{sta}⟧ ≤ 20
│ rng borrows = borrowed_books
│ catalogue_books = dom reserve_lists
│ dom borrows ⊆ library_users
│ ∀book: catalogue_books ·
│     rng(reserve_lists book) ⊆ library_users
```

overdue_books ⊆ borrowed_books
day_reserve ⊆ shelf_books

Reserved books can be currently missing or out on loan. Students are not allowed to borrow more than 10 books and staff are not allowed to borrow more than 20 books. Each borrowed book is borrowed on a particular day. Only books in the library catalogue can be reserved. Only registered library users are allowed to borrow books and reserve books. Books are only regarded as overdue if they have been borrowed. The books kept in the day reserve section of the library are regarded as being on the shelves.

$$\Delta\text{sys} \triangleq \text{inv\_sys} \wedge \text{inv\_sys}'$$

$$\equiv\text{sys} \triangleq [\Delta\text{sys} \mid \text{tuple sys}' = \text{tuple sys}].$$

The next section of a Z specification document should detail the operations on the system. The extract below is taken from part of the document dealing with the generation of unused book registration numbers

provide_book_nos
≡sys
success
no_of_book_numbers?: **N**
unused_book_numbers!: seq **N**

no_of_book_numbers? ≤ 1000
$^\#\{a: \mathbf{N} \mid a < 1\,000\,000 \wedge a \notin \text{catalogue\_books}\} \geq$
  no_of_book_numbers?
rng unused_book_numbers! ⊆
  $\{a: \mathbf{N} \mid a < 1\,000\,000 \wedge a \notin \text{catalogue\_books}\}$
$\forall i, j$: dom unused_book_numbers · $i < j \Rightarrow$
  unused_book_numbers! $i <$ unused_book_numbers! j
$^\#$unused_book_numbers! = no_of_book_numbers?

The operation of generating unused book registration numbers is carried out by a library assistant who provides the number of numbers to be generated. When successfully carried out this operation does not affect the library system. It provides the number of book numbers required. For this operation to be successful the number of numbers will be less than 1000, enough numbers should be available to satisfy the request, and they will not have been allocated to books in the library catalogue. The numbers will be printed out in ascending numerical order.

---

invalid_no_of_books
no_of_book_numbers?: $\mathbb{N}$
exceptions

---

no_of_book_numbers? > 1000
message! = too_many_book_nos

---

not_enough_book_nos
no_of_book_numbers?
exceptions

$\#\{a: \mathbb{N} \mid a < 1\,000\,000 \land a \notin \text{catalogue\_books}\} <$
  no_of_book_numbers?
message! = too_few_book_numbers_available_error

$$\text{Provide\_book\_nos2.5} \triangleq \text{provide\_book\_nos}$$
$$\lor \text{invalid\_no\_of\_books}$$
$$\lor \text{not\_enough\_book\_nos}.$$

Two errors can occur. The first is when an invalid number of required book numbers is provided. The second is when not enough unused book numbers are available.

12.5 Postscript

This section of the book has been an introduction to the Z notation. It has introduced about 80 per cent of the facilities of the language. The interested reader who wishes to examine other specifications of systems would be advised to read Sufrin and Morgan (1984) which contains a specification of the UNIX file system and Flinn (1986) which describes the use of Z in specifying a conference booking system. A full specification of Z can be found as an appendix to Flinn (1986).

Appendix: Definition of Z operators

This appendix contains a full specification of the Z operators found in the text of this book.

A.1 Mathematical notation

A.1.1 Definitions and declarations

Let x, x_k be identifiers and let T, T_k be sets.

LHS $\triangleq$ RHS	Definition of LHS as syntactically equivalent to RHS.
$x: T$	Declaration of x as type T.

$x_1: T_1; x_2: T_2; \ldots ; x_n: T_n$
          List of declarations.

$x_1, x_2, \ldots , x_n: T \triangleq x_1: T; x_2: T; \ldots ; x_n: T.$

$[A, B]$	Introduction of generic sets.

A.1.2 Logic

Let P, Q be predicates and let D be a declaration.

true, false	Logical constants.
$\neg P$	Negation: 'not P'.
$P \wedge Q$	Conjunction: 'P and Q'.
$P \vee Q$	Disjunction: 'P or Q'.
$P \Rightarrow Q$	Implication: 'P implies Q' or 'if P then Q'.
$P \Leftrightarrow Q$	Equivalence: 'P is logically equivalent to Q'.
$P \rightarrow Q, R$	Conditional: 'if P then Q else R'; $(P \rightarrow Q, R) \Leftrightarrow ((P \Rightarrow Q) \wedge (\neg P \Rightarrow R))$.
$\forall x: T \cdot P$	Universal quantification: 'for all x of type T, P holds'.

$\exists x: T \cdot P$ Existential quantification: 'there exists an x of type T such that P'.

$\exists!x: T \cdot P_x$ Unique existence: 'there exists a unique x of type T such that P'.
$\triangleq (\exists x: T \cdot P_x \wedge \neg(\exists y: T, y \neq x \cdot P_y))$

$\forall x_1: T_1; x_2: T_1; \ldots; x_n: T_n \cdot P$
'For all x_1 of type T_1, x_2 of type T_2, $\ldots$, and x_n of type T_n, P holds'.

$\exists x_1: T_1; x_2: T_2; \ldots; x_n: T_n \cdot P$
Similar to $\forall$.

$\exists!x_1: T_1; x_2: T_2; \ldots; x_n: T_n \cdot P$
Similar to $\forall$.

$\forall D \mid P \cdot Q \triangleq (\forall D \cdot P \Rightarrow Q)$.
$\exists D \mid P \cdot Q \triangleq (\exists D \cdot P \wedge Q)$.
$t_1 = t_2$ Equality between terms.
$t_1 \neq t_2$ $\triangleq \neg(t_1 = t_2)$.

A.1.3 Sets

Let S, T, and X be sets; t, t_k terms; P a predicate; and D declarations.

$t \in S$ Set membership: 't is an element of S'.
$t \notin S$ $\triangleq \neg(t \in S)$.
$S \subseteq T$ Set inclusion:
               $\triangleq (\forall x: S \cdot x \in T)$.
$S \subset T$ Strict set inclusion:
               $\triangleq S \subseteq T \wedge S \neq T$.
$\{\}$ The empty set.

$\{t_1, t_2, \ldots, t_n\}$ The set containing $t_1, t_2, \ldots$ and t_n.

$\{x: T \mid P\}$ The set containing exactly those x of type T for which P holds.

$(t_1, t_2, \ldots, t_n)$ Ordered n tuple of $t_1, t_2, \ldots$ and t_n.

$T_1 \times T_2 \times \ldots \times T_n$
Cartesian product: the set of all n tuples such that the kth component is of type T_k.

$\{x_1: T_1; x_2: T_2; \ldots; x_n: T_n \mid P\}$

> The set of n tuples $(x_1, x_2, \ldots, x_n)$ with each x_k of type T_k such that P holds.

$\{D \mid P \cdot t\}$	The set of t's such that, given the declarations D, P holds.
$\{D \cdot t\}$	$\triangleq \{D \mid \text{true} \cdot t\}$.
$\mathbb{P}S$	Power set: the set of all subsets of S.
$\mathbb{F}S$	Set of finite subsets of S: $\triangleq \{T: \mathbb{P}S \mid T \text{ is finite}\}$
$S \cap T$	Set intersection: given S, $T: \mathbb{P}X$, $\triangleq \{x: X \mid x \in S \wedge x \in T\}$.
$S \cup T$	Set union: given S, $T: \mathbb{P}X$, $\triangleq \{x: X \mid x \in S \vee x \in T\}$.
$S - T$	Set difference: given S, $T: \mathbb{P}X$, $\triangleq \{x: X \mid x \in S \wedge x \notin T\}$.
$\bigcap SS$	Generalized set intersection: given $SS: \mathbb{P}(\mathbb{P}X)$, $\triangleq \{x: X \mid (\forall S: SS \cdot x \in S)\}$.
$\bigcup SS$	Generalized set union: given $SS: \mathbb{P}(\mathbb{P}X)$, $\triangleq \{x: X \mid (\exists S: SS \cdot x \in S)\}$.
$^{\#}S$	Cardinality (number of distinct elements) of a finite set.
$\mid S \mid$	$\triangleq {}^{\#}S$.

A.1.4 Numbers

N	The set of natural numbers (non-negative integers).
N_1	The set of strictly positive natural numbers: $\triangleq \mathbf{N} - \{0\}$.
$\mathbf{Z}$	The set of integers (positive, zero, and negative).
$m..n$	The set of integers between m and n inclusive: $\triangleq \{k: \mathbf{Z} \mid m \leq k \wedge k \leq n\}$.
min S	Minimum of a set; for $S: \mathbb{F}\mathbf{N} \mid S \neq \{\}$, min $S \in S \wedge (\forall x: S \cdot x \geq \text{min } S)$.
max S	Maximum of a set; for $S: \mathbb{F}\mathbf{N} \mid S \neq \{\}$, max $S \in S \wedge (\forall x: S \cdot x \leq \text{max } S)$.

A.1.5 Relations

A relation is modelled by a set of ordered pairs; hence operators defined for sets can be used on relations.

Let X, Y, and Z be sets; $x: X; y: Y$; and $R: X \leftrightarrow Y$.

$X \leftrightarrow Y$	The set of relations from X to Y: $\triangleq \mathbb{P}(X \times Y)$.
xRy	x is related by R to y: $\triangleq (x, y) \in R$.
$x \mapsto y$	$\triangleq (x, y)$
$\{x_1 \mapsto y_1, x_2 \mapsto y_2, \ldots, x_n \mapsto y_n\}$	
	The relation $\{(x_1, y_1), \ldots, (x_n, y_n)\}$ relating x_1 to y_1, $\ldots$, and x_n to y_n.
dom R	The domain of a relation: $\triangleq \{x: X \mid (\exists y: Y \cdot xRy)\}$.
rng R	The range of a relation: $\triangleq \{y: Y \mid (\exists x: X \cdot xRy)\}$.
$R_1; R_2$	Forward relational composition: given $R_1: X \leftrightarrow Y$; $R_2: Y \leftrightarrow Z$, $\triangleq \{x: X; z: Z \mid (\exists y: Y \cdot xR_1 y \wedge yR_2 z)\}$.
$R_1 \circ R_2$	Relational composition: $\triangleq R_2; R_1$.
R^{-1}	Inverse of relation R: $\triangleq \{y: Y; x: X \mid xRy\}$.
$id\ X$	Identity function on the set X: $\triangleq \{x: X \cdot x \mapsto x\}$.
R^k	The relation R composed with itself k times: given $R: X \leftrightarrow X$, $R^0 \triangleq id\ X$, $R^{k+1} \triangleq R^k \circ R$.
R^*	Reflexive transitive closure: $\triangleq \bigcup\{n: \mathbf{N} \cdot R^n\}$.

R^+	Non-reflexive transitive closure: $\triangleq \bigcup\{n: N_1 \cdot R^n\}$.
$R[\![S]\!]$	Image: given $S: \mathbb{P}X$, $\triangleq \{y: Y \mid (\exists x: S \cdot xRy)\}$.
$S \lhd R$	Domain restriction to S: given $S: \mathbb{P}X$, $\triangleq \{x: X; y: Y \mid x \in S \wedge xRy\}$.
$S \lhd\!\!\!- R$	Domain subtraction: given $S: \mathbb{P}X$, $\triangleq (X - S) \lhd R$.
$R \rhd T$	Range restriction to T: given $T: \mathbb{P}Y$, $\triangleq \{x: X; y: Y \mid xRy \wedge y \in T\}$.
$R -\!\!\!\rhd T$	Range subtraction of T: given $T: \mathbb{P}Y$, $\triangleq R \rhd (Y - T)$.
$R_1 \oplus R_2$	Overriding: given $R_1, R_2: X \leftrightarrow Y$, $\triangleq (\mathrm{dom}\, R_2 \lhd\!\!\!- R_1) \cup R_2$.

A.1.6 *Functions*

A function is a relation with the property that for each element in its domain there is a unique element in its range related to it. As functions are relations, all the operators defined above for relations also apply to functions.

$X \nrightarrow Y$	The set of partial functions from X to Y: $\triangleq \{f: X \leftrightarrow Y \mid (\forall x: \mathrm{dom}\, f \cdot (\exists! y: Y \cdot xfy))\}$.
$X \rightarrow Y$	The set of total functions from X to Y: $\triangleq \{f: X \nrightarrow Y \mid \mathrm{dom}\, f = X\}$.
$X \rightarrowtail\!\!\!\!\!\!\cdot\, Y$	The set of one-to-one partial functions from X to Y: $\triangleq \{f: X \nrightarrow Y \mid (\forall y: \mathrm{rng}\, f \cdot (\exists! x: X \cdot xfy))\}$.
$X \rightarrowtail Y$	The set of one-to-one total functions from X to Y: $\triangleq \{f: X \rightarrowtail\!\!\!\!\!\!\cdot\, Y \mid \mathrm{dom}\, f = X\}$.
$X \nrightarrow\!\!\!\!\!+ Y$	The set of finite partial functions from X to Y. $\triangleq \{f: X \nrightarrow Y \mid f \in \mathbb{F}(X \times Y)\}$.

$f\,t$ The function f applied to t.

$(\lambda x\colon X \mid P \cdot t)$ Lambda-abstraction: the function that, given an argument x of type X such that P holds, the result is t.
$\triangleq \{x\colon X \mid P \cdot x \mapsto t\}$.

$(\lambda x_1\colon T_1; \ldots ; x_n\colon T_n \mid P \cdot t)$
$\triangleq \{x_1\colon T_1; \ldots ; x_n\colon T_n \mid P \cdot (x_1, \ldots, x_n) \mapsto t\}$.

A.1.7 Orders

partial_order X The set of partial orders on X.
$\triangleq \{R\colon X \leftrightarrow X \mid \forall x, y, z\colon X \cdot xRx \wedge$
$\qquad\qquad\qquad\qquad xRy \wedge yRx \Rightarrow x = y \wedge$
$\qquad\qquad\qquad\qquad xRy \wedge yRz \Rightarrow xRz$
$\qquad\qquad\}$.

total_order X The set of total orders on X.
$\triangleq \{R\colon \text{partial\_order } X \mid \forall x, y\colon X \cdot xRy \vee yRx\}$.

monotonic $X <_x$ The set of functions from X to X that are monotonic with respect to the order $<_x$ on X.
$\triangleq \{f\colon X \nrightarrow X \mid (\forall x, y\colon X \cdot x <_x y \Rightarrow f(x) <_x f(y))\}$.

A.1.8 Sequences

seq X The set of sequences whose elements are drawn from X:
$\triangleq \{A\colon N_1 \nrightarrow X \mid (\exists n\colon \mathbf{N} \cdot \mathrm{dom}\,A = 1..n)\}$.

$\#A$ The length of sequence A.
$[\,]$ The empty sequence $\{\,\}$.

$[a_1, \ldots, a_n]$ $\triangleq \{1 \mapsto a_1, \ldots, n \mapsto a_n\}$.

$[a_1, \ldots, a_n]^\frown[b_1, \ldots, b_m]$
       Concatenation: $\triangleq [a_1, \ldots, a_n, b_1, \ldots, b_m]$,
$[\,]^\frown A = A^\frown[\,] = A$.

head A The first element of a non-empty sequence:
$A \neq [\,] \Rightarrow \text{head } A = A(1)$.

last A The final element of a non-empty sequence:
$$A \neq [\,] \Rightarrow \text{last } A = A(\#A).$$

tail A All but the head of a sequence: $\text{tail}([x]^\frown A) = A.$

front A All but the last of a sequence: $\text{front }(A^\frown[x]) = A.$

rev $[a_1, a_2, \ldots, a_n]$

Reverse:
$$\triangleq [a_n, \ldots, a_2, a_1],$$
$$\text{rev}\,[\,] = [\,].$$

$^\frown/AA$ Distributed concatenation: gives AA: $\text{seq}(\text{seq}(X))$,
$$\triangleq AA(1)^\frown \ldots {}^\frown AA(\#AA),$$
$$^\frown/[\,] = [\,].$$

$;/AR$ Distributed relational composition: given
AR: $\text{seq}(X \leftrightarrow X)$,
$$\triangleq AR(1); \ldots; AR(\#AR),$$
$$;/[\,] = \text{id } X.$$

disjoint AS Pairwise disjoint: given AS: $\text{seq}(\mathbb{P}X)$,
$$\triangleq (\forall i, j\colon \text{dom } AS \cdot i \neq j \Rightarrow AS(i) \cap AS(j) = \{\}).$$

AS **partitions** S $\triangleq$ disjoint $AS \wedge \bigcup \text{rng } AS = S.$

A **in** B Contiguous subsequence:
$$\triangleq (\exists C, D\colon \text{seq } X \cdot C^\frown A^\frown D = B).$$

squash f Convert a finite function, $f\colon \mathbf{N} \nrightarrow X$, into a sequence
by squashing its domain. That is,

squash $\{\} = [\,]$, and if $f \neq \{\}$ then
squash $f = [f(i)]^\frown \text{squash}(\{i\} \lhd f)$
where $i = \min(\text{dom } f)$.

For example, squash $\{2 \mapsto A, 27 \mapsto C, 4 \mapsto B\} = [A, B, C].$

$S \upharpoonright A$ Restrict the sequence A to those items whose index is
in the set S:
$$\triangleq \text{squash}(S \lhd A)$$

$A \upharpoonright T$ Restrict the range of the sequence A to the set T:
$$\triangleq \text{squash}(A \rhd T).$$

A.2 Schema notation

Schema definition: a schema groups together some declarations of
variables and a predicate relating these variables. There are two ways of
writing schemas: vertically, for example

$$
\begin{array}{|l}
\hline
S \\\hline
x \colon \mathbf{N} \\
y \colon \operatorname{seq} \mathbf{N} \\\hline
x \le {}^{\#}y \\\hline
\end{array}
$$

or horizontally, for the same example

$$S \triangleq [x \colon \mathbf{N};\, y \colon \operatorname{seq} \mathbf{N} \mid x \le {}^{\#}y].$$

Use in signatures after $\forall$, λ, $\{\ldots\}$, etc.:

$$(\forall S \cdot y \ne [\,]) \triangleq (\forall x \colon \mathbf{N};\, y \colon \operatorname{seq} \mathbf{N} \mid x \le {}^{\#}y \cdot y \ne [\,]).$$

Schemas as types

> When a schema name S is used as a type it stands for
> the set of all objects described by the schema, $\{S\}$,
> e.g. $w \colon S$ declares a variable w with components x (a
> natural number) and y (a sequence of natural
> numbers) such that $x \le {}^{\#}y$.

Projection functions

> The component names of a schema may be used as
> projection (or selector) functions, e.g. given
> $W \colon S$, $x(w)$ is w's x-component and $y(w)$ is its
> y-component; of course, the following predicate
> holds: $x(w) \le {}^{\#}y(w)$.
> Alternative notations for $x(w)$ and $y(w)$ are $w.x$ and
> $w.y$, respectively.

tuple S The tuple formed from a schema's variables; e.g.
                  tuple S is (x, y). Where there is no risk of ambiguity,
                  the word 'tuple' can be omitted, so that just 'S' is
                  written for '(x, y)'.

pred S The predicate part of a schema: e.g. pred S is $x \le {}^{\#}y$.

Inclusion

A schema S may be included within the declarations of a schema T, in which case the declarations of S are merged with the other declarations of T (variables declared in both S and T must be of the same type) and the predicates of S and T are conjoined. For example,

$$T\underline{}$$
$$S$$
$$z: \mathbf{N}$$
$$\overline{}$$
$$z < x$$

is

$$x, z: \mathbf{N}$$
$$y: \text{seq } \mathbf{N}$$
$$\overline{}$$
$$x \le {}^{\#}y \land z < x$$

$S \mid P$

The schema S with P conjoined to its predicate part. For example,

$$(S \mid x > 0) \quad \text{is} \quad [x: \mathbf{N}; y: \text{seq } \mathbf{N} \mid x \le {}^{\#}y \land x > 0].$$

$S; D$

The schema S with the declarations D merged with the declarations of S. For example,

$$(S; z: \mathbf{N}) \quad \text{is} \quad [x, z: \mathbf{N}; y: \text{seq } \mathbf{N} \mid x \le {}^{\#}y].$$

$S[\text{new}/\text{old}]$

Renaming of components: the schema S in which the component *old* has been renamed to *new* both in the declaration and at its every free occurrence in the predicate. For example,

$$S[z/x] \qquad \text{is} \quad [z: \mathbf{N}; y: \text{seq } \mathbf{N} \mid z \le {}^{\#}y]$$

and

$$S[y/x, x/y] \quad \text{is} \quad [y: \mathbf{N}; x: \text{seq } \mathbf{N} \mid y \le {}^{\#}x].$$

In the second case above, the renaming is simultaneous. And as usual, the renaming in the predicate might entail consequential changes of bound variable.

Decoration

Decoration with subscript, superscript, prime, etc.; systematic renaming of the variables declared in the schema.

For example,

$$S' \text{ is } [x': \mathbf{N}; y': \text{seq } \mathbf{N} \mid x' \leq {}^{\#}y'].$$

$\neg S$ The schema S with its predicate part negated. For example,

$$\neg S \text{ is } [x: \mathbf{N}; y: \text{seq } \mathbf{N} \mid \neg(x \leq {}^{\#}y)].$$

$S \wedge T$ The schema formed from schemas S and T by merging their declarations (see inclusion above) and conjoining (and-ing) their predicates. Given $T \triangleq [x: \mathbf{N}; z: \mathbb{P}\mathbf{N} \mid x \in z]$, $S \wedge T$ is

```
┌─────────────────────────────────┐
│ x: N                            │
│ y: seq N                        │
│ z: PN                           │
├─────────────────────────────────┤
│ x ≤ #y ∧ x ∈ z                  │
└─────────────────────────────────┘
```

$S \vee T$ The schema formed from schemas S and T by merging their declarations and disjoining (or-ing) their predicates. For example, $S \vee T$ is

```
┌─────────────────────────────────┐
│ x: N                            │
│ y: seq N                        │
│ z: PN                           │
├─────────────────────────────────┤
│ x ≤ #y ∨ x ∈ z                  │
└─────────────────────────────────┘
```

$S \Rightarrow T$ The schema formed from schemas S and T by merging their declarations and taking pred $S \Rightarrow$ pred T as the predicate. For example, $S \Rightarrow T$ is

```
┌─────────────────────────────────┐
│ x: N                            │
│ y: seq N                        │
│ z: PN                           │
├─────────────────────────────────┤
│ x ≤ #y ⇒ x ∈ z                  │
└─────────────────────────────────┘
```

$S \Leftrightarrow T$ The schema formed from schemas S and T by merging their declarations and taking pred $S \Leftrightarrow$ pred T as the predicate. For example, $S \Leftrightarrow T$ is

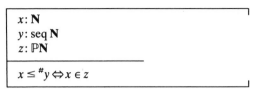

$S \backslash (v_1, v_2, \ldots, v_n)$

Hiding: the schema S with the variables $v_1, v_2, \ldots,$ and v_n hidden: the variables listed are removed from the declarations and existentially quantified in the predicate. For example,

$$S \backslash x \quad \text{is} \quad [y : \text{seq } \mathbf{N} \mid (\exists x : \mathbf{N} \cdot x \leq {}^{\#}y)].$$

(We omit the parentheses when only one variable is hidden.) A schema may be specified instead of a list of variables; in this case the variables declared in that schema are hidden. e.g. $(S \wedge T) \backslash S$ is

$$
\begin{array}{|l}
\hline
z : \mathbb{P}\mathbf{N} \\
\hline
(\exists x : \mathbf{N}; y : \text{seq } \mathbf{N} \cdot \\
\quad x \leq {}^{\#}y \wedge x \in z) \\
\hline
\end{array}
$$

$S \upharpoonright (v_1, v_2, \ldots, v_n)$

Projection: The schema S with any variables that do not occur in the list $v_1, v_2, \ldots, v_n$ hidden: the variables removed from the declarations are existentially quantified in the predicate.

For example, $(S \wedge T) \upharpoonright (x, y)$ is

$$
\begin{array}{|l}
\hline
x : \mathbf{N} \\
y : \text{seq } \mathbf{N} \\
\hline
\exists z : \mathbb{P}\mathbf{N} \cdot \\
\quad x \leq {}^{\#}y \wedge x \in z) \\
\hline
\end{array}
$$

(We omit the parentheses when only one variable is hidden.) The list of variables may be replaced by a schema as for hiding; the variables declared in the schema are used for the projection.

The following conventions are used for variable names in those schemas which represent operations—that is, which are written as descriptions of operations on some state.

undashed	state before the operation,
dashed	state after the operation,
ending in '?'	inputs to (arguments for) the operation, and
ending in '!'	outputs from (results of) the operation.

The following schema operations only apply to schemas following the above conventions.

pre S Precondition: all the state after components (dashed) and the outputs (ending in '!') are hidden, e.g. given

S
$$x?, s, s', y!: \mathbf{N}$$
$$s' = s - x? \wedge y! = s$$

pre S is

$$x?, s: \mathbf{N}$$
$$(\exists s', y!: \mathbf{N} \cdot$$
$$s' = s - x? \wedge y! = s)$$

post S Postcondition: this is similar to precondition except all the state before components (undashed) and inputs (ending in '?') are hidden. (Note that this definition differs from some others, in which the 'postcondition' is in fact the predicate relating all of initial state, inputs, outputs, and final state.)

$S \oplus T$ Overriding:
$\triangleq (S \wedge \neg \text{pre } T) \vee T$. For example, given S above and

T
$$x?, s, s': \mathbf{N}$$
$$s < x? \wedge s' = s$$

$S \oplus T$ is

$$x?, s, s', y!: \mathbf{N}$$

$$
\begin{aligned}
&(s' = s - x? \wedge y! = s \wedge \\
&\neg(\exists s': \mathbf{N} \cdot \\
&\quad s < x? \wedge s' = s)) \\
&\vee (s < x? \wedge s' = s)
\end{aligned}
$$

Because (given the declaration s: $\mathbf{N}$ above)

$$
\begin{aligned}
&(\exists s': \mathbf{N} \cdot s' = s \wedge s < x?) \Leftrightarrow \\
&(s \in \mathbf{N} \wedge s < x?) \Leftrightarrow \\
&s < x?,
\end{aligned}
$$

the predicate can be simplified:

$$
\begin{array}{|l}
\hline
x?, s, s', y!: \mathbf{N} \\
\hline
(s' = s - x? \wedge y! = s \\
\quad \wedge s \geq x?) \\
\vee \\
(s < x? \wedge s' = s) \\
\hline
\end{array}
$$

$S; T$ Schema composition: if we consider an intermediate state that is both the final state of the operation S and the initial state of the operation T, then the composition of S and T is the operation which relates the initial state of S to the final state of T through the intermediate state. To form the composition of S and T we take the state-after components of S and the state-before components of T that have a base name* in common, rename both to new variables, take the schema which is the 'and' ($\wedge$) of the resulting schemas, and hide the new variables. For example, $S; T$ is

$$
\begin{array}{|l}
\hline
x?, s, s', y!: \mathbf{N} \\
\hline
(\exists s^+: \mathbf{N} \cdot \\
\quad s^+ = s - x \wedge y! = \quad \wedge \\
\quad s^+ < x? \wedge s' = s^+) \\
\hline
\end{array}
$$

* base name is the name with any decoration (''', '!', '?', etc.) removed.

$S \gg T$ Piping: this schema operation is similar to schema composition; the difference is that, rather than identifying the state-after components of S with the state-before components of T, the output components of S (ending in '!') are identified with the input components of T (ending in '?') that have the same base name.

References

Bell, T. E., Bixler, D. C., and Dyer, M. (1977). An extendable approach to computer aided software requirements engineering. *IEEE Transactions of Software Engineering,* **SE-3** (1), 49–60.

Bjorner, D. and Jones, C. B. (1982). *Formal specification and software development.* Prentice-Hall, Englewood Cliffs, New Jersey.

Boehm, B. W. (1981). *Software engineering economics.* Prentice-Hall, Englewood Cliffs, New Jersey.

Cain, S. H. and Gordon, E. K. (1975). PDL—a tool for software design. *Proceedings National Computer Conference* **44**, 211–76.

Clarke, L. (1976). A system to generate test data and symbolically execute programs. *IEEE Transactions on Software Engineering* **SE-2** (3), 215–22.

Constable, R. L. and O'Donnell, M. J. (1978). *A programming logic.* Winthrop, Cambridge, Massachusetts.

Flinn, W. (1986). CAVIAR: a case study in specification. In: *Specification case studies* (ed. I. Hayes) Prentice Hall, Englewood Cliffs, New Jersey.

Gerhart, D. L., Musser, D. R., and 10 others. (1980). An overview of AFFIRM. A specification and verification system. In *Proceedings International Federation for Information Processing Congress,* pp. 343–7. North Holland, Amsterdam.

Guttag, J. V. and Horning, J. J. (1978). The algebraic specification of abstract data types. *Acta Informatica* **10**(1), 27–52.

Luckham, D., German, S., *et al.* (1979). Stanford Pascal verifier user's manual. AI Memo CS-79-731, Computer Science Department, Stanford University.

Miller, E. F. (1977). Program testing: art meets theory. *Computer* **10**(6), 42–51.

Osterweil, L. J. (1983). Toolpack—an experimental software development environment research project. *IEEE Transactions on Software Engineering* **SE-9** (6), 673–86.

Schoman, K. and Ross, D. T. (1977). Structured analysis for requirements definition. *IEEE Transactions on Software Engineering* **SE-3** (1), 6–15.

Stewart, I. and Tall, D. (1977). *The foundations of mathematics*. Oxford University Press, Oxford.

Sufrin, B. A. and Morgan, C. C. (1984). Specification of the UNIX file system. *IEEE Transactions on Software Engineering* **SE-10** (2), 128–42.

Teichrow, D. and Hershey, E. A. (1977). PSL/PSA: a computer aided technique for structured documentation and analysis of information processing systems. *IEEE Transactions on Software Engineering* **SE-3** (1), 41–8.

Weinberg, V. (1980). *Structured analysis*. Prentice Hall, Englewood Cliffs, New Jersey.

Index

abstraction, levels of 35, 270
addition operator 238–9
after operator 254
analysis, dynamic 10
analysis, static 10
antecedent operand 45, 53, 69
arbitrary set element operator 242
arithmetic operators 93, 238–9
arrays 123
axiomatic theories 127, 128, 129
axioms 127, 128, 129, 130

back-order system 254–65
   events in 260–5
   statement of requirements for 255–7
   static properties of 257–9
base case 213
base names 339, 340
boolean functions 94

cardinality of sets ($^{\#}$) 145, 207, 329
classes of objects 92, 97, 98, 102
closure operators, transitive 173–6, 244
   non-reflexive ($^{+}$) 174, 175, 244, 331
   reflexive (*) 174–5, 244, 330
coding 3, 8
composition, relation 162–5
concatenation operator ($^{\frown}$) 199, 209, 218, 250, 332
conclusions 65, 67–8, 71, 73, 111, 113
conjunction ($^{\wedge}$) 44, 52, 280
   of predicates 222, 270, 327, 335
consequent operand 45, 53, 69
constants 235
contradiction 53, 54
   law of 59
   proof by 75
cross-products 144–5
currying 196

data bases
   design of 7
   spare-parts 281–6
data requirements 18, 27
declarations 327, 334
   constant 235
   programming language 222
decoration 335–6
deduction 111
deduction, formal 128
design, detailed 3, 7–8
design directives 16, 27
design specifications 119–25
disjunction ($\vee$) 44, 53, 280, 327
   exclusive 44, 45
dom 159, 177, 178, 330
domain operator (dom) 159, 177, 178, 330

empty set 138–9, 140, 207, 328
equality
   law of 59
   operator 44, 45, 46, 280, 327
   set 141
   symbol ($\triangleq$) 223, 327
events 227, 228, 229
   in Z schemas 273, 277, 319
existence, unique 328

filing system, models of 147–54, 231–4
formal methods 11
   misconceptions surrounding 12–14
   problems with 38–40
formal specification documents 12, 13
for operator 254
front operator 198, 251, 333
functions 180, 331–2
   bijective 184–5
      partial 184
      total 184–5

functions (*cont.*)
  curried 196
  higher-order 189
  injective 182–3, 184
    partial 183, 224, 247
    total 183, 224, 247
  as lambda expressions 194–5
  mapping by 180
  partial 180–1, 224, 247, 331
  pred 186
  projection 268, 334
  sequences as 196–9
  succ 186, 239
  surjective 183, 184
    partial 184
    total 184
  symbols used to identify, in Z 224,
    247
  total 181–2, 224, 247, 331
  used in system specification 180–1,
    190–4
  use of operators with 186
  use of schemas to define 235, 246–8

goals 17, 27, 39
graphical notations 6, 10

hardware requirements 27
head operator 197–8, 218, 251, 332
hiding 337, 338, 339
hypotheses 111, 128

id 165, 177, 243, 330
identifiers 93, 98, 101, 135, 327
identity relation (id) 165, 177, 243,
  330
implementation directives 16, 27
implication
  form, transformation to 68–74
  law of 59
  operator 44, 45, 46, 53, 280, 327
inconsistencies, detection of 80–3
induction 210
  base case 213
  hypothesis 213
  on natural numbers 210–13
  sequence 217–18
  set 214–16
  step 213
  structural 214

inference
  rules of 75, 112, 113–14, 127, 146
  using invalid argument 74–9
informal theories 127, 129
integration 3, 8
invariants 228, 273–7
inverse operator ($^{-1}$) 161, 177, 178,
  179, 330
iterate operator 173, 244, 330

lambda expressions 194–5, 238, 267,
  268, 332
language, natural 10
  ambiguities in 22, 37
  in formal methods 12
  translations in Z specifications 320
last operator 198, 251, 333
laws 127, 128
laws, propositional 57–62
  of and simplification 60
  associative 58
  commutative 58
  of contradiction 59
  de Morgan's 58–9
  distributive 58
  of equality 59
  of the excluded middle 59
  exclusive or 60
  of implication 59
  negation 59
  of or simplification 60
logical operators and schemas 280–1

maintenance 3, 8–9, 27–8
mathematics
  in definition of Z operators 327–33
  and system specification 34–8, 39
members of sets 132
models of reality 37
modules 6, 8, 176
  implementation part 176
  specification part 176
multiplication operator 239

natural language, *see* language, natural
negation
  law of 59
  operator ($\neg$) 44, 280, 281, 327
numbers, natural (**N**) 117, 238, 329

induction on 210–13
minus zero ($\mathbf{N_1}$) 238, 329
set of consecutive 240

objects
  classes of 92, 97, 98, 102
  collections of 130, 131, 132; *see also*
    sets
  defined in terms of themselves 204–
    5; *see also* specification,
    recursive
  relationship between 93–4, 158; *see
    also* relations
  in Z specifications 319, 320–2
observations 227, 228, 229
operation of software system 3
operator, summation 121
operators, arithmetic 93, 238–9
operators, binary 238
  logical 280
operators, propositional 44–6, 112
  dyadic 44
  monadic 44
  precedence of 49
operators, relational 93, 239, 330–1
  domain (dom) 159, 177, 178, 330
  domain restriction ($\lhd$, $\lhd$) 168–9,
    243–4, 331
  with functions 186
  inverse ($^{-1}$) 161, 177, 178, 179, 330
  iteration 173, 244, 330
  override ($\oplus$) 169–70, 178, 244,
    331, 338–9
  range (rng) 159–60, 177, 178, 330
  range restriction ($\rhd$, $\rhd$) 168–9,
    243–4, 331
  set image ($\lVert\,\rVert$) 171, 177, 178, 244,
    331
  transitive closures 173–6, 244
    non-reflexive ($^{+}$) 174, 175, 244,
      331
    reflexive (*) 174–5, 244, 330
operators, schema 273, 334–40
  composition 339
  hiding 337
  overriding 338–9
  piping 340
  pred 273, 334
  projection 337
  tuple 273, 334
operators, sequence 197–9, 250–1,
  332–3

after 254
concatenation ($\frown$) 199, 209, 218,
  250, 332
for 254
front 198, 251, 333
head 197–8, 218, 251, 332
last 198, 251, 333
reverse (rev) 209, 218, 333
squash 333
tail 198, 209, 218, 251, 333
operators, set 132–3, 139–45, 207–8,
  215, 240–2
operators, unary 241
orders 332
override operator ($\oplus$) 169–70, 178,
  244, 331, 338–9

pairs, ordered 155, 243
parameters, program 121
piping 340
post-conditions 121, 338
power sets 140–1, 240–1, 329
pre-conditions 121, 338
predecessor function (pred) 186
predicate calculus 94
  and design specification 119–25
  used to define set operators 141
  see also predicates
predicate operator (pred) 273, 334
predicates 94, 111
  in comprehensive set
    specification 135
  conjunction of 222, 270, 327, 335
  interchangeable with schemas 267
  intermediate 111–12, 113
  in lambda expressions 194
  post-condition 121, 338
  pre-condition 121, 338
  propositions as 93
  quantified expressions as 101, 105,
    108
  quantifiers as 97
  in schemas 221, 222, 334
  in specification of relations 155
  using set operators 133
  see also predicate calculus
premises 65, 67, 68, 73, 111, 128
print spoolers 199–203
program proving 11
program units 119, 120, 121
projection functions 268, 334
projection on schemas 337

proof 111–14
  patterns in 113, 114
  in set theory 145–7
  in a theory 127
proof, indirect 75, 78, 81, 88, 111, 112
proof by contradiction 75, 111
proof systems, automatic 11
propositional calculus
  as an axiomatic theory 128
  laws of 57–62
  use of, in system specification 43,
    84, 90
  weaknesses of 92–3
  see also propositions
propositional operators, *see* operators,
  propositional
propositions 44
  consistent 80
  inconsistent 80–1
  as predicates 93
  from system specifications 71, 74
  see also conclusions; contradiction;
    implication; inference; laws,
    propositional; operators,
    propositional; premises;
    propositional calculus;
    reasoning; tautologies
prototyping 14, 39

quantification
  in pre- and post-conditions 123
  see also quantification, existential;
    quantification, universal
quantification, existential 97–102, 110,
  328
  relationship with universal
    quantification 107–10
  rules of inference involving 114
  see also quantifier, existential
quantification, universal 102–7, 327
  relationship with existential
    quantification 107–10
  rules of inference involving 114
  see also quantifier, universal
quantifier, counting 120
quantifier, existential 97, 120
  singular 120
quantifier, universal 97, 102, 235
queues 250, 251, 255

range operator (rng) 159–60, 177, 178,
  330

reasoning 65, 90
  chains of 36
  about natural numbers 117
  in set theory 145–7
  using invalid argument 74–9
  using transformation to implication
    form 68–74
  see also induction
recursive specification, *see*
  specification, recursive
reductio ad absurdum 75, 111
relational operators, *see* operators,
  relational
relations 155, 330–1
  composition of 162–5, 173, 243
  constructive specification of 155,
    156
  enumeration of 156
  homogeneous 164, 173
  identity (id) 165, 177, 243, 330
  less than 157
  over pairs of sets 156
  restriction of 167–71
  theorems involving 177–9
  use of schemas to define 236
  used for modelling computer
    systems 158
  in Z specifications 242
  see also functions; operators,
    relational
requirements, functional 4–5, 15–16,
  27
requirements, non-functional 4, 5–6,
  16, 27
requirements analysis 3–6, 23
  as construction of informal
    theory 129
  example of 28–34
  procedure for 25–8
  using mathematics 39
restriction operators ($\lhd, \rhd, \mathbin{\rlap{\lhd}-}, \mathbin{\rlap{\rhd}-}$)
  168–9, 243–4, 331
reverse operator (rev) 209, 218, 333
rng 159–60, 177, 178, 330
rules, scoping 101

schema inclusion 226, 269–70, 335
schemas 221–5, 334–40
  box-like form 221–2, 269, 334
  composite 319
  conventions for (in Z) 273–9
  definition of constants by 235
  definition of functions by 235

definition of relations by 236
definition of sets by 236
describing operations on
    system 319, 323–4
describing parts of system not
    changed by events (≡) 277–8,
    319
    examples 283, 294–5, 297–8, 300
example of use of calculus of 281–6
examples of use of 234–6
extension of 272
indicating invariant properties
    (△) 273–7, 319
    examples 283, 293–5, 297–8, 300
inputs to 230, 278–9, 338, 340
interchangeable with comprehensive
    set specifications 266, 267
interchangeable with lambda
    abstractions 267, 268
interchangeable with predicates 266,
    267
linear form 222, 223, 269, 334
logical operators and 280–1
as objects 266–9
outputs from 278–9, 338, 340
primed (dashed) 271, 338
quantification of 268
as types 334
see also events; operators, schema;
    schema inclusion; University of
    Lincoln Library system
sequences 196–9, 332–3
    cardinality of 218, 332
    definition of 197, 249, 332–3
    induction over 217–18
    never empty 250
    recursive specifications applied
        to 207, 209
    reversal of 209, 218, 333
    in specifications 199–203
    in Z specifications 249–54
    see also operators, sequence
set cardinality (#) 145, 207, 329
set difference 144, 240, 329
set image operator (⟦ ⟧) 171, 177, 178,
    244, 331
set inclusion, *see* subset operator
set induction 214–16
set intersection 142–3, 208, 215, 240,
    329
    generalized 240, 241, 329
sets 131–2, 328–9
    cross-products of 144–5, 328
    empty 138–9, 140, 207, 328

finite 132
generic 327
given, in Z specifications 319, 320
infinite 132
power 140–1, 329
use of schemas to define 236
set specification 134–6
    comprehensive 134–5, 136
set theorems 146
set theory
    reasoning and proof in 145–7
    role of 131
    typed 221
set union 142, 143, 240, 329
    generalized 240–1, 329
signatures 135, 221, 222, 223, 334
    variables in 278–9
simplification rules 55, 57–60
software engineering 37
software life cycle 3
software specifications, *see* system
    specifications
sorting procedures 124
spare-parts data base system 281–6
specification, recursive 204–9
    applied to natural numbers 204–6
    applied to sequences 207, 209
    applied to sets 206–8, 215
specifications, functional 119
squash operator 333
statements of requirements 4, 34
    for back-order system 255–7
    contents of 15–18
    deficiencies in 18–23, 30–4
        ambiguity 22
        contradiction 19–20
        incompleteness 20–1
        mixed requirements 21
        mixture of levels of
            abstraction 22–3
        naivety 21
        vagueness 19
    examples of 28–9, 191
    feasibility check 25, 27
    simplification of 63
    for spare-parts data base system 282
    for University of Lincoln Library
        system 287–92
states 227
    static properties of (invariants) 228,
        273–7
structure charts 6
subset operator (⊆) 139–41, 216–17,
    240, 328

subset operator (*cont.*)
  proper (⊂) 139, 142, 240, 328
successor function (succ) 186, 239
summation operator 121
symbolic execution 10
system design 3, 6–7, 119; *see also*
    design specifications
system specifications 3–6
  ambiguities in 54, 56
  as construction of informal
    theory 129–30
  contradictions in 55–6
  conversion into predicate calculus
    form 95, 99, 103, 133, 147
  conversion into propositional
    calculus form 46, 85–8, 90
  inconsistencies in 81
  mathematics and 34–8, 39
  in natural language 13, 85
  notations for 38, 40
  partitioning
    horizontal 24
    vertical 24
  qualities of good 23–5
  simplification of 54, 55, 63
  testability 25
  use of functions for 180–1, 190–4
  use of relations for 167, 176
  use of sequences for 199–203
  use of set theory for 147–54
  validation of 71, 73, 129
  see also formal methods;
      specifications, functional; Z

tail operator 198, 209, 218, 251, 333
tautologies 53–4, 57, 68–9, 113
technology transfer 39–40
terms
  in comprehensive set
    specification 135–6
  in lambda expressions 194
terms, primitive 127
testing
  acceptance 12, 15
  system 9–10, 12
theorems 127, 128, 129, 130
  involving relations 177–9
theories
  axiomatic 127, 128, 129
  informal 127, 129
truth tables 51–2, 112

tuple operator 273, 334
types, set theoretic 222, 240, 327

University of Lincoln Library
    system 287–324
  borrowing of books 291, 312–14
  changing an address or name 289,
    305–6
  error-processing in 288–9, 291, 292
  generating microfiche hard
    copy 290, 310–11
  generating unused book registration
    numbers 290, 307–8
  generating unused user registration
    numbers 290, 308–10
  modelling operations by means of
    events and observations in 302–
    19
  notification of found books 292,
    317–18
  notification of overdue books 291,
    311–12
  notification of return of reserved
    books 292, 318–19
  registering a new book 289, 306–7
  registration of new users 289, 301–3
  removal of existing users 289, 303–4
  return of books 292, 314–17
  statement of requirements in 287–
    92
  static properties of 293–300
    invariants 293, 294, 295, 296,
      297–8, 299
    schema describing changes
      (△) 293, 294, 295, 297, 298,
      300
    schema describing events leaving
      parts of system unchanged
      (≡) 294, 295, 297, 298, 300

validation 9–10, 27
  of specifications 71, 73
variables
  bound 101, 102
  free 101, 102
  global 121, 222
  in schemas 222
verification 9–10
version-control systems 190–4

Z 40, 221, 237
  definition of operators in 327–40
    mathematical notation 327–33
    schema notation 334–40
  full specification of 325
  functions in 246–7
  modelling a back-order system
    in 254–65
  modelling a spare-parts data base
    in 281–6
  operators on natural numbers
    in 238–40

operators on sets in 240
relations in 242
schema conventions in 273–9
sentences in 230
sequences in 249–54
structure of specifications in 226,
  230, 319–24
see also events; functions; objects;
  observations; schemas;
  University of Lincoln Library
  system